Teaching While White

Teaching While White

Addressing the Intersections of Race and Immigration in the Classroom

Laura A. Roy

ROWMAN & LITTLEFIELD
Lanham • Boulder • New York • London

Published by Rowman & Littlefield
An imprint of The Rowman & Littlefield Publishing Group, Inc.
4501 Forbes Boulevard, Suite 200, Lanham, Maryland 20706
www.rowman.com

Unit A, Whitacre Mews, 26-34 Stannary Street, London SE11 4AB

British Library Cataloguing in Publication Information Available

Library of Congress Cataloging-in-Publication Data

Names: Roy, Laura A., 1978– author.
Title: Teaching while White : addressing the intersections of race and immigration in the classroom / Laura A. Roy.
Description: Lanham, Maryland : Rowman & Littlefield, [2018]. | Includes bibliographical references.
Identifiers: LCCN 2018026445 (print) | LCCN 2018032258 (ebook) | ISBN 9781475840391 (electronic) | ISBN 9781475840377 (cloth : alk. paper) | ISBN 9781475840384 (pbk. : alk. paper)
Subjects: LCSH: Multicultural education—United States. | Minorities—Education—United States. | Teachers, White—United States.
Classification: LCC LC1099.3 (ebook) | LCC LC1099.3 .R69 2018 (print) | DDC 370.117—dc23
LC record available at https://lccn.loc.gov/2018026445

∞ ™ The paper used in this publication meets the minimum requirements of American National Standard for Information Sciences Permanence of Paper for Printed Library Materials, ANSI/NISO Z39.48-1992.

Printed in the United States of America

For my strong, kind-hearted mom, Dana—my first teacher.

Contents

Introduction ix

Part I: Disrupting the Single Story of Histories **1**

1 Who Are Americans?: Imagined Histories of Immigration 3

2 Race and Immigration: Intersections of Histories and Identities 25

3 Deficit and Microaggressive Discourses: Unmasking the Language of White Supremacy 47

Part II: Disrupting the Single Story in Curriculum **69**

4 Cultivating a Critical Classroom Community from Day One 71

5 Critical Approaches to Curricular Change 95
With Contributions From Drew Gingrich

6 Critical Media Literacy: Fake News, Trolls, and Memes 111
With Contributions From Drew Gingrich

Part III: What Disruption Looks Like: Supporting Teacher Activism **123**

7 Teacher Research as Activism 125

8 Allies and Accomplices: What White Teachers Should Know and Do 147

9 Making Your Case: Building Relationships, Not Walls 163
With Contributions From Drew Gingrich

Additional Recommended Resources 177

About the Author and Contributor 183

Introduction

AN INVITATION TO BE UNCOMFORTABLE

On the first day of any class I teach, I invite my students to be comfortable being uncomfortable—to live for a while in the disequilibrium that ultimately leads to real learning and transformation. This book is an invitation for White teachers to be uncomfortable. The intersection of race and immigration is the primary theme of this book and thus topics such as racism, White supremacy, White privilege, and citizenship—topics that White people often deem too controversial or divisive to discuss—are explored.

I argue in this book that avoiding authentic dialogue about racism and White supremacy is part of why these topics seem so challenging and divisive to begin with. But what is the cost of not talking about it? What is the cost of allowing racism to thrive? In order to solve the problem of racism and White supremacy, White teachers must be willing and able to name and identify the system of racism and White supremacy. For White teachers, this can evoke feelings of guilt, anger, fear, and discomfort—especially among White teachers who believe themselves well intentioned. This book invites White teachers to build from those good intentions by sitting with and unpacking their reactions to conversations about racism, White privilege, and White supremacy.

I advocate specifically for White teachers who are concerned with equity and social justice to address racism and White supremacy head-on—to get comfortable using words like *racism*, *White supremacy*, *White privilege*, for example, when naming the problem and teaching about the social, cultural, economic, and political realities of our history past and present. I urge teachers to reconsider terms such as *diversity* and instead actively work to decenter Whiteness in educational spaces and amplify issues of social justice and equity.

WHY WRITE A BOOK ABOUT WHITE TEACHERS TEACHING WHITE STUDENTS ABOUT RACE AND IMMIGRATION?

The US teaching population remains largely White, middle class, and female. The student population, however, is increasingly diverse. At the same time, school communities are becoming increasingly segregated and resegregated, especially in exurban areas that exist in and beyond traditional suburbs. Preservice and in-service teachers who grow up and live in predominantly White communities are less likely to interact with people of color, including new immigrant populations.

Chang (2016) asserts that this White isolation from communities of color is intentional. He states, "Whether through white flight, the optics of diversity, or metaphorical and actual wall building, the privileged spare themselves the sight of disparity, and foreclose the possibility of empathy and transformation" (p. 4). This isolation, segregation and resegregation, and distancing of White communities, physically, socially, and emotionally, allows biased, deficit, and racist polices, practices, and views to go unchallenged.

As such, White teachers and community members in predominantly White communities may not see or recognize the need for critical conversations or action, especially as it relates to the intersections of race and immigration. And, if the majority of the teaching population is White and the majority of books and curricula published are by White people, this means White teachers are teaching through curriculum and pedagogical practices that are grounded in White, Eurocentric, middle-class norms, further distancing Whites from the ways communities of color are marginalized and oppressed by the system. As a result, stories of people of color are misrepresented, silenced, or omitted in schools. I argue in this book that real teaching is about liberation and freedom for all students. As such, I urge White teachers to take an activist stance in decentering Whiteness in pedagogy and curriculum by educating White students, colleagues, and communities about the intersections of race, racism, and immigration.

WHAT'S THAT TITLE ABOUT?

The intention of this book is to engage White teachers in a critique of Whiteness, especially the notion of White as default—the norm, regular, or the standard. The title *Teaching While White* is to call attention to the permanence of the problem of Whiteness as a liability for both students of color and White students. What I mean by this is that, intentionally or unintentionally, White people, including White teachers, are complicit in perpetuating the larger system of White supremacy and racial oppression that is embedded in the US's history and social, economic, educational, and criminal justice systems.

This is not a call to remove White, European histories, practices, and experiences. Nor is it to suggest that White teachers can't be a part of the solution to racism. Rather, it is a call for White teachers to recognize, identify, and disrupt the ways current pedagogical practices and curricula privilege White, European histories, practices, and experiences as the primary narrative.

The aim of this book is to critique the system and to emphasize the role White teachers can and should play in disrupting it. As you will read in this book, a critique of the system, while sometimes challenging, does not have to be an unpleasant endeavor. The White teachers I have worked with find CRTA (critical race teacher activism), critical literacy, and liberatory education practices, all discussed in this book, to be rewarding for their students, families, and communities. I argue that White teachers have the potential to play a primary role in transforming the notion of "teaching while White" from a liability to an emancipatory act of radical love and critical consciousness (Freire, 1972).

THEORETICAL FRAMEWORK

Much scholarly work has been done to illuminate the mismatch between teacher and student demographics and to educate White teachers to better serve diverse student populations (see, for example, Howard, 2006; Ladson-Billings & Tate, 1995; Matias, 2013). This book works in concert with this endeavor by cultivating activism literacies in White teachers working in predominately White spaces. This book is designed to debunk the notion that White teachers working with White students are somehow absolved from engaging in critical conversations about the intersectional issues of race and racism. Rather, I argue White teachers in White educational spaces have an equally critical responsibility to call out racism when they see it and actively work to dismantle systems of oppression.

The theoretical framing of this book draws primarily from critical race teacher activism (CRTA) (Matias & Liou, 2015) to support teachers in taking an activist stance in disrupting the system of White supremacy and racial oppression. This framework has origins in critical theory, critical race theory (CRT) in education (see, for example, Krenshaw, Peller, Thomas, & Gotanda, 1996; Taylor, Gillborn, & Ladson-Billings, 2009; Ladson-Billings, 2006; Solorzano & Yosso, 2010; Vaught & Castagno, 2008), and critical Whiteness studies (CWS) (see, for example, Jupp & Slattery, 2010; Leonardo, 2009; Leonardo, 2013; Matias, Viesca, Garrison-Wade, Tandon, & Galindo, 2014; Picower, 2009).

Critical theory developed in response to a "presumed superiority and infallibility of scientific method, and raised questions about *whose* rationality and *whose* presumed objectivity underlies scientific methods" (Sensoy & DiAngelo, 2012, p. 4). Critical race theory, as Leonardo (2014) asserts, is a theory designed to "halt racism" through "anti-racism" approaches (p. 4), and critical Whiteness studies seeks to reveal how notions of White supremacy are structurally and institutionally embedded and reproduced.

CRTA extends this conversation to focus more closely on the relationship between teaching and activism, and the radical possibilities for teachers to dismantle systemic and institutional racism in schools. This book is designed to draw from CRTA as well as other critical perspectives to support teachers in developing activist literacies and cultivating activist literacies in their own classrooms. This calls for an intersectional understanding of race and requires teachers to take direct action in disrupting the system of White supremacy and racial oppression through antiracist work. I emphasize *anti*racist work over *non*racist work. Antiracist work places direct action at the center, while nonracist work implies passive neutrality, that is, the idea that if one is not committing an overtly racist act, one cannot be considered racist. I argue that unless antiracist action against the system is prioritized, racism will persist.

POSITIONALITY

In Chapter 7, I discuss and define positionality in depth and show how it serves as a pedagogical and research tool for teachers. I provide my own positionality statement here to share what brought me to this work.

As a White woman who grew up in a small town in Nebraska, I witnessed the tensions that occur when new and existing communities meet and intersect. In the early 1990s, during my middle school years, towns like mine across Nebraska experienced an influx of immigrants from Mexico and Central America as the meatpacking industry boomed. My small town of fewer than 10,000 people went from 99% White to nearly 60% Latinx. Racism that once lay dormant or hidden was swiftly unmasked by this demographic shift. Whites in my community who found it easy to appreciate "diversity" from afar on their vacations or business travel used thinly veiled, coded language to lament how the downtown was "changing" and neighborhoods were going "downhill" as a result of these new residents. "White flight," the phenomenon of Whites moving out of an area when people of color move in, was a reality as community members with means began to sell their homes and move to gated communities or larger towns for fear of falling real estate prices. I distinctly remember hearing a group adults at my church complain about the inconvenience of having to add a Spanish mass to the church schedule and how "those customers" standing outside the local grocery store made them feel unsafe.

At the same time, however, some community members stepped up and welcomed the newcomers. My Spanish and English teachers taught after-school English classes for adults and encouraged bilingual and bicultural activities at school. Teachers such as these served as role models for me and for my friends. Over time—more than 20 years later, my small town is increasingly integrated. Living bilingually and biculturally is now the norm. Nebraska is currently designated as a welcoming state for both immigrants and refugees, receiving more refugees per capita each year than any other state in the nation. That said, anti-immigrant rhetoric, including calls for English-only legislation, border walls, and tighter, more punitive policies for identifying and deporting undocumented immigrants, continues to permeate public and private discourse in small-town Nebraska and elsewhere.

For example, debates about Deferred Action for Childhood Arrivals (DACA) nearly shut down the US government in 2017–2018, the Muslim ban implemented by the Trump administration continues to divide families and deny asylum seekers, and while the majority of Americans do not support the wall between Mexico and the US, construction continues. And, on the international stage, the United Kingdom (UK) passed "Brexit"—a referendum for the UK to leave the European Union, which effectively closes its borders to Black and Brown immigrants and refugees. Meanwhile, people continue to be displaced throughout the world due to a long history of colonization and imperialism perpetrated by countries like the US and UK. This book emerges from these local, national, and global issues in addition to my experiences living and working in communities in Nebraska, Georgia, Texas, and Pennsylvania, both in K–12 and university settings.

As a scholar-activist and teacher educator, I continue to witness the fear, reluctance, avoidance, and resistance of many White peers, colleagues, family members, and students to authentically and openly talk about race and the legacy of racism in the US. I set my sights on writing a book to share my experiences and offer a framework for White teachers to get comfortable with addressing intersectional issues of race and immigration in the classroom. In this way, my hope is that White teachers can act as accomplices and coconspirators in creating schools that center social justice and equity.

I was fortunate growing up to be guided by my Quaker activist roots that presented a counternarrative to the interpersonal and systemic racism I witnessed in the community. I am also fortunate and grateful to the many students, friends, teachers, and mentors who shared their knowledge, experiences, and checked me on my privilege when it needed to be checked. I have spent most of my adult life earnestly, but sometimes imperfectly, advocating for communities of color and working to dismantle the system of racial oppression and White supremacy. This book is designed to educate White teachers and urge them to join in this endeavor.

Drew Gingrich, a contributor to this book, was a former student of mine who showed an interest in teacher activism work as an undergraduate and graduate student in some of my classes. He invited me to his classroom during his first year of teaching and demonstrated how he worked to understand his role as a White educator and interrogate Whiteness in his elementary classroom. Drew contributed activities from his own classroom to some of the chapters and provided input on his experiences teaching from a CRTA perspective in both Pennsylvania and Florida. I am grateful for his contributions to this book. He truly embodies an educator committed to justice, equity, activism, and radical love.

HOW TO USE THIS BOOK

Each chapter begins with a framing quote, goals, and essential questions for reflection and discussion. Most chapters are divided into two parts. Part 1 of each chapter is designed to provide definitions and background knowledge related to the chapter focus. Part 2 of each chapter focuses on specific curricular and pedagogical recommendations including relevant activities, text set resources, and references.

I envision educators using the framing quote as an introductory discussion prompt for the topic of each chapter. The essential questions for reflection and discussion are designed for educators to reflect on their own responses and make predictions about their students' responses. Each chapter also includes activities that can be modified for a variety of ages, grades, and content areas and a list of books and resources. This book is designed for teachers in pK–20 contexts. It requires teachers to use the books and resources in each chapter to expand and elaborate on the topics for their particular context, age, and grade level.

Part of activism, as you will read in Chapters 8 and 9, involves educating yourself and understanding that pedagogy and curriculum must be designed and developed at the grassroots level. To be a successful CRTA teacher, you have to read, read, read, and find outlets for discussion, planning, and action. Use this book as an opportunity to develop your network of partners, allies, and accomplices (see Chapter 8) to employ an activist approach to teaching.

A NOTE ON TERMS

In this book, I attempt to use labels and naming conventions in ways that reflect critical and liberatory practices. For example, "Latinx" is used instead of the gendered Latino or Latina. Additionally, White and Black are used instead of problematic terms such as "Caucasian." Caucasian is a problematic term because it is grounded in the notion that Whites are superior. The label was coined by Friedrich Blumenbach in the late 1700s and early 1800s. Blumenbach examined the characteristics of skulls and determined that those from the Caucus region were superior in shape and form. The skulls, to him, also represented a superior White race.

Pan-ethnic identities, like Asian, are not used unless it is a marker of identity included in a quote, because it implies that people from regions in Asia are homogenous. Instead, appropriate nation-state or ethnic identity such as Japanese or Hmong are used when possible. Because this book is about the intersections of race and immigration, racial labeling like Black, Brown, and White are used to describe the complex, nuanced, and often flawed ways we racialize human beings. Chapter 2 provides an in-depth discussion of race and racial labeling and how it is intertwined with histories, identities, regions of origin, and ever-evolving social conventions.

Finally, I recognize that the problem of racism and White supremacy is much greater than any one educator or school can solve, and that these systems may not be fixed or dismantled anytime soon. That said, I am confident that collective action in transforming pedagogy and curriculum through CRTA has the potential to fundamentally shift how both teachers and students value plurality, take antiracist action, and work toward justice.

REFERENCES

Chang, J. (2016). *We gon' be alright: Notes on race and resegregation*. New York, NY: Picador.

Freire, P. (1972). *Pedagogy of the oppressed*. New York, NY: Herder and Herder.

Howard, G. R. (2006). *We can't teach what we don't know: White teachers, multiracial schools*. New York, NY: Teachers College Press. Google Scholar.

Krenshaw, K., Peller, G., Thomas, K., & Gotanda, N. (1996). *Critical Race Theory*. New York: The New Press.

Jupp, J. C. & Slattery Jr., G. P. (2010), Committed White Male Teachers and Identifications: Toward Creative Identifications and a "Second Wave" of White Identity Studies. *Curriculum Inquiry*, 40: 454–474. doi:10.1111/j.1467-873X.2010.00493.x

Ladson-Billings, G. (2006). The evolving role of critical race theory in educational scholarship. *Race Ethnicity and Education*, *8*(1), 115–119. http://dx.doi.org/10.1080/1361332052000341024

Ladson-Billings, G., & Tate, M. (1995). Towards a critical race theory of education. *Teachers College Record, 97*, 47–68.

Leonardo, Z. (2009). *Race, whiteness, and education.* New York, NY: Routledge.

Leonardo, Z. (2013). The color of supremacy: Beyond the discourse of "White privilege." *Educational Philosophy and Theory, 36*(2), 137–152. http://dx.doi.org/10.1111/j.1469-5812.2004.00057.x

Leonardo, Z. (2014). *Education and racism: A primer on issues and dilemmas.* New York, NY: Routledge.

Matias, C. E. (2013). Check yo'self before you wreck yo'self and our kids: Counterstories from culturally responsive white teachers? . . . to culturally responsive white teachers! *Interdisciplinary Journal of Teaching and Learning, 3*(2), 68–81.

Matias, C. E., & Liou, D. D. (2015). Tending to the heart of communities of color: Towards critical race teacher activism. *Urban Education, 50*(5), 601–625. http://dx.doi.org/10.1177/0042085913519338

Matias, C. E., Viesca, K. M., Garrison-Wade, D. F., Tandon, M. & Galindo, R. (2014). What is critical Whiteness doing in our nice field like critical race theory? Applying CRT and CWS to understand the White imaginations of White teacher candidates. *Equity & Excellence in Education, 47*(3), 289–304.

Picower, B. (2009). The unexamined Whiteness of teaching: How White teachers maintain and enact dominant racial ideologies. *Race Ethnicity and Education, 12*(2), 197–215. http://dx.doi.org/10.1080/13613320902995475

Sensoy, Ö., & DiAngelo, R. (2012). *Is everyone really equal? An introduction to key concepts in social justice education.* New York, NY: Teachers College.

Solorzano, D. G., & Yosso, T. J. (2010). Critical race and LatCrit theory and method: Counter-storytelling. *International Journal of Qualitative Studies in Education, 14*(4) 471–495. http://dx.doi.org/10.1080/09518390110063365

Taylor, E., Gillborn, D., & Ladson-Billings, G. (2009). *Foundations of critical race theory in education.* New York, NY: Routledge.

Vaught, S. E., & Castagno, A. E. (2008). "I don't think I'm a racist": Critical race theory, teacher attitudes, and structural racism. *Race Ethnicity and Education, 11*(2), 95–113. http://dx.doi.org/10.1080/13613320802110217

Part I

Disrupting the Single Story of Histories

Chapter One

Who Are Americans?

Imagined Histories of Immigration

> I am the immigrant clutching the hope I seek—
> And finding only the same old stupid plan
> Of dog eat dog, of mighty crush the weak.
>
> —Langston Hughes, "Let America Be America Again"

This chapter invites educators to employ a critical race teacher activism (CRTA) lens to critique the single story of immigration that is present in school curricula. The changing nature of the US population and the largely unchanged demographic of the teaching population amplifies the need for White teachers to become well versed in the multiple and often silenced histories of immigration. At the same time that the US is becoming more diverse, it is also becoming increasingly segregated. For this reason, it is crucial for teachers and the public at large to engage in authentic, critical, and meaningful conversations about immigration, border crossing, citizenship, and transnationalism.

Read Langston Hughes's "Let America Be America Again" and explore the question "Who is American and who gets to decide?" What does Hughes mean by "the same old stupid plan"? This chapter urges teachers to consider the need for critical approaches to the study of immigration histories in order to challenge dominant ideologies represented in text and society that promote and reify the system of White supremacy and racial oppression.

This chapter seeks to do the following:

- Engage educators in reflection and active engagement in critiquing their views and narratives of immigration past and present

- Employ the tools of CRTA to ask questions of social studies and history curricula, including, how are immigration stories told in curricula, whose stories are forefronted, whose stories are foregrounded, and why? Who benefits from amplifying or silencing particular immigration experiences?
- Help educators identify and deconstruct the single story of immigration by considering the notion of "imagined histories"
- Problematize the notion that there is an ideal or model immigrant or immigrant experience and instead explore the ever-evolving nature of what is and has been considered "legal" immigration in the US
- Explore how counterstories can transform curricula
- Take action to include multiple histories and perspectives in the classroom

Key Ideas and Terms

- Imagined histories of immigration
- Single story
- Critical historiography
- The myth of the American dream

Prereading Questions

Answer the following questions before reading the chapter. Then, consider how your students might respond to these questions.

1. What do you recall about your social studies and history education in school? How did you feel about it? How do you explain your feelings about learning history?
2. How was immigration history discussed in your schooling experiences? What about in your own family and community?
3. Did you learn about your own ethnic group's immigration to the US in school, at home, in your community? How and in what way?
4. Have you ever been asked to trace your family's roots for a school project? Were you able to do so? What resources did you draw upon to complete this task?
5. What do you know about recent immigration patterns in the last 10 to 20 years? How do you perceive it to be alike or different than immigration in the early 20th century or prior?
6. How and when do you learn about and teach current immigration issues? What sources do you privilege most?

Next, complete Activity 3 at the end of this chapter. Revisit your responses to the Prereading Questions and the activity after reading the chapter. Part 1 of this chapter provides definitions and background related to the intersection of race and immigration. Part 2 provides activities for teachers and students to explore imagined histories through a CRTA lens.

PART 1: DEFINITIONS AND BACKGROUND

During the 2016 election, the issue of "the border" and immigration resurfaced in ways that amplified the constant ebb and flow of anti-immigrant rhetoric. Amidst promises to build a 70-billion-dollar wall between the US-Mexico border, an act that is as costly as it is ineffective, Donald Trump, during one of his first official bids for the presidency, made a statement about Mexican immigrants coming to the US. He stated, "They are not our friend, believe me. They're bringing drugs. They're bringing crime. They're rapists. And some, I assume, are good people."

While this quote and other quotes made during the 2016 election garnered shock and disbelief by some, this sentiment about Black and Brown immigrants is hardly new. The US has been historically biased against non–Western European, non-White immigrant groups through both de jure (by law) and de facto (by practice) racial segregation and resegregation policies and practices.

For example, between 1910 and 1920, President Woodrow Wilson sent 110,000 National Guardsmen to the Texas border in an effort to assuage Whites who made exaggerated claims about the so-called dangerous and economically burdensome immigrants arriving from Mexico. Thousands of people of Mexican descent, including US citizens, were displaced and murdered by border patrol agents and militia groups on the US side of the Texas-Mexico border in what was called "La Matanza," or "the Killing." This is but one example in the history of the US where people of Mexican descent experienced violence, murder, and forced expulsion from their homes, jobs, and communities in the southwest US from Texas to California as a result of the system of racism and White supremacy.

Seventy years prior, in 1848, as a result of the Treaty of Guadalupe Hidalgo, many Mexicans living in the border region of what is now south Texas in the Rio Grande valley became legal residents of Texas. In Texas, the saying for ancestors and descendants of these families is, "We didn't cross the border; the border crossed us." White settlers were encouraged through White affirmative action policies like monetary incentives and political backing to populate this region. The intermingling of these groups formed a complex interplay of bicultural and bilingual practices socially, economically, and politically. South Texas, in particular, continues to embody the intersecting and conflicting historical tensions of colonization and the richness of living in two (or more) languages and cultures.

The hegemony of English and the centering of Whiteness, however, cannot be underestimated. While the region continues to boast some of the best dual and bilingual language programs in the country, policies and practices are still fraught with histories of anti-Spanish, anti-Mexican, anti-indigenous practices of segregation, racial violence, and deculturalization. A legacy of fear, for example, reverberates among Latinx parents who are now in their 50s, 60s, and 70s as they were routinely punished and abused as children by White teachers for speaking Spanish in schools. These language tensions persist as a result of racial and economic segregation. For example, affluent White families in this region have better access to high-quality dual language, Spanish/English programs, while funding is limited for lower income, Spanish-speaking immigrants who seek proficiency in English and the maintenance of their heritage language(s). In this way, two languages are seen as an asset for affluent White families while Spanish is seen as a liability for working-class Mexican immigrants who have little opportunity to maintain Spanish in school.

The diverse landscape of the border region and the everyday realities of border crossing experiences in the southwest US are largely unknown or ignored in current public discourse. In Nuevo Laredo, Mexico, and Laredo, Texas, US, for example, children cross the border daily from both sides to visit friends and attend school on *el otro lado* (the other side). For residents in this region on both sides of the border, living in two languages, two cultures, and two worlds is an everyday reality.

The lack of awareness of this phenomenon compounded with other myths about immigration allows anti-immigrant sentiments to persist. For example, anti-immigrant rhetoric was popular among conservatives in the 2016 election, but the US has been experiencing negative immigration from Mexico. That is to say, more people are leaving than arriving, providing little rationale for harsher border protections.

Myths and misinformation about immigration are reproduced in the media, schools, criminal justice system, and voting booths, cultivating ongoing anti-immigrant hate rhetoric, biased curricula, and a shoring up of arguments for voter ID laws, immigration status checkpoints, and the detainment and mass incarceration of immigrants without trial, including children. This chapter seeks to illuminate stories that are often overlooked, silenced, or omitted in studying immigration and employ a CRTA lens to consider the intersectional issues of race and immigration in constructing and maintaining imagined histories. Atrocities related to immigration are grounded in the system of racism—racism that is all too often seen as a part of our distant past rather than our existing present.

Imagined Histories of Immigration: Critiquing the Single Story

An oft-cited African proverb states, "Until the story of the hunt is told by the lion, the tale of the hunt will always glorify the hunter." In other words, those in power will write history in their favor and likeness. I use the term *imagined histories* in this chapter to describe the "single story" (Adichie, 2009) and "grand narratives" of immigration that permeate public discourse and school curricula in the US.

Imagined histories of immigration are a form of historical revisionism created and controlled by those with social, political, and economic power. My use of imagined histories is couched in Benedict Anderson's (1983) notion of imagined communities, which is the idea that capitalism and mass media create single, grand narratives that subjects (people and groups) anchor their ideological stances and practices to. These grand narratives are woven into the fabric of social memory. When considering schools, the term *imagined histories* is helpful because it makes clear that the stories in school curricula are based on a limited set of decontextualized information that constructs a false majoritarian and colonialistic narrative about immigration.

These stories create a collective social memory loosely based on facts of what immigration was historically. These imagined histories then impact how the public views immigration today, pitting current immigration issues against a romanticized past. As Anderson suggests, both nationalism and capitalism play a primary role in constructing the imaginary.

Textbooks and the publishing industry are one such example. In Texas, textbooks are typically adopted universally across the state, which means a big profit for the publishers whose textbooks are chosen. For this reason, it behooves the publishers to print curriculum that is popular to the social and political orientations of one of their most lucrative customers. Also, because publishers are profit driven, they tend to produce what is in highest demand. So, the story of immigration Texas chooses to tell is often the story that gets told across the country.

In 2015, Texas history textbooks were called into question when enslaved Africans brought to the US via the transatlantic slave trade were referred to as "workers" rather than enslaved human beings. This discussion of African "workers" was positioned in a chapter focusing on immigration, implying that enslaved Africans had chosen to come to the Americas by their own free will. Implying that enslaved Africans were immigrants results in erasure of how the system of White supremacy impacted the movement of people. It took a parent complaint that eventually went viral on social media to push the publisher to edit the page.

Loewen (1995), in *Lies My Teacher Told Me*, suggests we learn the "twigs" of history: oversimplified, decontextualized lists of dates or events that rarely address the deep structures of why and how events occurred.

Rarely are we asked to question the short accounts or lists of facts on the page. Howard Zinn's work, most notably *A People's History of the United States* (2003), questions the learning and content of history curricula, emphasizing that stories are told from the perspective of the colonizer rather than the "people."

Immigration units in schools, for example, tend to center the experiences of White Europeans, especially the *Mayflower* Pilgrims in their quest for economic opportunity and religious freedom in the 17th century and Ellis Island arrivals seeking the "American dream" in the early 20th century. Other equally arduous and valiant immigrant stories are often omitted or addressed cursorily. Moreover, it is rare that immigration units reach modern-day experiences, especially those of immigrants of color.

One of my students, a White male teacher in suburban Philadelphia, shared how reading Loewen's and Zinn's work changed his mind about teaching immigration entirely. "I don't treat our history curriculum as the sole provider of information anymore. My second graders ask critical questions of the text and we seek multiple perspectives on historical events. They ask better questions than I do because they haven't been immersed in the single story for as long. We study current events related to immigration, including interviews with local community members." Providing multiple perspectives like this is vital as it reveals the ideologically constructed nature of text (Ciardiello, 2004; Freire, 1970; Giroux, 1992). "Text" meaning discursive events, oral or written, that are used in the process of meaning-making.

Who Is the Model Immigrant?

Imagined histories also construct a single story of who is the model or ideal immigrant. This romanticized portraiture is often envisioned as a European immigrant arriving through Ellis Island from 1892 to 1954. Stories from this "golden era" of immigration are permeated by accounts of brave stowaways, businessmen, and families scraping together their last pennies for a ticket to America.

In one of my graduate classes I plan an in-class activity where teachers are asked to design a mini-lesson on immigration. I do not specify a particular time period in history for the lesson. Only once in my eight years of assigning this in-class activity has a group developed a mini-lesson around current immigration issues. The activities always focus on Ellis Island.

The one exception was a mini-lesson created by a group of teachers with a large population of Nepali refugees in their community. Their mini-lesson focused on the theme of displacement and family. For these teachers, current issues of immigration were an everyday reality for the children and families in their school. What happens when teachers lack these firsthand experiences? Who benefits from a curriculum focused on Ellis Island narratives as the primary source of immigrant stories? If these stories represent the ideal immigrant story, how does it impact views of immigrants from Mexico or refugees from Syria, for example? What impact do imagined histories have on perceptions of immigrants?

In addition to the focus on European immigrant groups, history books tend to privilege the stories of those who are perceived to have assimilated, including an imagined voluntary and expedient process for learning English. While there is some agency involved in whether immigrant groups choose to retain linguistic and cultural practices of their home countries, how immigrants assimilate is largely based on their reception by their new community, and assimilation can look different depending on where in the US immigrants settle. For example, are neighborhoods in the new community largely segregated? Are language services available? Is the community accustomed to new arrivals or is it historically homogenous? In what way do the linguistic, cultural, religious, and familial practices align with the receiving community?

My research with Somali Bantu refugees in south Texas revealed a definition of assimilation that involved hybridity, that is to say, the receiving community valued aspects of living in two (or more) languages and cultures. For this reason, bilingualism and biculturalism were supported in ways that are not in other parts of the US. Somali Bantu refugees who were relocated to Michigan, for example, experienced different expectations for assimilation.

It still holds true that most immigrant groups lose their first language by the third generation regardless of where in the US they relocate. Race also plays a factor in whether immigrant groups are able to assimilate seamlessly. Immigrants of color are more likely to experience the same forms of discrimination as US-born people of color with the added, intersectional experience of being an immigrant (Rong & Brown, 2002).

The racialization of immigrants, or how they are perceived racially by Whites, makes it difficult for immigrants of color to assimilate, even if they work to take on the linguistic and cultural practices of the majority. In this way, depending on the racial views of the time, immigrants are subject to racism regardless of how much they attempt to assimilate. Irish and Italian immigrants experienced discrimination and hardship, but also benefited from the evolving definition of race over time. They were able to "become White" based on the socially constructed notions of race.

Immigrant quota laws have historically privileged European immigration and demonized immigrants that posed a perceived and typically unfounded fear of national security or economic burden (see, for example, the Immigration Act of 1924, which excluded Asian immigrants entirely). Most ancestors of White Irish and Italian immigrants today are viewed as White, even if it was not the case historically. Other immigrant groups such as the Japanese have been perpetually racialized. After the bombing of Pearl Harbor, for example, 120,000 Japanese immigrants, most of whom were citizens, were placed in internment camps in 10 different locations in the US in the interest of national security. They lost their homes, businesses, and belongings. German and Italian citizens were not placed in camps even though Germany and Italy were also considered threats to the US national security during this time period.

Another more recent example is the experience of Muslims after the 9/11 terrorist attacks in New York. Muslims and groups such as Sikhs, who are often mistaken for being Muslim, experienced increased threats of racial violence. Muslim Americans were targeted by Homeland Security through wiretaps and surveillance made possible by the Patriot Act signed into law in 2001. Islamophobia, the unfounded fear of people who practice Islam, was refueled during the 2016 election when then candidate Donald Trump cited Muslims as a danger to US national security, even though US-born White, right-wing extremists have committed more terrorist acts on US soil than Muslims (Neiwert, 2017).

During his first few weeks in office, President Trump's "Muslim ban," which was based on this unfounded fear, stranded or displaced hundreds of Muslim citizens and documented immigrants or refugees. Some were left stranded in the very locations they were fleeing to escape persecution.

Black and Brown immigrants continue to be characterized as perpetual Others in the US regardless of how many generations their families have been in the US or how much they attempt to assimilate. History textbooks do address the persecution and poor treatment of the Puritans, Quakers, Irish, and Italians, but when will our history books include the accounts of how Muslim children and families were impacted by Islamophobia after 9/11? Or, will children in other countries learn how Muslim families had to flee the US in order to escape religious persecution?

Citizenship: Who Are Americans?

The notion of citizenship is almost always at the center of conversations about immigration; however, the notion of citizenship has changed and does not apply to all groups in the same way. For example, as I write this chapter, the people of Puerto Rico, who are US citizens, are still without power and are being denied hurricane relief after experiencing both category 4 and a category 5 hurricanes in a few short weeks. Puerto Ricans have been US citizens since 1917 as a result of the Jones-Shafroth Act, which allowed Puerto Rican residents to retain their Puerto Rican citizenship while becoming US citizens.

Tens of thousands of Puerto Ricans were drafted into and served in World War II. Eventually, strategic military bases were built there. The process of giving citizenship in exchange for strategic access for military operations and resources is a common practice among colonizing nations. Colonialism, in general, is responsible for much of the world's ongoing migration, diaspora, and economic insecurity.

In *Harvest of Empire*, Gonzalez (2011) discusses how the US's involvement in the Caribbean, Central, and South America, including the support of dictators who promised to increase the economic bottom line of the US companies, decimated once thriving countries. Margarita Engle (2016), in *Silver People: Voices from the Panama Canal*, illuminates this phenomenon through a verse novel exploring how the intersections of race, immigration, economics, and capitalism stripped Panama of its economic resources and exploited workers in dangerous and sometimes deadly working conditions, all for the US strategic trading and profit for the building of the Panama Canal. Because it is written in verse, teachers can use this book or excerpts from it with any age group to discuss race, the movement of people, colonialism, and issues of environmental and social justice. See the resources at the end of this chapter for lesson plans using this text.

Few curricula address what it actually takes to become a citizen other than a cursory look at citizenship tests. What paperwork is needed to travel to the US? Can anyone get a visa? What if you want to work? How long can you stay? What if you are a refugee seeking asylum? How long is the process?

Also absent from this conversation about citizenship is the phenomenon of transnational migration or "transnationalism." Sánchez (2007) defines transnationalism as "various systems or relationships that span two or more nations, including sustained and meaningful flows of people, money, labor, goods, information, advice, care, and love" (Sánchez, 2007, p. 493). Sánchez and Kasun (2012) expand this definition in their work with transnational children and families, explaining that "transnationalism embodies social practices by people who engage more than one national context with some depth of familiarity, through activities that include maintaining family ties in multiple countries, possible visits to the sending country (and sometimes decisions for part or all of the family to return to the sending country), and the exchange of goods, information, and accumulated local knowledges between countries" (p. 75).

In this way, the notion of citizenship and belonging becomes less nation or territory based and instead, resembles a "people-state" (p. 71) of transborder communities, whereby mobility and movement are determined by social and economic opportunities and survival. Laws like Arizona SB 1070 seek to criminalize transnational practices in the US. The interests of the powerful, however, are served both by the movement of people, cheap labor, and the subsequent criminalization of migration with laws like Arizona SB 1070, which was partially written and received full political support from for-profit prisons. In this way, US corporations are free to benefit and function transnationally, but the workers who move from place to place to survive, and ultimately contribute to the wealth of these companies, are criminalized.

Children and families who live transnational lives bring much in the way of knowledge and experience to US classrooms, but rarely are these funds of knowledge taken up. Sánchez and Kasun (2012) explain that "the transnational social space in which these children and youth are raised is often filled with deep understandings of geopolitical contexts that span multiple national perspectives, personal navigation of physical borders (both with and without authorized documentation), and complex social networks in more than one country sustained through ever-changing media applications" (p. 72). In this way, the everyday lived experiences of more than 200 million transnationals across the globe are omitted from conversations about immigration experiences in schools.

In critiquing the imagined histories of immigration, it is important to recognize and acknowledge that immigration stories serve as a badge of honor for families of all racial and ethnic backgrounds. These stories are used to convey strength and perseverance to new generations. I use the term *imagined* not because the stories of White, Western European immigrants are without merit, truth, hard work, or sacrifice. I both value and respect my own European family histories of immigration and perseverance.

"Imagined" is not intended as an indictment of *individual* families' stories or experiences, but rather an indictment of the *system* of White supremacy that supports one story that is told and sold in most history curricula; the story that revises, omits, or misrepresents the stories of immigrants of color and contributes to deep-seated, anti-immigrant rhetoric that forms the foundation for xenophobia, Islamophobia, and other intersectional forms of racism and bias perpetrated against immigrants. In other words, I emphasize that I do not seek to erase stories, but to advocate for an equitable and critical telling of histor*ies*. I urge teachers to privilege the telling of histories in ways that acknowledge systems of power, plurality, and context.

Disrupting Imagined Histories of Immigration Through Counterstories

Counter-storytelling is one way to employ CRTA when teaching immigration. Counter-storytelling is "a method of telling the stories of those people whose experiences are not often told" (Solorzano & Yosso, 2002, p. 26). Counterstories challenge imagined histories of immigration by making space for new, parallel, or contradicting stories. Counterstories can be stories that have been silenced or omitted, or composite stories designed to illustrate an experience that contradicts the majoritarian narrative.

Adichie (2009) explains that when single stories of people or events are told over and over again, we develop narrow understandings of the world. It is only through counterstories (DeCuir & Dixon, 2004; Roy & Roxas, 2011) that we cultivate a more reflexive, pluralistic, and complex view of the world. Sleeter (2016) advocates for White teachers to engage in critical family histories to interrogate how their own stories align or disrupt the single story told in school. Zinn (1994/2002) advocates for putting the history of the people in conversation with majoritarian stories in order to show the power structures at work in whose story is told, why, and for what purpose. He emphasizes that the telling of histories is never neutral.

To accompany counter-storytelling, teachers working from a CRTA approach can draw from the study of critical historiography. Historiography is the study of how history comes to be. For example, who writes history books for schools? What is their educational background and interest? What sources are used? What and whose knowledge is privileged? Critical historiography, like other critical approaches, seeks to engage the readers of history in the process of questioning the power relationships at play when interacting with texts. This approach usurps the notion that students are passive learners of history, awaiting teachers or textbooks to deposit knowledge. Using this approach helps educators and students to ask why stories are omitted instead of whether one story is more important than another.

The challenge of critical approaches to history is that they require a relearning of that which some privilege as truth. This process of challenging long-held imagined stories can often place learners in a place of disequilibrium. Ultimately, though, it holds liberating possibilities for cultivating democratic dispositions.

The National Council for the Social Studies (NCSS, 2018) purports that "the aim of social studies is the promotion of civic competence—the knowledge, intellectual processes, and democratic dispositions required of students to be active and engaged participants in public life." Teachers employing CRTA meet and exceed this expectation. The sections that follow provide counterstories for common immigration stories told in schools and offer critical questions and approaches for using them in classrooms.

Angel Island and Immigration Detention Centers

The story of the Angel Island Immigration Station is an example of a counterstory to the commonly studied Ellis Island. The Angel Island Immigration Station operated off the coast of San Francisco, California, from 1910 to 1940 in order to monitor and detain immigrants from Asia. Unlike Ellis Island, which operated from 1892 to 1954 and only rejected 1–3% of arriving immigrants, Angel Island rejected at least 18%.

The monitoring system developed at the Angel Island Immigration Station is an example of an early immigration detention center. Many immigrants arriving to Angel Island spent days or months in detention while Ellis Island arrivals were released within days. A teacher working from a CRTA stance can integrate the story of Angel Island into the curriculum in ways that allow students to critique the privileging of Ellis Island stories. Teachers can also explore with their students the ways detention center models have evolved from Angel Island, to Japanese internment camps, to Braceros reception centers, to current detention centers like the one in Berks County, Pennsylvania.

Currently, the US detains approximately 300,000 to 450,000 immigrants per year. Most are detained without trial for weeks, months, or years.

Critical Questions for the Classroom

- Who is placed in immigration detention centers?
- Why and how long are they detained?
- How do detained immigrants seek help, support, or legal counsel?
- What rights are they afforded or denied?
- What happens to families and children who are placed in these centers?
- What are the conditions?
- Immigration detention centers have become a lucrative business that draws primarily from US tax dollars. Which companies and CEOs profit from the arrest and detainment of immigrants, documented or otherwise?

DNA Histories as Counterstories and Tracing Family Trees

Forty percent of Americans can trace their ancestry through Ellis Island. This may sound like a lot, but imagine this statistic applied to your classroom. If only 40% or fewer of your students can trace their roots through Ellis Island, *60%* of the class has other ancestral immigration experiences, forced or voluntary, to explore.

Consider for example, the students in your classroom whose ancestors were brought to the US through the transatlantic slave trade. Conversely, in a classroom with a majority of students with roots in Ellis Island, in what ways are they given the false notion that their families' history is the norm? How does this impact their views of other immigrant experiences? With advances in genetic testing, DNA has now become a way of discovering immigration and migration histories in new ways, especially for descendants of enslaved Africans, although not everyone has access to these expensive tests.

Unlike the detailed records kept of immigrants passing through Ellis Island, few records were kept detailing the names and dates of enslaved Africans who were brought to the US through the transatlantic slave trade. For this reason, genetic tests offer a way for some US Blacks to finally trace their roots. These tests also allow people with European ancestry to have expanded views of their ancestry beyond public records.

In the classroom, consider how genetic tests both inform or complicate discussions of race and immigration, especially when genetic tests attempt to address racial heritage.

Critical Questions for the Classroom

- Given the complicated nature of DNA genetic testing, how should we understand or make use of genetic test results?
- Does it build tolerance for Whites to learn they have ancestors of color?
- In what ways does it benefit Whites to learn of indigenous heritage?
- Does it inform or complicate understandings of White privilege?
- For example, can a White person who discovers a Navajo ancestor claim oppression or deny White privilege?
- How do these genetic tests benefit people of color?

In Chapter 2, the notion that race is socially constructed, not biological, is explored. If race is not biological, how does one make sense of recent trends of tracing racial heritage promoted by genealogical companies and television network series such as *Finding Your Roots*? In order to determine your racial heritage, these genetic testing companies trace migration patterns of humans by taking samples of DNA from regions of the world and comparing samples. These are compared with the DNA samples provided by customers and used to make an estimation about genetic origins. The accuracy and reliability of these tests has been questioned.

For example, in some regions few samples are taken, making it difficult to garner precise results. Additionally, the categories used to define and categorize ethnic origins are grounded in existing socially constructed labels. In other words, nonscientific, socially constructed labels are used to investigate race; thus, the findings make use of these nonscientific, socially constructed labels to describe racial heritage. Also, there are numerous examples of people receiving different results from different DNA testing companies.

On the other hand, access to DNA information has made it possible for people whose ancestors arrived to the US through the transatlantic slave trade to trace their roots back to specific regions of Africa. Few records were kept for enslaved Africans, and thus many US Blacks have difficulty tracing their ancestral roots and participating in family tree assignments in school. Part 2 continues this discussion by providing suggestions for conversations and activities with students. Given that family ancestry activities are often included in immigration units, these questions as they relate to race, biology, and history should be included.

Labor Exploitation and Human Trafficking: A Needed Counterstory

Teachers working from a CRTA perspective should consider the power dynamics at work when studying a particular topic. Labor exploitation and human trafficking are inextricably linked to immigration experiences past and present. Immigrants, because they lack protections under US policies and laws, are most vulnerable to labor exploitation.

The exploitation of human labor has and continues to fuel the US economy from chattel slavery to indentured servitude, to modern practices that surreptitiously entrap, imprison, and abuse vulnerable populations. The imagined histories of immigrations protect and feed labor exploitation by dividing the public through anti-immigrant sentiments that blame immigrants for their experiences or spread false narratives of crime or economic burden. If we study and are to be horrified, for example, by the abhorrent labor conditions and experiences of the Irish and Italians, then we should be equally horrified by the same practices that continue in the agricultural and manufacturing industry across the US.

Gabriel Thompson (2011) exposes immigrant labor exploitation in the lettuce fields, poultry factories, flower markets, and takeout delivery workers in his book *Working in the Shadows*. Working alongside both documented and undocumented workers, Thompson, a White journalist who speaks fluent Spanish with no experience in any of these jobs, was consistently offered higher-level positions when applying to work. Thompson debunks the idea that hard work and obeying the law leads to prosperity and upward social mobility. He also identifies the harsh treatment and low pay of workers who were often unable to seek medical care or were afraid to notify authorities for fear of their work visas being denied or revoked.

More recently, in 2017, the popular television series *American Crime* addressed how labor exploitation and human trafficking go hand in hand. Women have always been particularly vulnerable to sex trafficking and abuse as laborers throughout the world. The US is no safer. According to the American Civil Liberties Union (ACLU, n.d.-b), "In the United States, victims of trafficking are almost exclusively immigrants, and mostly immigrant women." There are 14,500 to 17,500 people trafficked into the US each year, although these figures do not account for the total number of people trafficked *within* the US. In order to prevent trafficking, the ACLU advocates for stronger legislative protections for workers, especially those who are most vulnerable, such as the undocumented. When false claims of immigrants taking US jobs speak louder than the ongoing issues of labor exploitation and human trafficking, these atrocities continue. In what ways are schools responsible for shaping the narrative toward justice? How can teachers help to educate the public?

The notion that immigrants take the jobs of US citizens is a false claim but tends to gain traction when economic times are hard. The imagined histories of immigration told in schools ignore how immigrants have been recruited through special government programs to come to the US and work when economic conditions were such that workers were scarce. From 1942 to 1964, the Braceros Program, which was part of the Mexican Farm Labor Agreement with US and Mexico and extended through an amendment to the Agriculture Act of 1949, brought more than 5.5 million workers to the US.

In the agreement between the US and Mexico, the US had to commit to healthy living conditions and exclusion from Jim Crow laws. The US's mistreatment of people of color was well known, and Mexico sought to protect its citizens who were coming to the US for employment. It did not take long for the US to skirt the agreement and subject workers to segregated, poor living conditions for little pay.

Additionally, the braceros (workers) from Mexico were subject to "reception centers" much like those on Ellis or Angel Island. As many of the workers extended their temporary visas and built lives and families in the US, changes in the economy and growing xenophobia led the Immigration and Naturalization Service (INS) to create Operation Wetback, which allowed for mass deportations of Mexicans, hundreds of whom were citizens or in the US legally.

The practice of deporting en masse continues today. I recall working with Latinx families in Nebraska. Children whose parents worked in the beef packing industry were often fearful of returning to their homes to find their parents deported. What was previously called INS (Immigration and Naturalization Service) until 2003, now called Immigration and Customs Enforcement (ICE), would arrive on a factory site and load workers into vans without allowing them to prove their citizenship or legal work status. This resulted in citizens detained in border prisons in the US, in Mexico, or in illegal deportations.

Some of these workers had never lived in Mexico or had only lived there as a child. Imagine being ripped from your job, placed in a detention center for weeks or months, and then ending up in a foreign country to which you have no connections or access to funds to return home. Later, when I became an ELL (English language learner) teacher, the fear instilled in immigrant families by anti-immigrant sentiments and ICE's illegal deportations made it difficult to connect with families.

Parents of my students were afraid to come to school even if they were documented. Home visits were also challenging as families were reluctant to open the door to school officials. Teachers can either work toward justice or contribute to this fear. One of my preservice teachers once asked, "Can I notify the police if I think a student is illegal?" What type of learning environment does it create when teachers become complicit in state violence? In what way does cultivating fear among immigrant families undermine the pursuit of a just and democratic society?

Learning about, celebrating, and fighting for workers' rights is one way teachers can engage CRTA practices that support immigrant children and families. A group of my graduate students created a unit on labor unions instead of using the district-provided curriculum on the Industrial Revolution. In the unit, elementary students studied how Irish and Italian immigrants fought for labor unions and child labor laws; how Jewish women fought for women workers' rights in the New York Shirtwaist strike; the story of Cesar Chavez's and Dolores Huerta's creation of the National Farmworkers Association, which later became the United Farm Workers (UFW); about the United Auto Workers in Detroit, Michigan; and about teachers union movements related to social justice in Seattle and Chicago. These movements were used to explore elements of the Industrial Revolution, the expansion of corporations and globalization, and the impact on workers and education. Students also had opportunities to interview local community members involved in workers' rights and unions to explore how organizing and grassroots movements contribute to justice and equity.

PART 2: CLASSROOM ACTIVITIES

Part 2 provides suggestions for educators to begin the work of addressing imagined histories of immigration through a CRTA perspective in the classroom. The primary challenge for educators is to first disrupt their own imagined histories of immigration and then seek resources to disrupt those present in the curriculum. Districts often look to quick-fix, standardized curricula to ensure all children obtain the same knowledge. Unfortunately, profit, not altruism or activism, is the primary goal of large publishing companies that produce these curricula.

Profits are made by manufacturing curricula that is general or meeting a current trend, not aspirational curricula that challenges the status quo. For this reason, it is unsurprising that companies like Scholastic, for example, tend to reproduce the same tropes in curriculum. On their website, for example, a collection of resources focused on "Immigration: Yesterday and Today" is advertised, but very little resources in the teacher's guide and resources provide in-depth information about "today's" immigrants, especially experiences of border crossing and transborder experiences. Resources related to Ellis Island, however, are abundant. The Grade 6–12 book list does offer *The Circuit* by Francisco Jimenez (1997) and *Ask Me No Questions* by Marina Budhos (2006), both of which are excellent books for teaching immigration; however, scores of books have been written in the last 10–20 years that are absent from Scholastic's collection.

Where are the stories of families arriving from El Salvador or Mexico? What are the real issues these immigrants encounter, and why do they come to the US? Which books address bilingualism, biculturalism, and border crossing? Where can teachers find information about what it means to be a refugee from Syria, Iraq, or Somalia? How do teachers who have little experience with undocumented children and families find resources to support these topics in the classroom? Given that Scholastic is one of the largest providers for teacher resources in the US, how do they set the tone for what is privileged in the teaching of immigration?

While classroom teachers may have little or no control over publishing decisions and the district-selected curriculum, they can strive to be careful consumers of these resources. Teachers working from a CRTA perspective can take action by serving on curriculum committees and seeking resources from peer-reviewed research, grassroots teacher-created curricula, and justice-oriented publishing companies like Rethinking Schools. Teachers can modify the existing curriculum to question imagined histories, monolingualism, assimilation, and deculturalization.

CRTA educators can also engage students in activities that address the intersections of race and immigration "yesterday and today" and problematize the myth of meritocracy and the American dream. Further, CRTA educators can honor all immigration stories by critiquing the single story. The following activities support teachers in this process. These activities can supplement or replace existing immigration units as all standards and competencies can be addressed.

Activity 1: Vetting and Citizenship: Past and Present

Using the two-part episode "It's Working Out Very Nicely" and "Heavy Vetting" from the podcast *This American Life* from February 2017 (https://www.thisamericanlife.org/609/its-working-out-very-nicely and https://www.thisamericanlife.org/609/its-working-out-very-nicely/act-two), explore how immigration issues played out after the 2016 election. The *This American Life* podcast provides details about the vetting process for immigrants and features stories of refugees and immigrants.

Consider the ways immigrants are currently "vetted" and compare the process with that of the Ellis Island Immigration Inspection Station, the Angel Island Immigration Station, and the Braceros reception centers. Include in this conversation current immigration vetting and detention centers in states such as Pennsylvania, Texas, New Hampshire, or Nebraska or ask students to research these centers on their own. On the US Immigration and Customs Enforcement (ICE) website, you can search for detention centers by state.

Incorporate literature such as Diane Guerrero's 2016 book *In the Country We Love*, *Super Cilantro Girl* by Juan Felipe Herrera (2003), and *Mama's Nightingale: A Story of Immigration and Separation* by Edwidge Danticat (2015) to discuss how families are often separated during immigration. *This American Life* also featured the story of a young man attempting to come to the US via a lottery process that places people who win on the short list for visas. Use this podcast episode to explore the multiple challenges people face trying to come to the US: https://www.thisamericanlife.org/560/abdi-and-the-golden-ticket.

Activity 2: Rewriting the American Dream

Use the full version of Langston Hughes's 1935 poem "Let America Be America Again" (2004) to introduce a unit on immigration. Find other poems and quotes related to the American dream.

- Discuss and define what the American dream is. Is it representative of all immigrant experiences?
- Do all immigrants have access to the American dream? In what ways is it possible, not possible?
- How do grand narratives like the American dream amplify some stories while silencing others?
- Do different generations of immigrants envision the American dream in new or different ways?
- How could we rewrite the American dream in a way that is more accurate?

Find first-person accounts from refugees coming to the US over the last several decades (e.g., refugees from Syria, Guatemala, Somalia). Interview families about their perceptions of the American dream or invite immigrants in your local community to speak on a panel in your classroom or at your school.

Activity 3: Immigration Privilege Survey

Use this survey to explore the intersections of race and today's immigration. Teachers should take the survey with their students.

Please place a check next to the statements that generally apply to you:

1. __ Immigrants from my family's ethnic group or country of origin are represented in history textbooks and/or curricula used in most schools.
2. __ I can access children's or young adult literature portraying stories of my family's ethnic group and their immigration experiences.
3. __ If my immigrant ancestors learned English, they were able to eventually blend in to American society.
4. __ My immigrant ancestors are portrayed in textbooks, films, and popular culture as hardworking people who persevered.
5. __ I can move to another community in the US and be relatively sure to find food, clothing, and music I'm used to.
6. __ If I am looking for a home to rent or buy, I can be sure a real estate agent will not discriminate against me based my accent, skin color, or religion.
7. __ If I speak a Standard English dialect, people assume I was born in the United States.
8. __ I can easily locate a place of worship near my home where I can practice my chosen faith in the language in which I am most comfortable.
9. __ I am able to wear an article of my own faith without fear of being called a terrorist or seen as different.
10. __ I can send my children to play at a friend's house without worrying about how their language, beliefs, or cultural practices will be perceived.
11. __ I can be sure that if I am pulled over, the police officer will assume I am a citizen.
12. __ As long as I have a driver's license, I can travel domestically in the US or get pulled over for a minor traffic violation without the fear of being deported or having my citizenship questioned.
13. __ I can go to work each day as a documented citizen without the fear of being illegally deported.
14. __ If I am the victim of a crime, I can feel safe contacting the police for help.

Follow-up activities to the Immigration Privilege Survey can include:

- Research Arizona Senate Bill (SB) 1070 and House Bill (HB) 2162, which is being challenged by the American Civil Liberties Union. Similar bills have been passed in 6 other states. These bills are considered to be some of the harshest anti-immigrant legislation in the country. According to the ACLU (n.d.-a), these bills "invite rampant racial profiling against Latinos, Asian-Americans and others presumed to be 'foreign' based on how they look or sound. They also authorize police to demand papers proving citizenship or immigration status from anyone they stop and suspect of being in the country unlawfully."

- Critiquing our curriculum: Talk to your students about how immigration is taught in school. Share your own experiences. With your students, research how immigration is taught in the school or district. What do you see and hear in politics and the media about immigration today? What images come to mind? Do these images differ from what you learned in school? If so, how? Ask students to do an inventory of immigration-related materials. Students can use the data in math lessons to explore percentages or other descriptive statistics. Based on the inventories, explore how schools, teachers, families, communities, textbooks, and media impact how we learn about immigration. Whose immigration stories get told? Why? Who gets to decide? What stories are missing? How do you know what's missing? In what ways do we romanticize the immigration past but critique the immigration present?

RECOMMENDED RESOURCES

Books and Articles

Budhos, M. T. (2006). *Ask me no questions.* New York, NY: Atheneum Books for Young Readers.

Danticat, E. (2015). *Mama's nightingale: A story of immigration and separation.* New York, NY: Dial Books for Young Readers.

Guerrero, D., & Burford, M. (2016). *In the country we love: My family divided.* New York, NY: St. Martin's.

Herrera, J. F. (2003). *Super cilantro girl.* New York, NY: Children's Book Press.

Jiménez, F. (1997). *The Circuit: Stories from the life of a migrant child.* Boston, MA: Houghton Mifflin.

Kendi, I. X. (2017). *Stamped from the beginning: The definitive history of racist ideas in America*. New York, NY: Nation Books.

Lai, T. (2011). *Inside out and back again.* New York, NY: HarperCollins.

Skerrett, A. (2015). *Teaching transnational youth: Literacy and education in a changing world.* New York, NY: Teachers College Press.

Vélez-Ibáñez. C. G., & Heyman, J. (2017). *The U.S.-Mexico transborder region: Cultural dynamics and historical interactions.* Tucson: University of Arizona Press.

Zinn, H. (2003). *A people's history of the United States*. New York, NY: Harper & Row.

Podcasts and Videos

Glass, I. (2017, February 3). *This American life: It's working out very nicely* [Audio podcast]. Retrieved from https://www.thisamericanlife.org/609/its-working-out-very-nicely

Websites

CIVIC End Isolation. (2017). *Immigration detention map & statistics.* Retrieved from http://www.endisolation.org/resources/immigration-detention/

Edman, J. (n.d.). Teacher's Guide: *Silver People: Voices from the Panama Canal* by Margarita Engle. Stanford Program on International and Cross-Cultural Education. Retrieved February

2018 from http://claspprograms.org/uploads/Silve_People_Teachers_Guide_Draft-cover-1471967718.pdf

REFERENCES

Adichie, C. N. (2009). *The danger of a single story* [Video file]. Retrieved from http://www.ted.com/talks/chimamanda_adichie_the_danger_of_a_single_story?language=en

American Civil Liberties Union. (n.d.-a). *Arizona's SB 1070.* Retrieved February 2018 from https://www.aclu.org/issues/immigrants-rights/state-and-local-immigration-laws/arizonas-sb-1070

American Civil Liberties Union. (n.d.-b). *Human trafficking: Modern enslavement of immigrant women in the United States.* Retrieved March 2018 from https://www.aclu.org/other/human-trafficking-modern-enslavement-immigrant-women-united-states

Anderson, B. (1983). *Imagined communities: Reflections on the origin and spread of nationalism.* New York, NY: Verso.

Ciardiello A. V. (2004). Democracy's young heroes: An instructional model of critical literacy practices. *The Reading Teacher, 58*(2), pp. 138–147.

DeCuir, J. T., & Dixson, A. D. (2004). So when it comes out, they aren't surprised that it is there: Using critical race theory as a tool of analysis of race and racism in education. *Educational Researcher, 33*(5) 26–31. Retrieved from https://eric.ed.gov/?id=EJ727581

Engle, M. (2016). *Silver people: Voices from the Panama Canal.* Boston, MA: HMH Books for Young Readers.

Freire, P. (1970). *Pedagogy of the oppressed.* New York, NY: Herder and Herder.

Giroux, H. (1992). Border pedagogy and the politics of postmodernism. *Education and Society, 9*(1), 23–38.

González, J. (2011). *Harvest of Empire.* New York: Penguin Paperbacks.

Hughes, L. (2004). *Let America be America again and other poems* (1st Vintage Books ed.). New York, NY: Vintage.

Loewen, James W. (2008)> *Lies my teacher told me: Everything your American history textbook got wrong.* New York: New Press.

National Council for the Social Studies. (2018). *National Curriculum Standards for Social Studies: Executive summary.* Retrieved from https://www.socialstudies.org/standards/execsummary

Neiwert, D. (2017, June 22). *Home is where the hate is.* Retrieved from https://www.theinvestigativefund.org/investigation/2017/06/22/home-hate/

Rong, X. L., & Brown, F. (2002). Socialization, culture, and identities of Black immigrant children. *Education and Urban Society, 34*(2), 247–273.

Roy, L., & Roxas, K. (2011). Whose deficit is this anyhow? Exploring counter-stories of Somali Bantu refugees in "doing school." *Harvard Educational Review, 81*(3), 521–541.

Sánchez, P. (2007). Urban immigrant students: How transnationalism shapes their world learning. *The Urban Review, 39*(5), 489–517. doi:10.1007/s11256-007-0064-8

Sánchez, P., & Kasun, G. Sue (2012). Connecting transnationalism to the classroom and to theories of immigrant student adaptation. *Berkeley Review of Education, 3*(1), 71–93.

Solorzano, D., & Yosso, T. J. (2002). *Critical race methodology: Counter storytelling as an analytical framework for educational research.* Retrieved from Qualitative Inquiry.

Sleeter, C. E. (2016). Critical family history: Situating family within contexts of power relationships. Journal of Multidisciplinary Research, 8(1), 11–23.

Thompson, G. (2011). *Working in the shadows.* New York, NY: Perseus.

Zinn, H. (1994/2002). *You can't be neutral on a moving train: A personal history of our times.* Boston, MA: Beacon.

Zinn, H. (2003). *A people's history of the United States.* New York, NY: Harper & Row.

Chapter Two

Race and Immigration

Intersections of Histories and Identities

> Washing one's hands of the conflict between the powerful and the powerless means to side with the powerful, not to be neutral.
>
> —Paulo Freire

This chapter addresses race and its relationship to teaching immigration through a critical race teacher activism (CRTA) lens. I advocate for a deep understanding of how racism and immigration are intertwined and assert that teaching about immigration should always involve a discussion of power and intersectionality. The introductory quote by Paulo Freire frames the primary goals of this chapter, which are:

- To define and dispel myths about race and racism
- To examine how White supremacy and White privilege impact education and society
- To explore the intersectional nature of race and immigration
- To disrupt the notion that education is (or can be) neutral in matters of race
- To explore how attempts to remain neutral in the classroom reify rather than dismantle the system of White supremacy
- To emphasize the historical, systemic, institutional, and evolving nature of race and racism
- To explore teaching race and immigration through a critical race teacher activism (CRTA) lens

Key Ideas and Terms:

- Race
- Intersectionality
- Racism
- White supremacy
- White privilege
- Color-blind racism

This chapter is divided into two parts: Part 1 provides definitions and background information on race, racism, and immigration. Part 2 provides specific considerations for what it means to teach about the intersections of race and immigration in the classroom. Within these sections, you are invited to reflect on your own experiences with race and racism in order to prepare to engage these topics with students. As I write this chapter, demonstrations of White supremacy are unfolding in Charlottesville, Virginia, as well as across the country. The urgency for White teachers to understand and address the system of racism cannot be underestimated. I use the phrase *system of racism* to avoid ahistorical assumptions about race. That is to say, the misconception that racism is simply composed of individual or isolated racist acts that occur detached from a history of racism.

The White supremacists' demonstrations and violence in Charlottesville, for example, are a symptom of unchecked racism over time, not an isolated incident perpetrated by a small fringe group. And, these events are not new. As Lozenski (2018) explains, "The fact that young adults and adolescents have been involved in these incidents is alarming to many because it runs counter to the liberal logic of racial progress: that racism is an old idea practiced by a dying generation of racists who will eventually take it to their graves" (p. 2).

I emphasize that while White educators may distance themselves from the acts of the White supremacists in Charlottesville and other historical and contemporary demonstrations of White supremacy, it is the silence and inaction of everyday citizens, including educators, about the system of racism that allows these groups to thrive. Further, events like Charlottesville are undoubtedly anti-Black, but they are also anti-immigrant.

Issues of race and immigration in America are inextricably linked. Notions of race, ethnicity, and citizenship are intertwined. And, while an immigrant from Guatemala may experience racism in a different way than US-born Blacks, the ideology that supports these varying forms of racism is at its roots the same, and must be intentionally dismantled both socially and institutionally.

While educators are not the sole arbiters of racial justice, they have a responsibility to work toward dismantling White supremacy at the pedagogical and curricular level. The White supremacists in Charlottesville and elsewhere sat in numerous classrooms throughout their lives. Who remained silent or neutral and missed the opportunity to engage them on the intersectional issues of racial justice?

Critical Questions for the Classroom

Begin by answering these questions for yourself. Then reflect on how your students might answer these questions.

- What and when have you learned about race and racism in school, in your family, in your community? What images come to mind when you hear "racist"? Who are racists and how do they get that way?
- What is power, and what role does it play in understanding race and privilege?
- What and when have you heard about the notion of White privilege? How do you feel when someone mentions White privilege?
- What is White supremacy? How does it function in society?
- How do conversations about race, power, and privilege relate to immigration? What's the connection?
- Who benefits from conversations about race? Who benefits when conversations about race are avoided or silenced? Is it possible to be neutral?
- Why are conversations about race sometimes difficult or controversial? What ideas do you have for effectively facilitating these challenging conversations in your family, community, or classroom?

Which questions were most difficult for you to answer? Why? Do you feel prepared to facilitate a conversation around these questions with students? The contents of this book are designed to support you in becoming adept in both your understanding and practice in discussing race and immigration through a CRTA lens. The following sections provide definitions that ground the notion of race in the social, historical, economic, educational, and political systems in which it is embedded.

PART 1: DEFINITIONS AND BACKGROUND

Race, Racism, and White Supremacy

Race is a complex and flawed way of labeling humans by their phenotypical characteristics. Phenotypical characteristics are defined as observed characteristics used to make assumptions about racial background (e.g., skin tone, hair texture, bone structure, facial features). Race is not biological, but rather a *socially constructed* term. When something is socially constructed, the definition is dependent on the beliefs, values, and interests of those who define it, rather than scientific evidence. The idea that race is socially constructed, however, does not mean that people's experiences of race and being *racialized* are not real. So, at the same time that we acknowledge the nonscientific, socially constructed nature of race, we cannot diminish the very real consequences and experiences of those who are impacted by rac*ism*.

Racism is a form of systemic and institutionalized discrimination based on the evolving and socially constructed notions of race. Racism is predicated on the notion of White supremacy, which holds that people of White, Western European ancestry are superior to other races and entitled to the power and privilege bestowed upon them. I emphasize again the importance of understanding racism and White supremacy as a system. By system, I mean embedded into social, economic, educational, and political policies and practices rather than isolated incidents or person-to-person discrimination; these are results of the system.

Dismantling the system of racism and White supremacy requires more than simply denouncing overt racist acts and racial violence. It involves changing the policies and practices that sustain it. Affirmative action policies, for example, were developed to serve as a set of checks and balances for the system of racism and White supremacy.

A helpful analogy might be to imagine society as a computer and the system of racism as a computer virus. Affirmative action policies are antivirus programs uploaded to the computer (society) to prevent the virus (racism). Affirmative action policies work to disrupt the system of racism, instead of depending solely on individuals to make sound, antiracist decisions. Consider how to extend this analogy. Who installs the virus? What happens if we ignore it on our computers? Who dismantles it?

When Whites attempt to remain neutral, ignore, or deny the existence of the system of racism, they are complicit in its proliferation and the retraumatization of people of color who continually have to identify, attempt to prove, and educate White people of its existence. Peggy McIntosh and Christine Sleeter are examples of White educator-scholars who research, write, and teach about the system of racism and White privilege in order to educate Whites.

McIntosh is most known for her seminal work "Unpacking the Invisible Knapsack" (1989). In this work, McIntosh provides a list of statements to which people can answer yes or no in order to illuminate the everyday privileges of Whites. For example, "When I am told about our national heritage or about 'civilization,' I am shown that people of my color made it what it is" or, "I can take a job with an affirmative action employer without having co-workers on the job suspect that I got it because of race," or questions as seemingly benign as, "I can choose blemish cover or bandages in 'flesh' color and have them more less match my skin."

Christine Sleeter's most recent work (2016) grounds the discussion of White privilege in the exploration of critical family history. The notion of critical family histories developed out of her own investigation into how her family benefited from official racist practices and policies such as the Homestead Act. Critical family histories involve the exploration of how family histories intersect with the social and political events of the time. Part 2 explores how critical family histories can be explored in immigration units with students in ways that honor family histories and critique the system of racism.

Conversations about racism, White supremacy, and White privilege are often seen as controversial, polarizing, or divisive. This is ironic given that the very premise of White supremacy, racism, and White privilege is to divide. Engaging in dialogue and direct action to dismantle the system of White supremacy, racism, and White privilege has solidarity and equity as its central goal. But what is equity when we understand racism as a system? Figure 2.1 is a popular Internet meme that was created to illustrate privilege and the difference between the goals of *equality* and *equity*.

On the left side of this image, equality is envisioned as all three people having a box. The tallest person, however, already possesses the opportunity to see over the fence. The other two people have a difficult or obscured opportunity to view even with the box. In a system designed for equality, this

Figure 2.1. Equality vs. Equity. Interaction Institute for Social Change Artist: Angus Maguire.

unleveled playing field goes unacknowledged or unaddressed. While all people in the equality graphic have a box, they do not have an equal opportunity to view the game. The shortest person, for example, must work much harder to have the same view as the tallest person.

In the equity image, however, the playing field is leveled by each person having equal opportunity to view the game. The image seeks to convey that fairness is not achieved by giving everyone a box; it is achieved by examining the roadblocks in place for each person (or group) and committing to an equitable solution.

Educators and students can question the meme further. For example, Sharif El-Mekki (2017), a school leader and educator in Philadelphia, suggested the real question should be less about the boxes and more about the presence of the fence. He asks, "Who put the fence there and who benefits from its existence?" Educators could extend El-Mekki's questions even more by asking who manufactured the boxes and do they have a vested interest in the existence of the fence?

If we relate these questions to the discussion of racism as a system, we can move the discussion away from the inherent qualities of people based on socially constructed notions of race and focus on the larger system of inequity that creates the need for the boxes in the first place. Critically analyzing images with students in this way is an example of how educators can engage in CRTA approaches in the classroom. Educators can search for memes and images such as this one that connect to a unit topic. Search for existing critiques and questions about the images online as a way to begin the process.

Intersections of Race and Immigration

Given the socially constructed and evolving nature of race, challenges emerge when race and other markers of identity, such as immigration status, intersect along axes of power. Distinguished law professor Kimberlé Crenshaw developed the concept of intersectionality to address these complexities. Crenshaw theorized an interplay between intersecting experiences of oppression within the system of White supremacy.

Intersectionality helps to deepen the conversation about power relationships within the system of racism because it makes visible the ways identities are inextricably linked to the historical, social, and political context. For example, consider the intersectional experiences of a US-born Black female who is also Muslim. Next, consider a US-born Black male. One might argue that a US-born Black male may benefit more than a US-born Black female who is Muslim because of the system of patriarchy that privileges men and Christianity. On the other hand, Black males experience other forms of racial violence and oppression, namely, stereotypes related to violence. How do we make sense of the system of racism that impacts people and groups in different ways? Who is impacted more by racism?

Arguing over who is more oppressed than whom is sardonically referred to as the Oppression Olympics. If one is concerned with dismantling racism, engaging in the Oppression Olympics is not a valuable exercise. What *is* valuable is recognizing the complex interplay between identities and how they relate to a given historical, social, and political context. So instead of debating who is more oppressed than whom, the better approach is to dialogue about how to dismantle a system of White supremacy and racial oppression that acts on people of color in complex and nuanced ways. Instead of trying to determine whether a Black person who emigrated from Kenya is more oppressed than a Muslim person who emigrated from Iran, ask questions like: In what ways does a racist system deny opportunities to either or both persons? How can I disrupt this system in my classroom, school, and community?

Other examples of intersectionality can be identified when considering race, immigration status, and religion. Sikhs, whether they are US born or not, sometimes choose to wear the *dastaar*, or turban, as one of the seven articles of their faith. They are often mistaken by Whites as Muslims. Basic knowledge of world religions would prevent such examples of mistaken identity and Islamophobia. And, while it is unacceptable to discriminate against Muslims too, Sikhs are often the target of anti-Muslim hate crimes because of this visible symbol. Sikhs have also been targeted, even when their attackers are aware of their religious affiliation.

The recognition of intersectional experiences of racism can serve as a call for Black and Brown solidarity; that is to say, groups who experience racism recognizing the intersectional nature of identity and supporting one another in the struggle. Sikhs, for example, have shown solidarity with other communities who have experienced racism including Muslims and the Black Lives Matter (BLM) movement. It is important to ground these conversations in uprooting xenophobia and Islamophobia rather than mistaken identity, as both groups should be free from experiencing discrimination.

Another example of a group experiencing intersectional racism is the Somali Bantu refugees who are racially Black, but may or may not identify with US Blacks because of their sociocultural and sociohistorical experiences. Unless the Somali Bantu are dressed in traditional clothing, speaking Maay Maay, or speaking with an accent that distinguishes them from US Blacks, they are often seen by Whites as being part of the US-born Black community.

I studied the experiences of Somali Bantu refugees in US schools and communities. It was common for Somali Bantu parents, for example, to attempt to distinguish themselves from US-born Blacks in order to avoid discrimination in White communities. According to the Somali Bantu parents in my study, they held no ill will toward US Blacks, but after living in the US for only a few short years, they observed and understood the way US Blacks were treated by Whites and sought to protect their children from these experiences by distancing themselves.

When anti-Muslim rhetoric increased after 9/11, Somali Bantu families were faced with another form of discrimination based on their religion. In this way, they experienced racism intersectionally by being Black, a refugee, and Muslim. One parent expressed, "In America, a lot is working against us. I cannot remove my black skin, so I am Black here. I am also a foreigner with an accent who practices Islam. These qualities are not always celebrated here. I will not hide who I am, but I am sometimes afraid for the children."

Intersections of Race and Immigration in History

In his final book, Martin Luther King Jr. (1967) wrote that Whites need to "reeducate themselves out of their racial ignorance." Part of that reeducation involves seeking out resources that provide multiple perspectives on history. The previous chapter explored how grand narratives or "imagined histories" prevent students from understanding the intersections of race and immigration. This section provides some historical touchpoints to understand how the system of racism and White supremacy is embedded in social, economic, educational, and political policies and practices of the US.

The use of race as a way to label, oppress, and enslave groups of people is a relatively new phenomenon in human history. Prior to the use of race, humans used other categories (e.g., language, education, tribal affiliation, class, religion). Race has remained a primary, but also intersectional, way of oppressing people in modern society.

Racialization on a global scale emerged in the 16th century, and race-based laws began to appear in the Americas in the latter half of the 17th century. Racializing humans and the notion of White supremacy was crucial in justifying European imperialism, colonization, and the enslavement of African people. The slave trade in particular formed the building blocks for capitalist and globalized economies, including that of the United States.

Europeans were the first and only group to turn race-based chattel slavery into a thriving economy. What is known as "Wall Street," for example, in the US was one of the first and largest slave markets in the Americas. Kidnapped and enslaved Black and Brown human beings were one of the first and most lucrative "stocks" bought, sold, and traded on Wall Street. The US economy thrived on slave labor.

Slave labor, whether through chattel slavery or indentured servitude, in the US economy has been dependent upon free or cheap labor since its inception. The signing of the Emancipation Proclamation proposed to free enslaved Africans, but contrary to popular belief, no slaves were freed as a result of its signing. Lincoln signed the Emancipation Proclamation in answer to Black organizers, activists, scholars, sympathetic politicians in Congress, and White abolitionists. The continued work of these antislavery activists as Sojourner Truth, David Walker, and Frederick Douglass helped the ideas of the Emancipation Proclamation come to fruition. It should be noted that Abraham Lincoln was a supporter of White supremacy and racial segregation. Indeed, most Whites at the time also supported these notions.

Reconstruction, the era after the Civil War, was a prosperous time in the sense that many Blacks were able to gain representation in business and politics, but a dangerous time as the system evolved to make up for the lack of free, enslaved labor. Jails and prisons became the primary way to ensure free labor. Whites who were opposed to racial integration and the dissolution of slave labor worked to pass laws that disproportionately targeted Blacks. These Black Codes, which evolved into what is now known as Jim Crow laws, justified anti-Black violence and imprisonment. It became illegal for Blacks to travel freely, work without restrictive contracts, and participate in civic responsibilities and privileges such as voting and serving on juries.

Laws related to harassing or assaulting White women, for example carried much harsher penalties for Black men than for Whites. Buying and selling goods and owning or possessing firearms were also restricted for Blacks. These racist laws allowed for the proliferation of the US prison system and a new form of free labor. The more Blacks arrested, the more labor opportunities for White farms and factories needing to recover from the devastation of the Civil War. This resulted in the re-enslavement of thousands of Blacks.

The reverberations from these early practices continue today. Currently, the US, which is only 5% of the world's population, now imprisons 25% of the world's total number of imprisoned persons, much more than any other country in the world. According to the United States Sentencing Commission (2017), people of color are more likely to be sentenced to imprisonment than Whites and serve longer sentences.

Indentured servitude, which largely affected immigrants from low socioeconomic backgrounds, including the Irish and Italians, also served as a form of free or cheap labor. Indentured servitude was often a form of punishment or way to pay off debts such as passage to America. Unlike slavery, indentured servants were often offered parcels of land or work after their release.

Practices of indentured servitude, like slavery, still exist today in both official and unofficial ways. For example, factory farms that primarily employ Latinx immigrants, both documented and undocumented, often require workers to live in camps where pay is often held for weeks or months in order to keep workers from leaving. Workers live in harsh and crowded conditions with little or no medical care for injuries from dangerous work environments.

Undocumented workers are particularly vulnerable to unpaid, harsh conditions because the assumption is they will not notify the police for fear of being deported. Construction companies, for example, have been known to bring large groups of workers to a site for weeks without pay and then make an anonymous call to the Immigration and Customs Enforcement (ICE). The workers are deported, and the company does not have to pay them. Many of the arrested immigrants end up in detention centers.

These for-profit prisons, including detention centers designed for undocumented immigrants, are a part of the system of White supremacy and racism of which most White Americans are unaware. For-profit corporations who own these prisons build wealth from public tax dollars to detain and deport undocumented people, even if their only crime is being undocumented.

Critical Questions for the Classroom

- How do for-profit prisons or the privatization of prisons keep the legacy of slavery and indentured servitude alive?
- Who benefits most from imprisoning undocumented immigrants?
- What is the rationale for incarcerating undocumented immigrants? Is the rationale valid?
- What is the social cost of imprisoning undocumented immigrants who have not committed a crime other than being undocumented?
- Who funds and writes legislation for immigration?
- Who benefits monetarily from imprisoned people?
- Who are the primary targets of anti-immigrant laws? In what way is race a factor?

RACE AND RACISM Q&A

The following questions and answers provide additional insight into inquiries educators have about racism and White supremacy. These are common questions from my courses and workshops. This section is designed to answer lingering queries and support dialogue about the intersection of race and immigration in the classroom.

Q: "Why spend so much time talking about race if it's socially constructed? Can't we simply quit using racial labels?"

A: While race is not real from a *scientific perspective*, racism *is* real and has very real consequences. During slave auctions on Wall Street, White men would prod, humiliate, and abuse Black people, including children, before a crowd of White traders, merchants, and onlookers. To determine the worth of Black women, for example, White men would run their hands through the hair of Black women while they stood before buyers. If the White man's hand easily combed through her hair, she garnered a higher bid. Women with this supposed "good hair" likely bore the genetic traits of women before her who had been raped by their White enslavers, accounting for looser curls or straighter hair texture.

How "good hair" is defined in modern society is largely based on these racist notions of White superiority. This is but one example of how racial oppression infiltrates contemporary society in ways that are often taken for granted. It is difficult to dismantle these ideas if we have little background knowledge or experience in talking about the system of racism and White supremacy and how it persists over time.

Q: "Why is it important for White teachers to talk about race in the classroom?"

A: Approximately 82% of the teaching population is White, while kids of color make up nearly half of the student population (United States Department of Education, Office of Planning, Evaluation, and Policy Development, 2016). What is more, one in five students speak a language other than English, while White teachers tend to be monolingual. That means, unless White teachers are working from an antiracist, CRTA perspective, they are reproducing and modeling the system of White supremacy in their pedagogy and curriculum. The impact on students of color is continued marginalization, and the impact on White students is affirmation of their position of power within the system of White supremacy.

Q: "If race isn't biological, what about diseases such as sickle-cell anemia, which seems to disproportionally affect Black people?"

A: The presence of sickle-cell anemia in people with African ancestry is largely tied to historical and environmental factors—namely, the prevalence of malaria in places like Africa. Scientists explain that sickle-cell anemia is a mutation of the blood cells that makes those infected less likely to die from malaria. For this reason, more people with sickle-cell anemia from these regions survived.

It stands to reason, then, that people with African ancestry, especially those whose ancestors survived the horrific conditions of the Middle Passage to the Americas, are more likely to have this disease, which is genetically passed down through generations. There are many other examples that explain the prevalence of diseases and conditions in certain races because of social distancing and environmental factors. There are more examples than can be addressed here of how the medical community has historically skewed and misused the notion of race as biologically significant. This has dire consequences for people of color through misdiagnoses, lack of care, and divestment in funding for diseases that are considered racially specific.

Racism, sexism, and other forms of discrimination in health care are still relevant topics for researchers. Immigrants and women of color in particular, regardless of their socioeconomic status, are most vulnerable in the US health care system. Black women in New York City, for example, "are 12 times more likely to suffer a pregnancy-related death than white women" (Howell, Egorova, Balbierz, Zeitlin, & Hebert, 2016, p. 143). The lack of representation of people of color in the health care field allows biased claims to go unchallenged, even in peer-reviewed academic journals. Imagine how the presence of Black scientists and journal reviewers would change the publication of biased studies. Chapter 3 elaborates on how racism and deficit-based thinking in psychology and education continues to marginalize people of color.

Q: "If labeling people by race is inaccurate, why do we continue to use these labels? Why can't we all just be 'American'?"

A: In an ideal world, we all would be "just American," but the question implies that all Americans (or those who want to become American) have equal opportunities and rights afforded to them. The system of racism is difficult to undo, especially when those in power continue to deny the existence of it or support it outright.

One way to begin to address the system of racism is to have data about race. Census documents, and anywhere people are asked to check a box, can help to ensure equity by providing data about how resources and opportunities are allocated or denied. At the time of writing this book, the Trump administration is working toward funding cuts for census data, making it difficult for civil rights organizations to advocate for underserved and underrepresented populations. This has also happened in schools.

School districts that abolished racial integration programs (like Philadelphia) stopped collecting data related to teachers' racial background. The absence of data related to equity is a strategy designed to keep the system of White supremacy thriving. In order to dismantle racism, an acknowledgment of the historical, systemic, and institutional roadblocks that the racialization of people has created is necessary. Instead of focusing on getting rid of the labels and data about race, the focus should be on dismantling the *system* that privileges Whiteness and created the labels in the first place.

Q: "I am White and I don't see color. It's not important to me whether you are Black, White, purple, or green. I don't judge people by their color."

A: Not judging people by their color is a worthy goal, but claiming to be color blind ignores the system of racism into which we are all born (Van

Ausdale & Feagin, 2001). In fact, claiming to "not see race" is another form of racism called color-blind racism. Color-blind racism is the false notion that people are capable of ignoring implicit racial biases. Saying you are color blind reifies rather than disrupts racism because it silences the very real experiences of people of color.

Keep in mind that people of color rarely claim to be color blind mainly because they are routinely faced with racism in their everyday lives. Moreover, adding colors like purple, green, and blue to conversations about race only succeeds in minimizing racism because these "colors" have not been used as a form of historical and institutionalized oppression. Can you imagine saying, "I don't see gender" when a woman remarks on an experience of misogyny? When you are a beneficiary of White privilege, it is a privilege to minimize the importance of race.

Q: "It seems like people of color discriminate against each other too. Why is it just White people who get singled out for being racist?"

A: In his book *Pedagogy of the Oppressed*, Paulo Freire (1968) theorizes the way systems of oppression infiltrate not only the minds of the oppressor, but also the oppressed. "Colorism," a form of within-group discrimination based on privileging or valuing shades of skin color, is another example of how the system of White supremacy acts on all who experience it. Chapter 8 elaborates on how White people can move beyond their concern about how communities of color talk about race and focus instead on how to challenge other White people to work from an antiracist position.

Q: "Why are White people the only group deemed racist? What about reverse racism: people of color who discriminate against Whites?"

A: Another product of the system of White supremacy is the myth of reverse racism. Reverse racism is based on the false premise that all races have equal potential to be discriminated against within the system of racial privilege, and also have the potential to experience this discrimination in the same way. The term *reverse racism* is a fundamental misunderstanding of the definition of racism.

Racism, by definition, is a system that is institutionalized in social, economic, educational, and political policies and practices. While racist acts can be perpetrated on an individual level, they are inextricably tied to the system that privileges Whiteness. For this reason, reverse racism is not possible, even in an alternate universe where Black people had instead been the creators of racial privilege; in this case it would still be defined as racism.

Q: "What about mixed-race people? If they are half-White, why do they identify as Black or Brown?" Related comments might be, " *I am one-*

quarter Cherokee" or *" My Irish ancestors were treated horribly, but I don't get any benefits from that."*

A: This question is also a misunderstanding of the systemic nature of racism and ignores how people of color experience this system. It is true that Irish and Italian immigrants, for example, faced persecution, but they were not part of the long-term, institution of chattel slavery. Additionally, they were not subject to long-term racist policies such as the "one-drop" rule, nor were they limited in the same ways from such freedoms as owning property, voting, and attending schools as Black and Brown people. The one-drop rule was the notion that "one drop" of African blood, meaning one ancestor of Black, African decent makes a person Black. The one-drop rule is grounded in notions of White superiority, which used the one-drop rule to justify racial violence and segregation.

Ignatiev's (1995) *How the Irish Became White* is helpful in clarifying the narrative of race-based oppression for groups like the Irish. Also important to this conversation is the idea of "passing." At different points in history, different phenotypical characteristics have allowed people to pass for White. For example, lighter skin or European features may allow individuals to be perceived and received as White and thus benefit from the system of White supremacy. At the same time, these persons may experience challenges in their own community by not having a sense of belonging or acceptance in either context. This too is a function of White supremacy.

Q: "Is racism really as much of a problem as it used to be? Isn't class or socioeconomic status the real issue?"

A: After the election of Barack Obama, the idea of a "postracial" America entered public discourse. The implied question is, "How can America still be racist it we elected a phenotypically Black president?" Holding up one example of a person of color in a position of power or leadership fails to account for how notions of White supremacy are still woven into the fabric of the US social, economic, educational, and political system.

It should be noted that White supremacist groups saw an exponential increase in membership and activity after the 2008 election, not to mention the racist remarks from President Trump regarding immigrants from "shithole African countries." Moreover, schools are more segregated today than they were in 1954 when *Brown v. Board* called for the desegregation of schools (Rothstein, 2017). Class alone cannot account for these inequities. When class is raised as a counterargument to racism it discursively signals a denial of the system of racism. If the concern is really about class it would be an "and" or "another" conversation rather than an "instead." Recall the discussion of intersectionality in this chapter and the relationship between race and other forms of oppression.

Q: "What about working hard? I was taught that if you work hard, you can succeed. Policies like affirmative action seem to give advantages to people who didn't have to work for it."

A: The notion that one can transcend the system of racism by working hard is a myth and a misunderstanding of how privilege works. Meritocracy is the term used to describe the notion that individuals are able to achieve success by merit, skill, and/or hard work only. A capitalistic society promotes the idea of meritocracy and the American dream because it is essential to the survival of capitalism as an economic system.

Also central to the survival of capitalism is that only a small group benefits from the wealth the system produces. Wealth depends on the exploitation of the larger population. In terms of affirmative action, White affirmative action has been the de facto practice in education, business, and government since the inception of the United States. People of color have been routinely denied wealth through an economic system that privileges Whites. For example, the benefits of the Homestead Act and the New Deal were accessible to Whites only, creating generations of potential wealth for White families. Jim Crow laws and anti-immigration laws not only marginalized and segregated people of color, but allowed for White privilege in all economic sectors.

To conclude Part 1, I emphasize that privilege is not pie. Pie is an inaccurate metaphor for privilege because it implies that privilege is finite (i.e., one pie to be divided among all). That is to say, taking one piece of the "privilege pie" does not imply that someone else gets less, unless you choose to design the system as such. In a just society, privilege is infinite (pies are abundant), but it requires that all individuals recognize and work toward dismantling the system of racism and White supremacy.

PART 2: CLASSROOM ACTIVITIES: TEACHING ABOUT WHITENESS, POWER, AND PRIVILEGE

A CRTA perspective requires educators to take action in matters of race at the individual (person-to-person), pedagogy and curriculum, and institutional levels. Part 1 of this chapter provided some background and content. Part 2 provides strategies for preparing, planning, and engaging in the work of dismantling the system of racism and White supremacy.

I begin by asking, how can White teachers become proficient in teaching White students about the system of racism? How do teacher preparation programs, professional development workshops, curriculum, and the textbook industry impact how race, racism, and immigration are explored in schools?

Matias and Liou (2015) advocate for critical race teaching, which "disrupts the centrality of Whiteness in teaching by questioning what constitutes normalcy and how teachers implicitly and explicitly participate and reproduce it" (p. 610). What does it mean to disrupt the centrality of Whiteness? In order to teach from a critical race teacher-activist position, White teachers must do their homework to prepare for dialogue in the classroom.

How to Prepare for Conversations About Race in the Classroom

- Do your research: Find resources that focus on antiracist and critical perspectives in education (see, for example, the resources at the end of this chapter) rather than diversity or tolerance approaches. Read books, blogs, and news articles written by people of color and use their work in your classroom.
- Racism audit or antiracist rubric: Create a racism audit or antiracist rubric for evaluating your pedagogy and curriculum. Engage your students in the evaluation process, including recommended changes. Examples of antiracism and equity rubrics and audits can be found at the following links: Mid-Atlantic Equity Consortium, Criteria for an Equitable Classroom: https://maec.org/wp-content/uploads/2016/04/Criteria-for-an-Equitable-Classroom.pdf; Crossroads Ministry, Continuum on Becoming an Anti-Racist Multicultural Organization: http://www.aesa.us/conferences/2013_ac_presentations/Continuum_AntiRacist.pdf.
- Anticipate questions: After doing your research, consider the questions that might arise when talking about the system of racism and White supremacy in the classroom. For example, are you prepared to respond to a White student who asks, "Why do the Black kids in the class get to use the 'N-word' and I don't?" Or, a colleague who asks, "Why should tax dollars pay for undocumented students to go to public school?" Investigate the antiracist responses to these questions.
- Rehearse and practice: Rehearse, rehearse, rehearse. Practice, practice, practice. If you have limited experience talking about race, find ways to practice alone or with friends or colleagues who can support you. Practice in the car, in front of a mirror, and with a knowledgeable friend, colleague, or mentor. Chapter 9 addresses how to build a network of partners, allies, and accomplices to support CRTA approaches.
- Get comfortable with being uncomfortable: Invite yourself, students, parents of your students, your friends, family, and colleagues to be uncomfortable. Discuss the benefits that accrue (namely, learning) when we allow ourselves to feel discomfort and disequilibrium. Learning rarely occurs in our comfort zone. I always begin my class with an invitation for students to be uncomfortable. It helps to lower the anxiety in the room and acknowledges that people make mistakes when learning how to discuss race. Additionally, it supports the idea that in a community of learners, we learn from mistakes and missteps. Keep in mind that while the system of

White supremacy might feel challenging for White people to discuss, people of color have the trauma of experiencing racism and also having to continually justify its existence at the same time.

- Listen, hear, and honor: Sometimes, White people are uncomfortable with the tone, delivery, or language people of color use when they talk about racism, White supremacy, and White privilege. As a White teacher, it is also important to set ground rules for conversations, and one of those ground rules should be listening—listening even when the tone or delivery of the message feels harsh or uncomfortable to you. Given the dire, painful, and traumatic experiences of racism, speaking through pain, silence, or anger should be honored. Is it really possible to have "polite" conversation about racism? Whose feelings are being privileged or considered most when conversations about racism have to be polite or void of authentic emotion?

Where Do Race and Immigration Appear in Curriculum?

Conversations about racism most often appear in units about slavery or the civil rights movement. Immigration units tend to focus on tracing European ancestry during the early 20th century. In these units about slavery, civil rights, or immigration, however, the history of systemic racism and White supremacy and how it functions, evolves, and endures is rarely discussed.

When I ask my in-service and preservice teachers about teaching from an antiracist perspective, most White students express the desire to remain neutral: "I try to stay away from politics in my class." Attempting to remain neutral reifies the system of White supremacy. To teach from a critical race teacher activism perspective, justice and equity are at the center, not the periphery, of pedagogy and curriculum. The following recommended classroom activities and resources provide examples of how to address intersectional issues of race and immigration with students.

Activity 1: Implicit Bias Visualization

This activity can be used to introduce a conversation about implicit bias. Engage your students in a visualization activity. Read the following passage to your students and ask them to illustrate the story on a piece of paper:

> I visited my doctor's office after experiencing pain in my chest. My doctor checked my neck, throat, blood pressure, and listened to my heartbeat using a stethoscope. Then my doctor asked me a long list of questions related to my exercise routine and eating habits. After more tests, I should find out if there's anything wrong by next week.

After all students have finished their illustration, ask them the following questions in small groups or as a class:

- Is the doctor a man or woman? Why?
- Is the doctor young or old?
- What race is the doctor?

Depending on the makeup of your class, the activity may garner different responses. Follow up with additional questions:

- Why do we make assumptions? Where do these assumptions come from?
- How do our personal experiences influence how we read books, watch movies, or interact with people?
- How can we check these assumptions and stereotypes?

As a follow-up activity, read a book or watch a film that is familiar to your students. Explore how the film would be perceived if the characters were different (e.g., gender, race, religion). What does "typecasting" in film, for example, say about our implicit biases?

Activity 2: Discourse Analysis as a Tool for Identifying the System of Racism

The notion of White supremacy, even if rejected by individual Whites, is built into the US economy, school system, and criminal justice system in ways that are both subtle and overt. The pervasiveness of White supremacy and White privilege can be identified in how and when racial labeling is used. For example, when describing a White person, White people rarely use a racial label; however, when describing someone who is a person of color, they often describe them by their race. This subtle language choice positions White as the norm or default and other groups as non-White or different.

Matias and Liou disrupt this idea, stating, "We are not non-white, you are just non-colored" (Matias & Liou, 2015). This reframing of language helps to disrupt the system of White supremacy by positioning people of color as the norm rather than the exception. In this way, "language in use" is a window into our ideas about race.

- What other examples of coded language can you identify in everyday discourse?
- What about terms such as illegals, limited English proficient (LEP), diverse, urban, or at-risk?
- How are these terms used, who do they describe, and why?

To reflect on your own labeling process, write three words to describe each of your students' identities as you perceive them. Then, add any official labels used by the school to describe each student. What patterns do you see? What changes would you make?

Activity 3: Hashtags for Racial Justice

One way racism has evolved is through distancing. For example, you may hear a White person say, "I wasn't alive during slavery; I'm not responsible for the actions of my ancestors." Another example of distancing occurred on social media during the White supremacists' rallies in Charlottesville. Twitter hashtags such as #NotMyAmerica #ThisIsNotUs attempted to distance the White supremacists' acts and portray them as a small segment of America separate from well-meaning White people. These proclamations, however, ignore the reality that racism is a system in which all Whites are involved whether they actively perpetuate it, ignore it, or actively work against it. From that perspective, #This**IS**Us.

How could you rewrite these hashtags through a CRTA lens to more accurately reflect the reality, and at the same time, work to uproot racism as a White person? With your students, search for hashtags related to race and immigration. Create examples of hashtags that acknowledge, rather than distance White people from, racist-based hashtags such as #buildthewall. Explore how racism exists and is supported beyond White supremacist groups.

Activity 4: "I Am" Poems (Any Grade/Age)

"I am" poems serve a variety of purposes in the classroom. "I am" poems can reveal the identities individuals and groups choose to foreground and background. In a study conducted by Clark and Flores (2001), where participants were asked to write the top 10 words that relate to who they are, students of color were more likely to place racial, ethnic, and cultural descriptors at the top of their list. Use "I am" poems to explore in what ways this occurs/does not occur in your own classroom. Ask students to write "I am" poems for characters in a book. Discuss intersectionality through their poems and chosen identity markers for the characters. "I am" poems can be used with any age group. Ada and Campoy's (2004) book *Authors in the Classroom* provides a guide for teachers and students to "author themselves" and their own lives. Also, Ada's website, almaflorada.com, provides additional resources for poems with children. The Public Broadcasting Service (PBS) has a sample lesson for exploring identity and intersectionality with advanced "I am" poems. Other resources, including Galbraith and Vogel's (2008) book *Voices of Teens: Writers Matter*, provide examples of how to extend "I am" poems and how to connect literacy across the curriculum.

Activity 5: Immigration and Genealogy Across the Content Areas

Chapter 5 addresses modifying the curriculum. The first steps may involve an add-on approach to address race and immigration through classroom activities. Topics related to race and immigration can be addressed interdisciplinarily across content areas. For example, select a focal text like Rebecca Skloot's *The Immortal Life of Henrietta Lacks*, 2010.

English language arts: Create a text set to accompany the focal texts that includes picture books, novels, films, and first-person accounts. Also include dystopian novels and films related to genetic engineering or caste systems based on colorism. Use a critical literacy framework (see Chapters 5 and 6) to analyze how Henrietta Lacks is portrayed by a White author.

Also, view the film starring Oprah Winfrey. Compare and contrast representation, voice, and perspective. (Who gets to tell the story, why, how, and for what purpose? Is Mrs. Lacks or the author the focal protagonist? How is Whiteness centered in the book and film? Whose journey and experiences get more play?) Select a menu of films for students to watch related to genetic engineering or eugenics-based segregation and race biology such as *Divergent* or *Gattaca*.

Science: Explore DNA and genes. Teachers can order DNA kits or access results and examples from other classrooms to study biology and question the use of race biology to justify state-sanctioned eugenics laws. Explore race and how nonscientific ideas infiltrate scientific research.

Social studies: Study the history of eugenics in the US. What social, economic, educational, and criminal justice practices and policies continue threads of the eugenics legacy? Watch the PBS documentary *No Más Bebés* to study reproductive justice and eugenics-based sterilization practices that impacted Puerto Ricans. Study the implications of the "one-drop rule" and how this connects to race-based segregation, the study of biology, and pseudoscientific notions of race.

Math: Explore how sample sizes impact genetic testing data. Explore percentages related to ancestry. Study bias in statistics and how statistics can be manipulated to favor particular results.

The Facing History and Ourselves website (https://www.facinghistory.org/resource-library/theory-classroom-eugenics-and-education) has additional resources for exploring eugenics and race in the classroom.

Reflective Activities for Teachers

1. Using the definitions from this chapter related to the White privilege and reverse racism, explain, in your own words, why a "Black power" organization is not fundamentally racist, but a "White power" organization is.

2. Explain how issues of racism (historically, socially, and politically) are connected to teaching about immigration in classrooms with predominantly White students.
3. Use the concepts of systems of power and intersectionality to answer the following question: "I am White, but I didn't have a privileged life. My parents worked blue-collar jobs and refused to take welfare unless we absolutely had to. How can you say I have White privilege?"
4. How is racism bad for White people?

RECOMMENDED RESOURCES

Books and Articles

Alexander, M. (2010). *The new Jim Crow: Mass incarceration in the age of colorblindness.* New York, NY: New Press.
Barnes, R. (1990). Race consciousness: The thematic content of racial distinctiveness in critical race scholarship. *Harvard Law Review, 103*, 1864–1871.
Bonilla-Silva, E. (2018). *Racism without racists: Color-blind racism and the persistence of racial inequality in America.* Lanham, MD: Rowman & Littlefield.
Ignatiev, N. (1995). *How the Irish Became White.* New York, NY: Routledge.
Leonardo, Z. (2009). *Race, Whiteness, and education.* New York, NY: Routledge.
Leonardo, Z., & Grubb, W. N. (2013). *Racism and education.* Hoboken, NJ: Taylor and Francis.
Skloot, R. (2010). *The Immortal Life of Henrietta Lacks.* New York, NY: Crown.

Podcasts and Videos

Crenshaw, Kimberlé (2016). *The urgency of intersectionality* [Video file]. Retrieved from https://www.ted.com/talks/kimberle_crenshaw_the_urgency_of_intersectionality
Gold, J. (2017). *Sickle cell patients endure discrimination, poor care and shortened lives* [Audio podcast]. Retrieved from https://www.npr.org/sections/health-shots/2017/11/04/561654823/sickle-cell-patients-endure-discrimination-poor-care-and-shortened-lives

Websites

Ferguson: https://sociologistsforjustice.org/ferguson-syllabus/; https://www.theatlantic.com/education/archive/2014/08/how-to-teach-kids-about-whats-happening-in-ferguson/379049/
Social justice resources: https://www.cultofpedagogy.com/social-justice-resources/

REFERENCES

Ada, A. F., & Campoy, F. I. (2004). *Authors in the classroom: A transformative education process.* Boston, MA: Allyn and Bacon.
Clark, E. R, & Flores, B. (2001). Who am I? The social construction of ethnic identity and self-perceptions in Latino preservice teachers. *Urban Review, 33*(2), 69–86.
El-Mekki, S. (November, 2017). Teach us all film screening and talk back. Panel presentation at La Salle University, Philadelphia, PA.
Freire, P. (1968). *Pedagogy of the Oppressed.* New York: Bloomsbury Publishing.

Galbraith, M., & Vogel, R. (2008). *Voices of teens: Writers matter.* Westerville, OH: National Middle School Association.

Howell, E. A., Egorova, N. N., Balbierz, A., Zeitlin, J., & Hebert, P. L. (2016). Site of delivery contribution to Black-White severe maternal morbidity disparity. *American Journal of Obstetrics & Gynecology*, Reports of Major Impact, 143–152.

King, M. L., Jr. (1967). *Where do we go from here: Chaos or community?* New York, NY: Harper & Row.

Lozenski, B. (2018, March). On the mythical rise of White nationalism and other stranger things. *Journal of Language and Literacy Education.*

Matias, C. E., & Liou, D. D. (2015). Tending to the heart of communities of color: Towards critical race teacher activism. *Urban Education, 50*(5), 601–625. http://dx.doi.org/10.1177/0042085913519338

McIntosh, P. (1989). *Unpacking the invisible knapsack.* Peace and Freedom, pp. 10–12.

Rothstein, R. (2017). *The color of the law: A forgotten history of how our government segregated America.* New York, NY: Liveright.

Sleeter, C. E. (2016). Critical family history: Situating family within contexts of power relationships. *Journal of Multidisciplinary Research, 8*(1), 11–23.

United States Department of Education, Office of Planning, Evaluation, and Policy Development. (2016). *The state of racial diversity in the educator workforce.* Retrieved from https://www2.ed.gov/rschstat/eval/highered/racial-diversity/state-racial-diversity-workforce.pdf

United States Sentencing Commission (2017). *Demographic differences in sentencing: An update to the 2012 Booker Report.* Retrieved from https://www.ussc.gov/sites/default/files/pdf/research-and-publications/research-publications/2017/20171114_Demographics.pdf

Van Ausdale, D., & Feagin, J. R. (2001). *The first R: How children learn race and racism.* Lanham, MD: Rowman & Littlefield.

Chapter Three

Deficit and Microaggressive Discourses

Unmasking the Language of White Supremacy

> Schools operate in contradictory ways with their potential to oppress and marginalize students which co-exists with their potential to emancipate and empower.
>
> —Daniel Solorzano and Tara Yosso

This chapter focuses on how White educators can work to recognize and disrupt deficit and microaggressive discourse in educational thought and practice. Drawing from a critical race teacher activism (CRTA) lens, this chapter addresses how to promote antideficit and antiracist practices in the classroom and school, especially around the teaching of race and immigration.

Key Ideas and Terms

- Deficit-model thinking
- Discourse(s)
- Deficit and microaggressive discourse
- Eugenics and race biology

This chapter is divided into two parts. Part 1 explores how deficit-model thinking and microaggressive discourses have been produced and reproduced in educational thought and practice. Examples from the K–12 and university classroom are used to illustrate how well-intentioned educators can still contribute to the system of White supremacy and racial oppression. Part 2 explores how to recognize and dismantle deficit-model thinking and microaggressive discourse through a CRTA approach. I begin the discussion of deficit-model thinking with an illustrative example from one of my teacher education courses.

* * *

"WE DON'T MEAN IT IN A BAD WAY"

Early in my university teaching career, I taught a curriculum class for future administrators. I tasked the students to work in groups to create a visual representation of a "school ecosystem." One group created a poster with an illustration of a flower garden with a sun, clouds, smog, and rain. When they presented their school ecosystem poster, I asked them to explain the significance of each object in the poster. They began: "The flowers are the children who need nourishment from the sun and rain. The sun and rain represent the teachers, and the garden, as a whole, is the school." "And, the dark clouds and smog, what do they represent?" I inquired. "The dark clouds are like storms or smog, representing the challenges in schools, like ESL [English as a second language] students, for example."

"The ESL students are the smog?" I responded, unsure of whether I heard them correctly.

"Well, it's difficult. We can't just teach when we have them. We have to make accommodations and it changes things, it disrupts the ecosystem," they clarified.

I again questioned their choice to depict children as smog. "I'm wondering if you've considered what this would convey to ESL children or parents. What message would this send if they saw your poster?" I questioned.

There was a clear tension in the room as their metaphor choice became clear. They were quick, however, to defend their choice. "We don't mean it in a bad way. We care about all students, but they really change schools and create challenges," they responded.

* * *

This example represents a group of educators and future administrators who firmly believe themselves to be caring, well-intentioned stewards of their school ecosystem. Many shared stories throughout the course of their commitment to serving the needs of all children and families. Good intentions aside, the group of educators who created the poster and the rest of the educators sitting in class chose not to verbalize opposition to comparing ESL children to smog. Instead, they defended their choice by claiming care for all students ("We don't mean it in a bad way. We care about all students. . . .").

Analyzing this event discursively suggests something different than care. It reveals deep-seated, deficit views of students who arrive speaking a language other than English. The ESL students in the poster were depicted as pollution, impeding the growth of the flowers, which were presumably White, English-speaking students. In this metaphor ESL students were dehumanized, that is, they were not even considered children. Moreover, the educators justified their choice of comparing ESL students to smog by positioning ESL students as a problem, impeding the normal practices of a school, and thus justifying, to these educators, their smog status. This conveys the message that not all students are seen as deserving of nourishment if they require modifications beyond the status quo.

What philosophy of education does this ecosystem support? What philosophy of education do the teachers' words support? And, can educators—even well-intentioned ones who compare ESL students to smog—make sound and equitable decisions for immigrant and refugee children and their families? How do they actually treat these students in their classrooms? What messages do they convey about immigrant and refugee students in a predominantly White classroom? Will the White monolingual students learn to approach the world through an antiracist lens if their teacher works from a deficit-based orientation?

The following sections provide some insight into how deficit-model and microaggressive discourses come to be and what teachers can do about it. Part 2 provides practice activities to disrupt deficit-model and microaggressive discourses in the classroom, school, and social world.

PART 1: DEFINITIONS AND BACKGROUND

What Is Discourse and Where Do Deficit Discourses Come From?

Gee (2014) defines discourses as "ways of enacting and recognizing different sorts of socially situated and significant identities through the use of language integrated with characteristic ways of acting, interacting, believing, valuing, and using various sorts of objects (including our bodies), tools, and technologies in concert with other people" (pp. 156–157). Discourse is both a product of the sociohistorical, cultural, and political context and a producer of structures and institutions within those contexts. Examples of "discourses" could include medical discourse, mainstream media discourse, or teacher discourse.

This chapter focuses on deficit discourses that live within these larger discursive structures. In particular, the ways language, one component of discourse, implicitly and explicitly reveals and reifies deficit thought and practice, is addressed. Embedded in this discussion is the notion of language ideologies.

Deficit-model discourses are ever present in educational thought and practice. Deficit-model thinking promotes the idea that people fail based on inherent, individual, or cultural group deficits without considering the larger systemic issues. The opposite of deficit-model thinking is antideficit, antiracist-model thinking, which questions the power relationships and social inequities that produce deficit discourses and create social, economic, and political circumstances that oppress some groups and privilege others. The challenge is that deficit-model thinking becomes so normalized that it is often difficult to recognize. Examples of policies and practices founded on deficit-model principles are compulsory ignorance laws, de facto and de jure school segregation (Rothstein, 2017), and high-stakes testing such as intelligence tests.

Menchaca (1997) explains that "the roots of deficit thinking are inextricably tied to racist discourses that evolved from the early 1600s to the late 1800s. Out of these discourses came beliefs that racial minorities were physically, cognitively, or culturally inferior to Whites." She goes on to say, "Such deficit thinking was used to justify the economic exploitation of people of color and to deny them the social and political rights enjoyed by whites" (p. 37). Menchaca further argues that while deficit-model thinking has been prevalent throughout history, the intelligence testing movement, beginning in 1905 with Binet and Simon in France, institutionalized deficit-model thinking in science and education. These tests posited that intellectual ability is determined by biology and thus, people who score lower on intelligence tests are inherently intellectually inferior. Menchaca described this as a genetic pathology model, which emerged in part from the eugenics movement.

The eugenics movement began in the late 19th century with British scholar Francis Galton. Galton believed in the superiority of the White race and sought ways to prove his claims. His ideas were extended and adopted by US scientists, some of whom were connected to the intelligence testing movement. US scientists used the study of eugenics in the early 20th century to not only expand intelligence testing, but also to create policies to stop the transmission of so-called undesirable genes.

Undesirable "genes" or qualities, to eugenics promoters, included criminal behavior, alcoholism, blindness or deafness, feeblemindedness, intellectual dullness, and promiscuity. These qualities were typically assigned to low-income Whites and people of color. The label of promiscuity included women and children who had been raped and become pregnant. When seeking medical care for their injuries or pregnancy, doctors, through official state policy, were legally able to sterilize the woman or child without consent. Some US states still retain eugenics-based laws. Court cases as recent as 2017 have been heard in states like North Carolina for women seeking justice for sterilization without consent. Prominent eugenics supporters in the US historically include Alexander Graham Bell and John Harvey Kellogg. Some intellectuals and scientists of color also supported ideas related to eugenics, but not based on racial categories. The popularity of the eugenics movement in the US spread to Germany. Adolf Hitler used this pseudoscience to promote his notion of the Aryan race and justify the genocide of the Jewish people.

The insidious nature of deficit-model thinking within the system of White supremacy and racial oppression is evident in the way it still impacts educational thought and practice. The eugenics movement, for example, engendered support for school segregation and the tracking of students into trade schools and vocational tracks. Chang (2016) explains:

> Segregation is still linked to racial disparities of every kind. Where you live plays a significant role in the quality of food and the quality of education available to you, your ability to get a job, buy a home, and build wealth, the kind of health care you receive and how long you live, and whether you will have anything to pass on to the next generation. (p. 72)

Common tropes such as "We have to have bricklayers too" or "Not everyone is cut out for college," for example, are grounded in this notion of biological determinism that ignores the social and economic impact of segregation.

Standardized tests such as the ACT, SAT, and other college entrance exams were born out of these ideas. They continue to serve as gatekeeping mechanisms for postsecondary education, even though they have been shown to be inadequate in predicting college success (Hiss & Franks, 2014). Still, the standardized test industry is booming, costing students, families, and schools millions, if not billions, of dollars each year. A CRTA reading of these tests includes, "How did these test come to be? Who benefits most from intelligence tests and standardized testing? Who is hurt by testing? Who decides who the 'bricklayers' are, and does everyone have equal opportunity to choose to be a bricklayer or to go to college?"

Deficit-model thought and practice also pervades current educational research. Valencia (1997) explains that in science, deficit-model thinking is "a form of pseudoscience in which researchers approach their work with deeply embedded negative biases, pursue such work in methodologically flawed ways, and communicate their findings in proselytizing manners" (p. 10). Valencia explains that the cycle of deficit thinking is still prevalent and works like this:

1. A social problem is identified.
2. A study is conducted to show how the advantaged and disadvantaged are different.

3. These differences are defined as the problem.
4. An intervention plan is designed and implemented with the differences as the premise.

An example of deficit-model thinking in educational research is the popular and widely shared "word gap" study. The notion of the word gap was first coined by Hart and Risley who investigated the vocabulary differences between low-income and high-income families in 1995. To illustrate how the cycle of deficit-model thinking in research works, I present a summary and critical analysis of the word gap study and how it reinforces and normalizes the cycle of deficit-model thinking in education.

Hart and Risley began by identifying a social problem. Namely, that children from poor neighborhoods performed lower in literacy skills tests—including vocabulary tests—upon entering kindergarten. The children they studied were enrolled in what they, and other researchers at the time, considered to be a high-quality language and literacy skills intervention program. Even with the support of this program low-income children were still performing much below their high-income peers on measures of literacy.

Naming a social problem is not in itself an example of deficit thinking; however, Hart and Risley failed to consider another possible problem: the assumed quality of the intervention program and the validity of the vocabulary assessments. Literacy skills intervention programs, especially those designed for low-income children, are historically deficit in nature as they present decontextualized approaches to literacy instruction rather than rich exposure to authentic texts. Further, vocabulary assessments test words out of context. Children who have "test literacy" (practice interacting with the discourse of testing) often perform better. In this way, familiarity with the format of vocabulary tests, not vocabulary knowledge alone, can contribute to better test scores.

Studies such as Heath's (1983), Purcell-Gates's (1995), and Smith and Wilhelm's (2002) seminal literacy ethnographies show how school-based practices are skewed toward White, middle-class norms. Middle- and high-income parents are often privy to the norms of "doing school" and thus train their children accordingly. Heath (1982 and 1983) challenged the notion of reducing literacy to vocabulary lists and other White middle-income practices of doing school. Heath suggests that schools fail to recognize the full range of linguistic resources in a community or household by focusing on a narrow set of discrete literacy skills and thus perpetually position low-income students and students of color as having a deficit.

Hart and Risley's study and those who sought to replicate it (e.g., Hart & Risley, 1995; Isaacs, Brookings Institute, 2012) unsurprisingly affirmed the notion of the word gap because their studies were based on the same premise: that low-income families and children were the problem, not the literacy program, the system that privileges White middle- and upper-class students, or the studies themselves.

As a result of these deficit-model approaches, interventions were developed. These interventions focused on "fixing" the families through parent literacy trainings and federal programs such as "Too Small to Fail," a program designed to address school readiness for low-income families. No funds were committed to housing discrimination, desegregation, or economic and social policies that would change a system designed for White middle- and upper-class families and would likely do much more to "fix" low literacy.

Lisa Delpit was also writing about literacy at the same time as the Hart and Risley word gap study but gained less traction in public discourse, mainly because the solution to the perceived problem, as Delpit proposed, is complex and nuanced. This is the challenge with studies based on deficit-model thinking. Solutions to educational problems that arise out of deficit-model thinking seem simple and solvable, but addressing the "culture of power," as Delpit calls it, seems much more nebulous and complicated.

A complicated problem requires a complicated solution, not a quick fix. Delpit asserts that schools privilege particular repertoires and pathologize those that diverge from norms and practices of the powerful rather than focusing on the inequities that place low-income families at a disadvantage (Dudley-Marling & Lucas, 2009; Dudley-Marling, 2007; Foley, 1997). Pathologizing children and families is the process of blaming inequities on individual families and communities as if their social and cultural practices are diseases rather than pathologizing the system that creates social and economic inequities like highly segregated neighborhoods with little promise of upward mobility.

A recent article published in *The Washington Post* explores the expense of being poor in the US (Weese, 2018). Addressing the particular issue described by Hart and Risley involves a focus on the system, not fixing families. In order to dismantle an inequitable system, those in power have to assume an antideficit, antiracist stance. Classrooms and schools are a good place to start.

Deficit discourses evolve and are largely shaped by the attitudes, policies, and social movements of the time (DeCuir & Dixson, 2004; Ladson-Billings & Tate, 1998; Menchaca, 1997; Parker & Lynn, 2002; Solorzano, Ceja, & Yosso, 2000; Taylor, 1998; Valencia, 2010). Antideficit approaches are related to, but should not be confused with or reduced to, strength- or asset-based approaches.

Strength-based and asset-based approaches in schools focus on identifying particular skills that are perceived to be valuable for the existing system (e.g., reading for information or fluency). Antideficit approaches are focused on questioning the nature of that system, who has the power to define educational failure including which skills are valued, and what can be done to change the system, not the child, family, or community.

How Notions of Standard English Perpetuate Deficit Thinking

Exploring the intersections of language and power is inextricably linked to the process of dismantling deficit-model thinking and discourse. When discussing race and immigration, in particular, language(s) and language ideologies are central to the conversation, especially in contexts like the US where English is the preferred linguistic medium of instruction. Language ideologies are "people's ideas about language and speech" and "what language is like and what it should be like" (Philips, 1993, p. 557).

Language ideologies form and are made visible through discursive practices of educational policy and practice. For example, while many varieties and forms of English are spoken in the US and one in five children in US schools speak a language other than English, monolingualism remains the focus in curriculum for most schools. Children and families who arrive in the US without a strong foundation in English are seen as having a deficit needing to be remedied, typically through English-only curricula. Monolingualism, however, is the exception rather than the rule globally, and the US has a troubled history of punitive approaches, erasure, and denial of linguistic rights to both indigenous peoples and immigrants.

Systems of power determine whether a code system is considered a language, dialect, or a standard or nonstandard form. To linguists, what constitutes a language or dialect—grammatically speaking—is inconsistent. The distinction is largely dependent upon who is in a position of decision-making power to label something a "language" or a "dialect." This is also true for so-called standard forms of languages.

Gee (2014) uses the example of the "naked be" often present in African American forms of English: "My sister, she be always bothering me." When this phrase is typed into word processing software, a blue line appears underneath, suggesting a need to "resolve subject verb agreement." The identification of this "mistake" is common among those who speak what is often thought of as the standard form of US English. As Gee asserts, however, "it is not a mistake. It is what linguists call a 'durative aspect marker,' that is, a form that means that an action or event is a regular event, happens over and over, and is characteristic or typical. Lots of languages have a durative aspect marker, even though Standard English does not" (p. 9).

Delpit (2006) argues that this propensity for labeling legitimate linguistic forms as a mistake is much more about who uses the forms, rather than the forms themselves. Consider, for example, the general US public's attitude toward someone speaking British English. What is assumed about this person based on his or her accent and language use? Are the linguistic forms the same as US English? If not, why are these acceptable deviations from the US standard form of English, but African American forms of English are not? Would you correct a student using a form of British English in your literacy classroom? What about a student speaking an African American form of English?

Accessing both the "politically popular" dialect and studying a variety of linguistic forms is key. In the same way that official and standard forms of English and Spanish, for example, can be taught, multiple dialects can be explored. White teachers in a predominantly White context have a critical responsibility to disrupt deficit-model thinking toward marginalized linguistic forms. Through a reflective, CRTA approach educators can work to first interrogate their own biases and then address those of their students and colleagues. The following is an example from my experience as an ELL teacher in the southern US. This example illustrates how educators who hold deficit views of linguistic forms impede learning.

* * *

THE COT SOT ON THE MOT

One afternoon, I visited the reading specialist's room to observe one of our ELL students, Andrea. Andrea was in third grade. I found Andrea sitting intently next to the reading specialist with a basal reader text designed to teach the short "a" sound.

Andrea read, "The cat sat on the mat." She read it with perfect fluency, but pronounced the words with a Spanish accent, with her "a" sound resembling something similar to the English short "o" sound. I was not surprised by Andrea's fluency as Andrea had read fourth-grade-level books in my classroom. In fact, I was in the process of recommending that Andrea begin to transition out of the ELL program.

To my surprise, the reading specialist asked Andrea to read the book again, "but pay attention to the 'a' sound." She turned to me and said, "I hope you are working with Andrea on her reading in your classroom." The reading specialist then modeled for Andrea what she believed to be the correct way to pronounce the words. Given our location in the South, the reading specialist had a distinct White, southern accent. Her pronunciation of the short "a" sound was reflective of her own linguistic norms, with the short "a's" having more than one syllable—"ca-yuht"—and sounding slightly more like a standard long "a." This is a common characteristic of southern US English.

* * *

In this example, neither the student nor the reading specialist was using a standard form of US English, but context and power played a primary role in whose linguistic forms were considered correct or conventional. Much time was wasted in the reading specialist's classroom on pronunciation rather than comprehension. The reading specialist had the power to determine that Andrea's accent was wrong and in need of remediation, thus depriving Andrea of valuable literacy time that could have been spent reading authentic texts for comprehension (or fun).

Consider the following questions: In what ways are you reproducing deficit attitudes toward particular linguistic forms in your classroom? In what ways are you disrupting them? If your students speak a standard variety of a language, how are you exposing them to the ways language and dialect relate to power?

Language attitudes can be explored both locally and globally. While there are between 6,000 and 7,000 languages spoken in the world, these numbers do not account for the multitude of codes that are classified as dialects or nonstandard forms of official languages. In Taiwan, for example, Taiwanese is recognized as a language. China claims Taiwan as a territory, but recognizes Taiwanese as a dialect of Mandarin Chinese, rather than an official language.

Some challenge this designation as there are issues with mutual intelligibility. Even speakers of the same dialect rarely produce linguistic forms in precisely the same way. For example, Cassidy and Hall produced a series of books titled *Dictionary of American Regional English*, cataloging in great detail the accents and dialects used regionally across the US. These dialect dictionaries, which are published in large, alphabetized volumes with thousands of pages, have taken more than 10 years to compile. The process is ongoing because language evolves faster than the research can be conducted, compiled, and published.

I engage both K–12 and university students in activities to explore their own regional dialects using these texts and students' own experiences. For example, I grew up in Nebraska using the word *pop* for carbonated drinks. My grandmother, who grew up in Kansas, used the general term *Coke*. In the region of Pennsylvania where I currently reside, *soda* is used. All of these forms are correct, but the preferred convention depends on where one lives.

To explore this, I engage students in an autogeography and linguistic landscape activity where students interview parents and community members using some of the regional dialect characteristics to trace their linguistic roots. In Philadelphia, I worked with students on a parts of speech minilesson using the word *jawn*, a flexible term that can be used to describe a person, place, thing, or event, depending on the context. Jawn is currently considered a "slang" word specific to Philadelphia, but it is likely to show up, if it has not already, in more official spaces soon.

Language is ever evolving and thus it is difficult to pinpoint a solid definition of the standard. Words we might consider to be staples of Standard English, like the word *aviation*, were once considered an abomination of the language (Yule, 2016). Consider the ways to explore American regional dialects with your students and how power plays a role in determining which are considered standard forms and which are not.

When language and literacy is reduced to a list of discrete language units and vocabulary lists, it fails to acknowledge the full range of linguistic resources in communities and households and the impact of language ideologies on how we view and teach language(s). If we return to the word gap notion, for example, what vocabularies or Englishes were missed in the testing and cataloging of children's language? Were standard and nonstandard forms "counted" or were they perceived as deficits impeding children's ability to use standard forms? In what ways do we value the linguistic skills required for code-switching between languages? As Lyiscott poetically proclaims, "The English language is a multifaceted oration; subject to indefinite transformation" (2014).

Microaggressions: How Deficit Discourses Play Out Through Language

Microaggressions are considered unconscious discursive acts committed by the majority that perpetuate stereotypes and "wound" marginalized individuals or groups (Lawrence, 1995, as cited in in DeCuir & Dixson, 2004; Sue, Capodilupo, Torino, Bucceri, Holder, Nadal, & Esquilin, 2007). In this section, we move our discussion from specific language code systems (e.g. English, Spanish, Taiwanese) to ways of using language to convey or perpetuate deficit or microaggressive views inherent in everyday society, including schools.

Derald Wing Sue (2010), who has written extensively about racial microaggressions, defines them as

> the brief and everyday slights, insults, indignities, and denigrating messages sent to people of color by well-intentioned White people who are unaware of the hidden messages being communicated. These messages may be sent verbally ("You speak good English."), nonverbally (clutching one's purse more tightly) or environmentally (symbols like the confederate flag or using American Indian mascots).

Microaggressions reveal the ingrained deficit-model thinking grounded in the system of White supremacy and racial oppression.

Here are some examples of microaggressions:

- "Where are you really from?"
- "You are so articulate."
- "What are you?"
- "When I talk about Mexicans, I don't mean you. You're different."
- "You're from Puerto Rico and you don't speak Spanish? What a shame."
- "He's an illegal."

An extensive list of microaggressions is included in the resources section of this chapter. The question "Where are you really from?" is used as an illustrative example to explore how microaggressions reinforce deficit-model thinking:

* * *

I'M FROM NEW JERSEY!

Ravinder is a Sikh man in his 20s. He wears the dastaar, or turban, and has a long beard, as is customary with some Sikh men. Ravinder, who is a tech entrepreneur, travels across the US and throughout the world frequently. "Wherever I go in the US, I get the question, 'Where are you from?' My answer is always the same, 'New Jersey.' But people are rarely satisfied with this answer. They usually follow up with, 'No, where are you really from?' And I repeat again: 'New-Jer-sey!'" (He laughs.)

* * *

This question of "Where are you really from?" seems innocuous to most Whites, but has at its roots a racially microaggressive subtext. The implied question is, "But, you don't look American to me, so you must be from somewhere else." People of White, European descent rarely get these follow-up inquiries unless the conversation is specifically focused on ancestry. This is what is called "Othering," a discursive act that separates and defines someone as different than the perceived norm. A popular YouTube video circulated a few years ago that parodies this experience. Teacher can use this resource to spark conversation about microaggressions with students: https://www.youtube.com/watch?v=crAv5ttax2I.

Another example of a common microaggression is the perceived compliment about being articulate. When a White person says to a person of color, "You are so articulate," it is implied that the White person is surprised by the person of color's ability to be articulate or an eloquent speaker. This relates to the discussion earlier in this chapter about the perceived deficits of African

American forms of English, namely, that White people often hold the notion that these forms equate to an educational deficit.

Jamila Lyiscott (2014), in her TED Talk *Three Ways to Speak English*, critiques and shatters the conventional notion of "being articulate" by positioning monolingualism and monodialectalism as the deficit. This TED talk, along with Lyiscott's research in literacy and code-switching, is one way to begin the conversation in your classroom about disrupting racial microaggressions related to language, race, and immigration status.

With my colleague Kevin Roxas (Roy & Roxas, 2011), I studied how deficit-model and microaggressive discourses directly impact students through our research with Somali Bantu students in a newcomer program in south Texas and Michigan through a critical race theory (CRT) lens. Findings revealed that educators focused on perceived behavioral issues, perceived deficits in motivation, and perceived cultural deficits as the reason for students' academic challenges rather than interrogating the school's proficiency in addressing the needs of refugee families and children. The planned interventions focused on ways to ameliorate the perceived problematic practices among the children and families rather than reevaluating the welcoming and unwelcoming aspects of the school.

Reframing of Essential Questions to Disrupt Deficit-Model Thinking

How you frame a question drives the types of answers you will receive. Essential Questions are designed to frame your lessons thematically and ask big-picture question about lessons and units. The following Essential Question was used for a lesson on homelessness. The teacher designed the lesson to address issues of social justice in the classroom. While the materials, resources, and intent were sound, the Essential Question was grounded in deficit-model thinking. Read the Essential Question. What makes it deficit based? How could it be revised?

Essential Question: In what ways does homelessness impact individuals and how do they overcome it?

On the surface, this Essential Question seems innocuous. It frames a conversation about homelessness, which is indeed a social justice topic. The problem with this question is that it focuses on individuals, not systems, and seems to suggest that homelessness is something that can be "overcome" by the individual homeless person. The individual human, rather than society, is implicated as the problem.

A teacher working from a CRTA lens might ask the following of this Essential Question: Can individuals overcome homelessness and what would this require? What are the structural, system, and institutional factors that cause homelessness? What structural, system, and institutional factors create barriers for overcoming homelessness in general? What are the biases or stereotypes people hold about the homeless? How can we disrupt those biases and change the system?

I Trust Your Judgment

I was recently observing one of my student teachers in an English language arts classroom. Mr. Kelley is White and his students are Black and Brown. One of his students asked, "Can I use slang and swear words in my essay for tomorrow since the article is about censorship?" Mr. Kelley's response was, "In this particular case, we're focusing on argument, so when we're trying to convince people of something, we have to think about how the audience will relate to it. I trust your judgment."

Mr. Kelley's classroom is a place where students study the craft of writing through multiple forms for multiple purposes. Grammar mini-lessons happen in his classroom, but instead of teaching "this is what's right about language," Mr. Kelley focuses on how language is used for different purposes to reach particular audiences. Multiple repertories are privileged in his classroom and students make their own choices in their writing. He really does trust their judgment and grammar is taught within larger units grounded in authentic literature and content.

Teachers like Mr. Kelley recognize that language is fluid and ever evolving. New words and phrases enter lexicons with regularity; some are accepted and others are discarded. How many times have you heard (or said), "It's not a word because it's not in the dictionary!"? Begin a lesson with the following questions: Who gets to decide which new words are added to the dictionary and how do they get this power? What factors are considered when adding a new word to the dictionary? If different people had the decision-making power, would different words be added? Hold language forums and attempt to replicate the process for entering a new word into the dictionary.

Also, explore how young people and pop culture play a large role in reshaping how language is used. Instead, young people are often held up as destroyers of language ("kids these days!"). Engage in a linguistic research project with your students instead of teaching grammar. Study how language changes and evolves over time and youths' impact on turning invention into convention. Study how other languages have impacted English historically.

The invention of the printing press had a lasting impact on privileging the written word. The printing press also helped to create standard forms of languages that were widely circulated. The printed forms often varied greatly from the spoken ones. For example, when printing presses were invented, there were many dialects of English and the printers had to choose one.

Dutch printing presses, for example, used Dutch orthography to spell words such as *ghost* with the silent "h."

Traditional grammar teaching typically involves holding up what is right and what is wrong about a language. This is not to say that conventional norms of language should not be taught, but a CRTA lens makes space for critique and innovation when learning about language. Students can question what systems and institutions get to decide whose way of using language is privileged. Students can also explore issues around relegating languages to dialect status or why certain words and phrases are characterized as slang. A CRTA lens supports exploring how code systems are marginalized based on the historical, social, and political context.

While microaggressions are described as slights by well-intentioned speakers, this definition can sometimes minimize the impetus and collective impact of deficit and microaggressive discourse in that it generously gives the microaggressors the benefit of the doubt. At what point are White educators held accountable for perpetuating or dismantling the system of White supremacy? Once it is revealed, what responsibility do White teachers have in taking action against it? Part 2 supports teachers in taking this action.

PART 2: CLASSROOM ACTIVITIES: UNMASKING WHITE SUPREMACY AND DISMANTLING DEFICIT-MODEL AND MICROAGGRESSIVE DISCOURSES

Dismantling deficit-model thinking and microaggressive discourse is an exercise in unmasking White supremacy. This section focuses on how educators can take action to dismantle deficit-model and microaggressive discourse in their classrooms, schools, and communities. The activities below are designed for both teachers and students.

I use discourse analysis in both my higher education and K–12 classroom to help students identify deficit discourses and microaggressions. Analysis of discourse can take multiple forms, which could involve more discrete analysis of linguistic practices—such as the use of pauses and tone—to content analysis, which could focus on word choice, for example. Use the exercises below to begin exploring the possibilities of analyzing discourse.

Activity 1: Transforming Our Questions: Moving Teachers From Deficit to Antideficit Questions

This exercise in transforming questions from deficit to antideficit-model thinking comes from an assignment in one of my graduate courses focused on teaching ELL students. In this assignment, I asked my graduate students, who were all in-service teachers, to write a reflection paper in preparation for a research project. The research project had to address a question they had about teaching ELLs or working with immigrant and refugee families. I asked them to begin by writing potential research questions. Examples A, B, and C are examples of questions my graduate students produced:

a. "My ESL students aren't motivated to use English. I want to study how to increase motivation in ESL students."
b. "The ESL student in my class is labeled oppositional defiant because when we ask him to participate in class and do his assignments, he just puts his head on his desk and refuses to do his work. I don't have a lot of extra instructional time to deal with him."
c. "The parents of our ESL kids aren't really involved in school and they rarely attend conferences and school events. I want to study how to motivate immigrant families to be involved in school."

In order to practice identifying deficit-model and microaggressive discourse, begin by underlining the deficit and/or microaggressive aspects of each example above. Pinpoint the particular words or phrases that index deficit-model and microaggressive discourse. Next, rewrite the questions from an antideficit perspective. Below are the edited, second drafts the graduate students produced after an in-class activity on transforming deficit thinking:

a. "In what ways can teachers or schools create an environment that is motivating for ELL students?"
b. "It must be incredibly difficult to live in a new language every day as a child. In what ways can I create a connection with the ELL students in my class and use their interests as pathways to learning?"
c. "What can schools do to be more flexible, creative, and welcoming in the process of involving parents? What programs have been successful in engaging families of ELL children?"

The first draft of the questions my graduate students produced are examples of deficit-model thinking. If the students had moved forward with their research projects based on their initial questions, it is likely they would have produced findings that pathologized or blamed ELLs and their families for challenges in school.

For example, in the first draft of Example A, the teacher assumed the students were unmotivated, but how did the teacher identify motivation? What indexed motivation? How can the teacher be sure it is not something else like the challenges of moving to a new country and living in a language that is unfamiliar? Focusing on motivation limited the study and potential findings for why the students were struggling.

Example B is problematic on a number of levels. First, is the ELL student really labeled oppositional defiant because he puts his head on the desk or chooses not to participate? This seems like inadequate evidence for such a weighty label. Research consistently shows an overrepresentation of ELLs in special education, including behavior-related intervention programs. Second, the use of the phrase "deal with him" positions the child as a problem to be fixed or perhaps even ignored, in this case. The idea of having to "deal with" ELL students aligns much more closely with the school ecosystem example at the beginning of this chapter.

The new version acknowledges the challenges faced by an ELL student and places the teacher as having the onus in creating pathways to learning. Still, the reframing of the question ignores the reality that the student has an oppositional defiant label. A teacher working from a CRTA approach might critique how BD (behavior disorder) labels are inequitably applied to children of color and the potential consequence of entering a child into the school-to-prison pipeline.

The first draft of Example C represents a blaming of parents rather than the system and its rigid approaches to parent outreach. The second draft of the question seeks to draw from what is working in parent outreach and focuses on ways to make school practices more permeable to parents.

Teachers can use the first drafts of these deficit-model research questions in professional development settings with colleagues. Begin with a description of deficit-model thinking and microaggressive discourse. Then, ask colleagues to revise the research questions themselves. As a follow-up activity, ask teachers to find examples of deficit-model and microaggressive discourse in their own classroom, curriculum, and school.

Activity 2: Identifying the Deficit Labels in Schooling

In addition to analyzing the questions we ask about students in our classroom, teachers can also analyze the specific discursive practices involved in "labeling" in schools. Identifying and critiquing the labels through a CRTA lens can reveal how language positions certain students in deficit ways.

Begin by making a list of terms or labels used to describe students in your school. Explore how these labels contribute to deficit-model thinking or microaggressive discourse. Here are some examples of labels you might encounter:

At-Risk

The label "at-risk" emerged in the 1980s after a report called *A Nation at Risk* was published by the National Commission on Excellence in Education. While the "system" was the primary target of this report, the warnings were quickly translated and transformed into deficit views of students and families. CRTA questions about this label might include, "Are students themselves 'risky' or does the system position them to be at risk of failure? If the system is to blame, why do we label the students as such? Could we identify at-risk policies and practices that harm students and families rather than labeling students?"

LEP (Limited English Proficient)

The use of the word *limited* in this label renders it easily identifiable as a deficit label. If monolingualism is the exception globally, most children coming to the US speaking a language other than English are multilingual. People who are bilingual or multilingual have been found to possess cognitive and linguistic skills beyond that of their monolingual peers, but schools rarely measure bilingualism; thus, these skills and knowledge are undervalued or ignored. Schools that privilege and value bilingualism focus instead on the continuum of language learning. Labels that identify students on a continuum, rather than a deficit of language learning, could include English language learners (ELLs) or English learners (ELs).

English as a Second Language (ESL)

This term is becoming less and less common, but it is still used to label students arriving in the US with little or no background in English. It is also used to describe the particular type of class or instructional delivery method for teaching English to immigrant and refugee students. Since most immigrant and refugee students arrive speaking more than one language, English is not always their "second" language. The use of the word *second* reveals and contributes to the hegemonic nature of English, that is, the assumption that if their first language was not English, then it must be the second. This also fails to recognize and value the multitude of ways humans use language.

Illegals or Illegal Aliens

Using the term *illegal immigrant* or *illegal alien* is considered a microaggression because it characterizes individuals and groups as illegal, rather than labeling the action or crime. No human is illegal or *Ningún ser humano es ilegal*. Why, for example, are other individuals or groups not labeled illegal for committing a crime? Describing someone as undocumented or unauthorized is preferred.

Language Barrier

This is not a label, per se, but is a common issue that is raised when talking about immigrants and refugees. A teacher might say, for example, "Students are struggling in my class because they have a language barrier" or "We can't communicate with parents because of the language barrier." It is not to say that this barrier is nonexistent, but a teacher working from a CRTA perspective might ask, "Do children and families have a language barrier or do schools create barriers by offering few language services? In what ways could schools build bridges through language? What systemic or institutional factors create language barriers?"

Activity 3: Honoring Multiple Voices

Use the following quote by Gloria Anzaldúa (1999):

> Until I am free to write bilingually and to switch codes without having always to translate, while I still have to speak English or Spanish when I would rather speak Spanglish, and as long as I have to accommodate the English speakers rather than having them accommodate me, my tongue will be illegitimate. I will no longer be made to feel ashamed of existing. I will have my voice: Indian, Spanish, white. I will have my serpent's tongue—my woman's voice, my sexual voice, my poet's voice. I will overcome the tradition of silence. (p. 81)

Ask your students, "What does Anzaldúa mean by 'tradition of silence'? How does this relate to deficit and microaggressive discourses? How does language relate to, anchor, guide, and inform our identities and histories? What 'voices' do you have and how are they perceived, uplifted, valued, marginalized, or silenced in society?"

RECOMMENDED RESOURCES

Books and Articles

Bonilla-Silva, E. (2018). *Racism without racists: Color-blind racism and the persistence of racial inequality in America*. Lanham, MD: Rowman & Littlefield.

University of Minnesota, School of Public Health. Adapted from Sue, Capodilupo, Torino, Bucceri, Holder, Nadal, & Esquilin. (2007, May–June). Racial microaggressions in everyday life: Implications for clinical practice. *American Psychologist, 62*(4), 271–286. Retrieved from http://sph.umn.edu/site/docs/hewg/microaggressions.pdf

Podcasts and Videos

Lyiscott, J. (2014). *Three ways to speak English* [Video file]. Retrieved from https://www.ted.com/talks/jamila_lyiscott_3_ways_to_speak_english

Tanaka, Ken [Kentanakajapan]. (2013, May). *Where are you from?* [Video file]. Retrieved from https://www.youtube.com/watch?v=crAv5ttax2I

Websites

Education Studies: Thinking Beyond the Deficit Model: http://debsedstudies.org/thinking-beyond-the-deficit-model/

REFERENCES

Anzaldúa, G. (1999). *Borderlands: La frontera*. San Francisco: Aunt Lute Books.

Chang, J. (2016). *We gon' be alright: Notes on race and resegregation.* New York, NY: Picador.

DeCuir, J. T., & Dixson, A. D. (2004). So when it comes out, they aren't surprised that it is there: Using critical race theory as a tool of analysis of race and racism in education. *Educational Researcher, 33*(5) 26–31. Retrieved from https://eric.ed.gov/?id=EJ727581

Delpit, Lisa. 2006. *Other people's children: Cultural conflict in the classroom*. New York: New Press.

Dudley-Marling, C. (2007). Return of the deficit. *Journal of Educational Controversy, 2*(1).

Dudley-Marling, C., & Lucas, K. (2009). Pathologizing the language and culture of poor children. *ERIC, 86*(5), 362–370.

Foley, D. E. (1997). Deficit thinking models based on culture: The anthropological protest. In Valencia, R. R. (Ed.), *The evolution of deficit thinking: Educational thought and practice* (pp. 113–131). Abingdon, England: Routledge.

Gee, J. (2014). *How to do discourse analysis.* Abingdon, England: Routledge.

Hart, B., & Risley, T. (1995). *Meaningful differences in the everyday experience of young American children*. Baltimore, MD: Paul H. Brookes.

Heath, S. (1982). What No Bedtime Story Means: Narrative Skills at Home and School. *Language in Society, 11*(1), 49–76.

Heath, S. B. (1983). *Ways with words: Language, life, and work in communities and classrooms.* Cambridge, England: Cambridge University Press.

Hiss, W., & Franks, V. W. (2014). *Defining promise: Optional standardized testing policies in American college and university admissions.* Retrieved from https://offices.depaul.edu/enrollment-management-marketing/testoptional/Documents/HISSDefiningPromise.pdf

Issacs, J. (2012). *Starting school at a disadvantage: The school readiness of poor children.* Brookings Institute: Center on Children and Families.

Ladson-Billings, G., & Tate, W. F. (1998). *Toward a critical race theory of education.* Retrieved from http://www.unco.edu/education-behavioral-sciences/pdf/TowardaCRTEduca.pdf

Menchaca, M. (1997). Early racist discourses: Roots of deficit thinking. In R. Valencia (Ed.) *The evolution of deficit thinking: Educational thought and practice, 1st ed.*, (pp. 13–40). London: Routledge Falmer.

Parker, L., & Lynn, M. (2002). What's race got to do with it? Critical race theory's conflicts with and connections to qualitative research methodology and epistemology. *Qualitative Inquiry, 8*(1)7–22. https://doi.org/10.1177/107780040200800102

Philips, S. (1993). *The invisible culture*. Prospect Heights, IL: Waveland Press.

Purcell-Gates, V. (1995). *Other people's words: The cycle of low literary*. Cambridge, MA: Harvard University Press.

Rothstein, R. (2017). *The color of the law: A forgotten history of how our government segregated America*. New York, NY: Liveright.

Roy, L., & Roxas, K. (2011). Whose deficit is this anyhow? Exploring counter-stories of Somali Bantu refugees in "doing school." *Harvard Educational Review, 81*(3), 521–541.

Smith, M., & Wilhelm, J. (2002). *Reading don't fix no Chevys: Literacy in the lives of young men.* Portsmouth, NH: Heinemann.

Solorzano, D., Ceja, M., & Yosso, T. (2000). Critical race theory, racial microaggressions and campus racial climate: The experiences of African American college students. *Journal of Negro Education, 69*(1/2), 60.

Sue, D. W. (2010). Racial microaggressions in everyday life: Is subtle bias harmless? *Psychology Today.* Retrieved from https://www.psychologytoday.com/us/blog/microaggressions-in-everyday-life/201010/racial-microaggressions-in-everyday-life

Sue, D. W., Capodilupo, C. M., Torino, G. C., Bucceri, J. M., Holder, A. M., Nadal, K. L., & Esquilin, M. (2007, May–June). Racial microaggressions in everyday life: Implications for clinical practice. *American Psychologist, 62*(4): 271–286.

Taylor, E. (1998). A primer on critical race theory. *Journal of Blacks in Higher Education, 19*, 122–124.

Valencia, R. R. (1997). Conceptualizing the Notion of Deficit Thinking. In R. R. Valencia, (Ed.), *The Evolution of Deficit Thinking: Educational thought and practice, 1st ed.*, (pp. 1–12). London: Routledge Falmer.

Valencia, R. R. (Ed.) (2010). *Chicano school failure and success: Past, present, and future* (3rd ed.). Abingdon, England: Routledge.

Weese, K. (2018, January 25). *Why it costs so much to be poor in America.* Retrieved from https://www.washingtonpost.com/news/posteverything/wp/2018/01/25/why-it-costs-so-much-to-be-poor-in-america/?utm_term=.51f2fcf9b9df

Yule, G. (2016). *The study of language. 6th ed.* London: Cambridge University Press.

Part II

Disrupting the Single Story in Curriculum

Chapter Four

Cultivating a Critical Classroom Community from Day One

> We cannot seek achievement for ourselves and forget about progress and prosperity for our community. Our ambitions must be broad enough to include the aspirations and needs of others, for their sakes and for our own.
>
> —Cesar Chavez

Cultivating classroom community begins on day one and is an ongoing, iterative process. This chapter focuses on cultivating classroom community through a critical race teacher activism (CRTA) lens. This chapter invites teachers to consider the benefits of liberatory and consciousness-raising practices in the classroom in order to build a more just and democratically minded society. Supporting teachers in developing an authentic ethos of care (Noddings, 2013) grounded in Freire's (1968) notion of dialogue is the primary focus in addition to the merits of restorative practices over traditional classroom management frameworks.

Key Ideas and Terms

- Classroom community
- Classroom management
- School-to-prison pipeline
- Authentic ethos of care
- Dialogue
- Restorative and consciousness-raising practices

Nouri and Sajjadi (2014) assert "that education should play a fundamental role in creating a just and democratic society" (p. 78). To this end, teachers should play a fundamental role in disrupting systems of oppression by engaging in liberatory pedagogy and restorative, consciousness-raising practices in the classroom. Consciousness-raising practices or developing critical consciousness is the act of critically "reading the word and the world" (Freire, 1968).

Freire contends that liberatory pedagogy happens at the intersection of love and critical consciousness in the classroom. Love, meaning an authentic dialogue and ethos of care that is grounded in deep respect for the funds of knowledge of students and their community, and critical consciousness raising, meaning the process of cultivating critical awareness of systems of oppression that hinder justice and democracy. This love and critical consciousness is grounded in dialogue whereby multiple perspectives and "ways of being" are honored and heard.

The following sections guide teachers in considering the radical possibilities for cultivating classroom community through a CRTA lens. This involves abandoning the traditional notions of classroom management and ensuring that students, families, and communities have power and voice in determining the culture of a classroom, school, or district community. It also means critiquing and transforming the ways classroom management practices in predominantly White spaces reify systems of oppression. Instead, I advocate for White teachers to lead the charge in modeling and teaching White students how to dismantle systems of oppression. Part 1 of this chapter provides background information and definitions that call into question traditional classroom management practices. Alternative approaches are offered to show how teachers can make changes. Part 2 of this chapter provides examples and strategies for cultivating community through authentic care and dialogue.

PART 1: BACKGROUND AND DEFINITIONS

Teachers employing a CRTA approach are reflective and action oriented. They work to question and change policies and practices in the classroom, school, and world that marginalize students. Begin by answering the following Critical Questions for the Classroom below.

Critical Questions for the Classroom

Answer the following questions and reflect on your own notions of classroom management and classroom community:

- What factors do you consider when deciding on how to manage your classroom?

- What input do students, parents, caregivers, and community members have in how you create classroom community?
- What is your philosophy of teaching and education, and how does that philosophy influence your decisions about classroom management?
- What fears, challenges, and possibilities do you anticipate in changing the way you manage or cultivate community in your classroom?
- How do you communicate your expectations about the classroom community on day one? In what ways do you check in with your students about these expectations throughout the year?

The following is an example from one of my first teaching experiences. It illuminates the inequities in how White, Black, and Brown students experience forms of behavior management differently in schools.

* * *

SCHOOLS THAT LOOK LIKE PRISONS

Before I took my first teaching job, I substituted for a few months. One of my first jobs was in an urban middle school with mostly US-born Black students and immigrant students from Mexico and countries in Central America. In my own middle school experience, I recall the noisy chatter and meeting up with friends between classes. In this school, however, the students were required to line up single file in the hallways with their hands behind their backs. Absolute silence was expected.

When this rule was inevitably violated (they were teenagers, after all!), all students were required to place the tip of their nose up against the wall until silence was once again restored. This often resulted in students being sent to the office for noncompliance. The next day, I substituted at a predominantly White school. Students were allowed to walk freely through the hallways between class periods. Students who were yelling or acting up were met with mild reprimands and side-smiles from their teachers. It was clear that expectations for behavior and freedom were markedly different for students of color and White students.

* * *

The first school in this example resembled a prison where teachers played the role of warden. The management practices were dehumanizing and only succeeded in setting students up for failure by increasing the number of possible rules to be broken. Put into a historical context, these in-school practices resemble Black Codes and Jim Crow laws established after Reconstruction, which were designed to unfairly punish people of color. In the second school, kids were seen as kids, and minor misbehavior was viewed as normal or even humorous. White students were free to be kids. They were trusted and given the benefit of the doubt.

The difference in how White children versus children of color experience discipline in schools sends a powerful message to children about who is trusted, loved, and valued in school and society. CRTA teachers ask, "What is oppressive and what is liberatory about the classroom environment? What is punitive and what is restorative and humanizing in my classroom? What are the real educational and social consequences for students, and would the outcomes be the same for a White middle-class student?"

"IT'S NOT YOU, IT'S US": RETHINKING POWER AND CONTROL IN THE CLASSROOM

"It's not you, it's us" frames how I hope teachers can begin to take responsibility for changing the system, not the kids. I advocate for White teachers to focus on building relationships and cultivating community instead of exercising power and control in the classroom. I advocate for White teachers to acknowledge to their students that it's not them, it's us, teachers who are complicit in perpetuating systems of oppression through the discipline practices they support in schools.

It is not surprising that school practices reflect and reinforce White, Eurocentric practices, especially in how teachers manage and interpret students' behaviors. The teaching population in the US is overwhelmingly White at approximately 80%, and predominantly female. The student population, however, is increasingly diverse.

The incongruence between classroom norms and expectations between White teachers and students of color has been well documented (see, for example, Philips, 1992; Heath, 1983). Recent studies (Gilliam, Maupin, Reyes, Accavitti, & Shic, 2016) show that White teachers' implicit bias of students of color begins as early as preschool. Calls for punitive-based discipline practices, including zero-tolerance policies, are most fervent in schools with predominantly Black and Brown students. In these spaces, classroom management is designed to punish and control rather than restore and heal. These practices have a profound impact on how students of color experience school, including entrance into the school-to-prison pipeline.

The American Civil Liberties Union (ACLU, 2018) defines the school-to-prison pipeline as the "disturbing national trend wherein children are funneled out of public schools and into the juvenile and criminal justice systems." Iselin (2010) found that expulsions and suspensions were associated with lower academic achievement, increased dropout rates, delayed graduation, and decreased academic engagement. Students of color are five times more likely to be suspended from school for the same infractions as White students (Camera, 2017), and thus more likely to enter the US criminal justice system through the school-to-prison pipeline.

The proliferation of zero-tolerance policies in the 1990s, White teachers' implicit bias, and the increase in school resource officers on school campuses have all contributed to the overrepresentation of students of color in the school-to-prison pipeline. School resources officers, the number of which has increased exponentially after the school shooting at Columbine High School in 1999, have been ineffective in preventing subsequent school shootings. Instead, the presence of these officers has increased in-school violence perpetrated against Black and Brown children by law enforcement. The presence of school resource officers has also dramatically changed the environment for both documented and undocumented students who fear that interactions with resource officers will lead to deportation. This has led to coining the school-to-prison-to-deportation pipeline, where school resource officers and even teachers act as an unofficial arm of immigration enforcement and state violence (Marquez & Prandini, 2018).

For-profit prison companies that lobby for the imprisonment of undocumented immigrants benefit financially from everyday citizens as informants. Recall when one of my students asked, "Can we turn students in to immigration if we know they are illegals?" How do teachers acting as unofficial immigration enforcers impact community, learning, and students' rights? How does the presence of law enforcement, metal detectors, and punitive practices impact classroom and school community? What is the purpose of schooling? What is the role of the teacher? Use the following vignette to consider how management practices impact the lives of immigrant students.

* * *

WHEN MANAGEMENT HINDERS COMMUNITY

Mr. Martin is a middle school science teacher. To Mr. Martin, order and discipline have to be present before learning can occur. In October, Horatio joined Mr. Martin's class. Horatio's family was displaced after a recent hurricane destroyed his town in the Dominican Republic. His uncle lives near the school and offered to take him in until Horatio's family could rebuild their life back home. Mr. Martin is unaware of Horatio's background and experiences.

Horatio has been in school for about two weeks and is struggling in school. His conversational English is pretty good, but he's accustomed to using Spanish to learn content. One day, when Horatio sits with friends who also speak Spanish, instead of sitting in his assigned seat, Mr. Martin marks him down for a point. In Mr. Martin's class, students are given points (demerits) each time he feels students are out of line. Once students receive three points, they are assigned to after-school detention.

Mr. Martin informs Horatio that he has "earned" one point and asks him to move back to his seat. Horatio reluctantly complies but rolls his eyes and makes a comment to his friends in Spanish as he does so. Mr. Martin sees the eye roll and the use of Spanish as disrespectful and marks Horatio down for another point. "Show respect in this class and speak English, please. That's another point for you. One more and you have detention," Mr. Martin says as he records the point.

Later, toward the end of the class, Mr. Martin asks students to complete a worksheet on the relationship between electricity and magnetism. Horatio glances around the room. It is clear he's the only one struggling with the worksheet. He drops his pen and uses it as an opportunity to jokingly swap worksheets with a girl sitting near him. She laughs and shushes him, glancing up at Mr. Martin, who is watching from his desk. "Hor-ay-sho," Mr. Martin calls out sternly. Horatio responds by correcting Mr. Martin on the pronunciation of his name, then laughs. Mr. Martin responds, "That's it. Third point. You have detention."

Since Horatio helps in his uncle's store after school, he skips detention, not knowing the implications. The next day, Mr. Martin refuses to allow Horatio in class since he skipped detention. Horatio is visibly frustrated and unclear as to why Mr. Martin is asking him to leave. He talks over Mr. Martin and tries to explain himself and his after-school responsibilities, but Mr. Martin calls the campus resource officer to address the issue. Horatio struggles when the officer attempts to escort him out of the room for what Mr. Martin calls "being combative." Because Horatio did not immediately comply with the resource officer, he is suspended from school.

* * *

Put aside for a moment whether you believe Horatio should have complied or reacted differently to Mr. Martin in this situation. Instead, focus on the idea of "it's not you (students), it's us (teachers)." How did the centering of power, management, control, and punishment set the stage for this interaction between Horatio and Mr. Martin? What can we assume about Mr. Martin's philosophy of teaching? If learning is the goal, what is the intended outcome of Mr. Martin's approach to management in removing Horatio from the learning environment? What are the unintended, but very real, consequences for Horatio? For example, what if Horatio or members of his family are undocumented? Should this matter to teachers? Would this scenario play out in a different way for a White middle class student in a suburban school? If so, how? How did the classroom community, or lack thereof, hinder learning?

The example of Mr. Martin's class demonstrates the potentially dire consequences for classroom management practices that may seem benign for many teachers. The system Mr. Martin was using to control behavior in his classroom resembles a token economy system. Token economy systems work from an extrinsic rewards system, designed to identify and reinforce positive behavior. Some token economies, such as the one used in Mr. Martin's classroom, include a demerit system designed to punish students for undesired behaviors.

Teachers may intend for token economies to shape the classroom community, but they fail to cultivate authentic community. Token economies presume that community and behavior can be commodified or bought. They work from the least common denominator, assuming that prizes or "tokens," rather than responsive pedagogy, motivate students to behave or stay engaged. One of Laura's graduate students lamented the token economy system in her school with predominantly Black and Brown students.

* * *

BUYING COMMUNITY?

"It's silly, really, giving out these rewards tickets for regular things like helping a friend or turning in homework—things students would probably do anyway, or not do, depending on the day and the circumstances. The tickets were supposed to entice students by allowing them to do things like eat their snacks in the classroom or buy things from a prize box in the office. The thing is, the behavior issues in my classroom, and we did have issues, weren't because kids weren't motivated to behave. They were because of the trauma my students experienced every day. Some had parents who were incarcerated, for example, or had to work long hours to supplement their family's income. I tried to create community in my classroom, but the school dictated much of the curriculum and it wasn't very engaging. All in all, the school was really set up like a prison. The students had to earn tokens for things my own kids could do anytime they wanted in their predominantly White suburban school."

* * *

Authors like Alfie Kohn (1993, 2006, 2015) have long critiqued the use of rewards and "bribes" in school to raise grades or behavior standards. Kohn contends that the focus on bribes for controlling behavior only "breeds the need for more control" and does little to create community. He emphasizes the paternalistic nature of these practices that succeed only in showing who teachers do or don't trust to be self-reliant and free. It becomes a self-fulfilling prophecy. Marinak and Gambrell (2008) found that tokens and bribes fail to motivate children unless the reward is directly related to the activity in question. Their study revealed that children who received books for reading were much more motivated to continue reading than children who received tokens or prizes. The authors still, however, caution against solely relying on a system of rewards to achieve a desired behavior. Token rewards systems are the antithesis to cultivating classroom community through a CRTA perspective. CRTA values a shared and negotiated definition of community, not one simply based on a teacher's predetermined set of ideas, rules, or guidelines. CRTA privileges community agreements between students and teachers that promote authentic care and dialogue and at the same time, value resistance and dissent.

Policing Language: Criminalizing the Language of the Community

The criminalization of Black and Brown students in the classroom extends beyond general expectations for behavior. Students who speak languages other than English have the added risk of being punished for using their language(s) in ways monolingual teachers see as inappropriate. In the example of Mr. Martin's classroom, Horatio's use of Spanish contributed to his demerit. Imagine if Mr. Martin had focused on building community rather than punishing Horatio for his use of Spanish. In what way did Mr. Martin's attitudes about language use in his classroom impact Horatio's school trajectory? These so-called linguistic infractions add up, even if they are not included in the official rules. For example, Mr. Martin's reaction led to resistance from Horatio. The resistance was seen as disrespect. In a classroom with an authoritarian orientation, resistance to the authority figure is forbidden and thus, punishable.

Horatio lived his entire day in a language that was new to him, a language in which he was unable to express the full range of his personality or academic knowledge. When "Speak in English!" becomes part of a punishment, students' linguistic resources are seen as criminal acts rather than normal linguistic practices. When teachers assume students are using linguistic forms to talk about them and then use it as a subsequent punishment, they create an environment of suspicion rather than one of interest in students' linguistic resources. Time is focused on controlling behavior rather than cultivating community.

Immigrant and refugee students often get punished for using their home language while affluent schools promote the value of bilingual and foreign language education for White students. Research consistently shows that using two (or more) languages is not a hindrance, but in fact a social and cognitive advantage (see, for example, Marian & Shook, 2012) and that teachers are actually the ones at a deficit in working with multilingual students; however, the culture of punishing students for using their home language in school is ongoing.

Classroom management based on an authoritarian orientation seeks to police and criminalize the everyday linguistic practices of a classroom community. Freire (1968) suggests that "those who have been denied their primordial right to speak their word must first reclaim this right and prevent the continuation of this dehumanizing aggression" (p. 88). Whose linguistic practices are privileged in your classroom? What linguistic practices are privileged or silenced, and how does this hinder classroom community? How can White teachers make space for students to reclaim their rights to speak a language other than English?

Policing language is not always about using a language other than English like Spanish or Tagalog, for example. It is sometimes about the use of variations of English or words that are considered inappropriate, by some, in school. I was working with a White student teacher placed in a school with a predominantly Black and Brown student population. I was encouraging the student teacher to use critical literacy practices in the elementary classroom when the following exchange occurred:

* * *

Student teacher: *I can't even begin to think about doing this creative stuff when I can't even get the kids to stop swearing.*

Laura: *What do you mean?*

Student teacher: *They are little kids and they are constantly saying the "N-word" to each other.*

Laura: *Are all the children Black?*

Student teacher: *Yes.*

Laura: *Give me more context. Could you explain a situation where the kids are using the N-word and how it prevents you from teaching?*

Student teacher: *But they should* never *use it. I can't teach them when they are using that kind of language. It's just not appropriate.*

Laura: *I hear what you're saying, but can you give me an example of how and when the students are using the word? I want to understand more about the context.*

Student teacher: *Like, just all the time. They are just talking to each other—almost like, "Hey, buddy," except the N-word. The teacher [cooperating teacher] doesn't do anything. She never writes them up or punishes them for it.*

* * *

In this example, the children, third graders, were using the N-word as a gesture of affinity. The teacher was right; they were using it like "hey, buddy." There were no disruptions, no resistance to instruction, only children engaging in the linguistic practices of their community and a student teacher who was uncomfortable. The cooperating teacher did not prevent the children from using the word in this way because she grew up in the same neighborhood as the children. She didn't see it as an impediment to the learning process; rather, she valued how students were building community in small-group conversations.

The White student teacher, however, saw the use of the N-word, under any circumstance, as a roadblock to her teaching. She believed the students should be punished for using it and chose to focus on the students' use of the word instead of good teaching practices. She missed the opportunity to learn about the linguistic practices of her students and the multiple repertories they draw from in building relationships and community with one another. Ironically, she saw the students' linguistic repertoire as a roadblock to using critical literacy practices, even though critical literacy asks the teacher and students to critique power relationships, such as the privileging of certain language practices.

Imagine how a teacher working from this perspective impacts students' life and learning trajectories. I worked with the student teacher, asking her to first put her views of the word aside for one week and focus instead on her prepared lessons and building relationships with the children. I also asked the student teacher to research the difference between White people and Black people using this word. Finally, I asked the student teacher to talk to the cooperating teacher about her perspectives on the use of the N-word and how punishing students might impact the classroom community. In this case, the student teacher's initial views of students interrupted classroom community because she privileged her own discomfort and misunderstanding over teaching.

Price (2011) recommends teaching about the N-word, but cautions that White teachers need to do their homework before engaging in this tough conversation. "Talk about language, about words and emotion, about words and pain," says Price. Talk about the history of the word and why students might choose to use it or not. If policing of language needs to happen, focus on the White students and White colleagues. What are the larger social and psychological consequences of Whites using this word? In what ways does it disrupt or damage community? White teachers can also focus on calling out deficit-model and microaggressive discourse used by White students and colleagues. In this way, White teachers are holding other White people accountable for participation in the system of racial oppression and White supremacy.

Restorative Justice Practices

What are the alternatives to classroom management practices that are grounded in punishment and control? The overrepresentation of people of color in the criminal justice system, as well as the complicity of school discipline practices in entering children into the school-to-prison pipeline, has led to calls for reform at all levels. Restorative justice has taken center stage in offering both a framework and set of strategies for changing the system. According to the International Institute for Restorative Practices (IIRP, 2006), "Restorative Justice is a process whereby those most directly affected by wrongdoing come together to determine what needs to be done to repair the harm and prevent a reoccurrence." IIRP suggests that "restorative practices are about working *with* people rather than doing things *to* or *for* them." Restorative justice practices are also about fair process, free expression of emotions and dialogue, and restorative questions that seek to privilege acknowledgment, reflection, and growth.

When order is privileged, the need for punitive practices increases. This speaks to the ingrained nature of authoritarian, banking practices that historically pervaded education and society (Freire, 1968). The banking concept positions teachers as the authority and holders of knowledge and students as empty vessels that need to be controlled and deposited with information.

Restorative justice practices in classroom are an alternative to traditional classroom management practices that focus on control and punishment. Instead, restorative practices center community and focus on humanizing principles where students' lived experiences are authentically valued and integrated into the classroom and school.

The basic tenets of restorative justice practices include an acknowledgment of issues that disrupt the classroom community and a collective effort to right those disruptions. Restorative practices are designed to engender the need to heal and right wrongs. Gardner (2016) explains, "Similar to the way critical pedagogy provides an alternative to the traditional 'banking' model of education, restorative justice gives us an alternative framework for the one-size-fits-all punitive model of school discipline" (p. 2).

Schools that implement restorative justice practices observe a decline in school disciplinary actions and improved school climate, improved school attendance, and increased student performance and academic engagement (Fronius, Persson, Guckenburg, Hurley, & Petrosino, 2016). As with any approach, the fidelity of implementation determines how effective it is in transforming the classroom or school. Implementing restorative justice management practice without training and support (for faculty, students, and community members) can hinder the aims of implementation.

Hiring a restorative justice expert or consultant that can support schoolwide implementation is key. It takes time for administrators, teachers, students, parents, and community members to adjust to a new framework. For White teachers teaching in predominantly Black and Brown spaces, restorative practices, if implemented correctly, have the potential to radically shift the school-to-prison pipeline. For White teachers teaching in predominantly White spaces, restorative practices can model for White students ways to reject authoritarian approaches in society and center antiracist ways of being. For all classrooms, restorative practices can provide a framework for reevaluating the overuse of labels such as behavior disorder (BD) and oppositional defiant (OD). And, if these labels are warranted, create better and more humanizing ways to support everyone in the classroom community. Restorative practices prepare all students for an increasingly diverse world and create more democratically minded citizens.

The challenge for many teachers choosing to rethink the notion of classroom management is the fear of loss of control. Authoritarian principles and practices are so ingrained that anything outside of receiving "due punishment" may feel like chaos or a lack of rigor. I argue that restorative practices are by definition rigorous because they require critical thinking, dialogue, and the consideration of multiple perspectives and positions. Traditional classroom management that privileges power and control is by its very nature anti-intellectual. The following is an example of a teacher who moved away from punishment and control and instead considered the merits of restorative practices.

* * *

RESTORATIVE POSSIBILITIES

Alex is a White teacher with three years of teaching experience. She teaches in an urban, predominantly Black elementary school in a midsized city in Pennsylvania. Alex's school has a behavior management system that functions much like a token economy. Students are written up with demerits and receive rewards when they follow the rules.

Alex's principal noted that demerits reached a peak the previous year. The principal recommended that teachers become clearer in enforcing and reinforcing the rules. Around the same time Alex received this message from her principal, she was reading about restorative practices and culturally responsive pedagogy in one of my graduate courses. She decided to implement some of these practices in her classroom for a research project.

She began by saying to her third graders, "I'm going to make some changes in our classroom. I read about some things in my university class and I'd like to try them out." Alex was determined not to give out a single demerit during the fall semester. "This didn't mean I ignored bad behavior or threw structure out the window. I simply thought about how I wanted my classroom community to look. We talked about it as a class. When issues arose, I tried to focus on my relationship with the student. We also talked about it as a community. The thing is, I didn't even implement all the practices I read about (I'm going to work toward that!), but it was shocking how a simple shift in how I viewed my classroom and students changed the classroom community entirely. The classroom was calmer and we had more fun. I think I gave out one or two demerits that semester. I'm hoping to get rid of the token merit/demerit system entirely in the spring. Of course, my principal asked what I was doing differently, so I provided resources from what I read."

* * *

The example from Alex's classroom shows how restorative and responsive practices have the potential to cultivate classroom community by elevating, not abandoning, expectations of community-oriented behavior. Instead of focusing on punishing individual students for behavior and infractions, Alex and her class asked each other, "How does this contribute to our community? How could we do better together? What is our community agreement?" Alex emphasized that change did not happen on day 1, 2, or even 20, it happened gradually over time. "I committed to the idea. I knew if I reverted back to the punitive practices or demerit system, I wouldn't know if restorative practices could really work. It takes time for everyone, both students and teachers to make the shift."

PART 2: CLASSROOM ACTIVITIES: CULTIVATING CLASSROOM COMMUNITY THROUGH CRTA

This section focuses on how to cultivate community in ways that are liberatory, restorative, and grounded in a CRTA. I emphasize again the importance of abandoning the idea of "managing" your classroom and, instead, focusing on coconstructing a community that engenders consciousness, love, and restorative, humanizing practices.

I ask teachers to begin by considering "frameworks before strategies." What I mean by this is that teachers are often asked to implement strategies or initiatives without a firm understanding of where these strategies and initiatives come from. In what philosophy of teaching, learning, or being are they grounded?

For example, traditional guides to classroom management often include such notions as student-centered practices; positive reinforcement; preparation; teacher and student dispositions; building relationships; nonverbal cues, patterns, routines; and modeling. These are potentially valuable concepts, but why? Where do these notions come from and why should we use them? In order to effectively cultivate community, teachers should understand the framework and philosophy in which strategies are embedded. Teachers should also reflect on their own teaching philosophies.

Is your teaching philosophy grounded in power and control or agreed upon, coconstructed notions of community? Are you the only knower or expert in your classroom or are you a colearner and expert with your students? Do you work from the banking concept of education, viewing your role as a knowledge depositor and rule maker/rule enforcer? Or, do you believe knowledge is coconstructed among members of the classroom, school, and community (Freire, 1972)? In your own classroom, how do you decide which rules, guidelines, patterns, and practices govern your classroom?

In order to consider how to cultivate classroom community through a CRTA lens, teachers should reflect on their definitions of justice and how those views align or conflict with their philosophy of teaching and education. I ask teachers to consider whether they are colonizers or liberators in their classrooms. In other words, do you teach in ways that impose punitive action on students or do you teach to liberate and dismantle systems of oppression? Notions of justice and democracy, in particular, influence teachers' perspectives on how teachers design their classroom. These notions underpin what teachers believe about how rules are created and what happens when students break those rules.

A focus on regulating behavior through punitive measures reflects an authoritarian orientation to classroom management. Many classroom management strategies that privilege behaviorist notions of rewards and punishment also draw from an authoritarian orientation. This orientation places authority in the hands of the teacher and school officials. Students are expected to respect authority and comply without question.

Even classroom management strategies that appear to include student voice seem like a smokescreen for teachers' predetermined sets of rules. A teacher in one of my courses once explained: "I let students help me construct the rules of the classroom during the first week of the school year. They volunteer ideas and we write them on chart paper. I help them to synthesize their ideas to match the character pillars of our school like respect and responsibility. I already know what pillars and rules I'm guiding them to." In what way is this authentic care and dialogue? What ideas from the class members were missed based on the teacher's predetermined set of rules? Review the Critical Questions for the Classroom in the textbox below with your students to begin developing your community agreements.

Critical Questions for the Classroom

Here are some questions you can ask yourself and your students before creating rules and guidelines for your classroom.

- How do we decide who gets to make decisions about how the classroom functions? Is this equitable? Why? Why not? What opportunities exist to engage democratic ideas?
- What rules, guidelines, practices, or agreements could help us to learn from one another?
- When do we want the classroom to be loud, quiet, serious, silly?
- How do we support each other in mistakes and missteps?
- How do we ensure everyone is given respect, dignity, and a voice in our classroom?
- How do we learn? Do we all learn the same? What rules, guidelines, practices, or agreements help us to support each other when we are challenged, unchallenged, feeling creative or uncreative, feeling lost?
- How do we define and celebrate success in this classroom?

Dialogue and Community

Conversations about the role classroom management practices play in contributing to the inequities in education will inevitably be political. This may make some teachers feel uncomfortable. Ada and Campoy (2004) emphasize the need for teachers to show their students who they are. Sometimes showing who you are involves sharing some of your personal, familial, political, or religious beliefs and practices. Freire argues that teaching is never neutral and that choosing to teach, or not teach, a topic is still a political act. In other words, continuing to use practices that privilege punishment and control is, whether you state it explicitly or not, a political act. Choosing to not talk about it is action through inaction and complicity through compliance. So, what happens when your politics are incongruent with those of your students? How do you cultivate authentic dialogue? What happens when you want to present multiple perspectives in the classroom?

The physical landscape of a classroom (and school), both visual and spatial, conveys particular messages about the types of activities you expect and the ideas you support. How are desks situated and what does this convey about dialogue? What type of posters, guides, and resources are present? Chapter 7 takes a closer look at how schools convey welcoming and unwelcoming messages to students and families through the visual landscape of the classroom and school.

Drew, who contributed to this book, carefully considers the visual print in his classroom. He strives to highlight justice-oriented writers, teachers, historians, and activists—both their lives and ideas. He uses the images in his classroom to create opportunities for questions and dialogue. During the 2016 presidential election, Drew's students were particularly curious about his political beliefs and who he was going to vote for. He knew that his students' families affiliated with a diverse range of political perspectives. Drew's students attempted to guess his political orientation based on the environmental print and spatial landscape of his classroom.

"You're too nice to vote for Trump," one student suggested. "You wouldn't vote for Trump because you want everyone to be treated fairly," another student ventured. Some students suggested that the posters of Mother Teresa, Nelson Mandela, Gandhi, and Martin Luther King Jr. signaled a vote against Mr. Trump. Drew used these inquiries to facilitate a conversation about his own political orientation, teaching philosophy, and how to critically read the word and world.

For example, he asked his students to do a critical visual literacy activity of their school and neighborhood. What political messages appear in our everyday lives? Who produces, pays for, or benefits from those messages? He also used students' inquiries to share his philosophy of teaching, asking students to suggest other images, people, or ideas that might correspond to the existing visual landscape of the classroom and his orientation. He asked his students, "What are benefits of knowing someone's politics?" And, "What would you like me to add to the visual landscape of the room?"

Drew also changes the visual and spatial landscape of his school and classroom by bringing the community into the classroom. The community-school model, which varies somewhat in structure and implementation, is grounded in the notion that schools should be hubs for building relationships and providing resources for the community. The idea is that the school is open to the community and used by the community for purposes other than just academic and extracurricular activities. For example, some community schools in Philadelphia offer space for health care or financial services through nonprofit organizations. Families have open access to the school and participate regularly in the shared cultivation of the community.

When topics arise related to race, immigration, and other intersectional issues, Drew invites parents, families, and community members to visit his classroom. For example, in a lesson for Drew's fifth-grade classroom designed to address immigration through a critical literacy lens, Drew asked students to study how immigrants are depicted in the school curriculum and the local and global media. This prompted a student to share that his father was an immigrant from Africa and moved to Florida for a better life with his family. The student chose to share this experience because Drew created a classroom community where students felt safe sharing their personal and familial experiences.

The student's story of his father's life made the immigration discussion more personal and relevant to the other students in the classroom. Drew invited the student's father to come to the classroom and share his experience as an immigrant in the US. The father was able to elaborate on the challenges of being an immigrant in the US and at the same time share the ways he and his family have adapted to their new country. For students with little experience or interactions with immigrant families, the father's counterstory transformed some of the students' previously held deficit views of immigrants, namely, the false notion that immigrants are criminals or a drain on the economy. In this way, the personal connection to another class member helped to shift views.

While inviting parents and community members to school is important, not all parents and community members are able to visit the school. Teachers can create community by spending time in the communities where their students live. When I taught in Georgia, I learned that one of my students' father owned a small market in a rural area about 45 minutes outside of town. I made it a point to drive there on a Saturday and purchase my produce for the week. It really strengthened my relationship with the student and his family. Spending time in the community helps teachers to understand what they are missing in the classroom. Sometimes, there is a tendency for teachers to view their students' families through a deficit lens. When teachers can shed that deficit lens and visit students' neighborhoods, they often learn that a commitment to education is already there. Gonzalez (2001) suggests that teachers often miss the rich educational, cultural, and linguistic resources of their students' communities.

Creating a Culture of True Dialogue

How do teachers prepare students and parents for an education grounded in a CRTA approach? Teachers can begin on day one of the school year with something like this:

> Our classroom is a community. In this community, we talk openly about complex and sometimes controversial issues. Sometimes, talking about certain issues can make us feel uncomfortable. I want us to support one another in feeling uncomfortable because that means we are learning. Sometimes, you may disagree with me or your peers. Disagreeing and talking about it is a way for us to develop our critical thinking skills. We learn to listen to someone else, think about their ideas, and decide whether they persuade us to change our minds. We also do the work to research our own opinions and ideas so that we can defend our stances or what we believe. Let's begin to set some guidelines together for disagreeing and listening to multiple viewpoints. Let's think about how we want our community to look. We are going to do that by writing a list of "community agreements." Before we do that, let me show you some examples of what those agreements might look like.

This initial introduction can be followed by books, film clips, or other demonstrations of options for classroom community. See the recommended resources at the end of the chapter for suggestions. If the school already has restorative practices in place, teachers can use this time to practice and model the tenets of restorative work.

For all students, teachers should be clear about how the community of the classroom works. Practice and demonstrate routines that reflect shared power among teachers, students, families, and community members. A shared understanding and the opportunity for dialogue, dissent, resistance, and action within the classroom community demonstrates what Freire (1968) calls a "profound love for the world and for people" (p. 89). In order to have true dialogue, critical reflection and action are paramount. A note or conversation with parents, families, and other community members can mirror the introduction you give to students. For example:

> Dear______, In our classroom we prioritize building community. In this community, we practice talking openly about complex and sometimes controversial issues. We acknowledge that sometimes, talking about certain issues can make us feel uncomfortable or cause concern among parents. We ask for your support allowing us to feel appropriately uncomfortable because feeling uncomfortable means we are learning. We acknowledge that we will sometimes have disagreements. We value disagreeing and suggest that talking about our disagreements is a way for us to develop our critical thinking skills. We learn valuable listening skills, how to process and synthesize information, consider multiple perspectives, and make informed decisions about whether we should be persuaded to change our minds or remain firm in our stances. We develop

research skills to study our own opinions and ideas so that we can defend our stances or what we believe. We begin each school year by setting some guidelines as a class for disagreeing and listening to multiple viewpoints. We envision how we want our community to look and write a list of "community agreements." Before we do that, I provide examples of different ways other schools build community and facilitate conversations that allow all members of the classroom, school, and community to have a voice. We invite you to join our discussions and contribute to our classroom community.

Writing a note prevents parents from being caught off guard when their children share the discussions they have in school. It also explicitly shows that community-building is the goal, not indoctrination to certain ideas. That said, you should be clear on your stances related to justice and equity. Use this book and the resources cited to help justify your decisions. The final chapter, Chapter 9, provides a more comprehensive process for making your CRTA case.

Another tenet of true dialogue to consider is allowing for the community to explore how dissent, resistance, and critique should look. Henry Giroux has written for some time, and continues to write, about the power of dissent in the classroom and school (see, for example, Giroux, 1983, 1988, 2014). Providing opportunities for students to disagree with each other and their teachers, investigate and work to solve social ills, and have ongoing conversations about the merits of new and differing ideas is at the heart of cultivating critical thinkers. It also allows students to practice, in a safe space, how to work out real-world problems like the school-to-prison pipeline.

When engaging in controversial conversations, consider how emotions are policed or silenced. Does dissent have to be courteous? Does dialogue imply politeness? Is dissent still authentic if it is courteous? I argue perhaps not, or at the very least, the answer is nuanced. Can students get angry about the issues they care about? How can they express this anger and in what way? Do students have an out? For example, is there a process in place for when students need to step back? Can the classroom community allow someone space if a conversation seems stressful? In what ways does the community learn to recognize and hear the pain of others? Can students use profanity? Why and in what way? In my classroom, words that are considered profanity are allowed if it is not directed toward a person (e.g., name-calling). She allows her students to negotiate how language is or is not policed, and the community decides on how to support each other in using language for emphasis or check one another when language is used to hurt others.

The question about polite dialogue also relates to activism. Engage students in a conversation about the advantages and disadvantages of peaceful dissent or protest. This is not to say that you advocate for violence, rather, that you support students in understanding their role as allies and accomplices; to understand that dialogue can still exist with anger and resistance;

and that the severity of racial violence in the US may require an understanding of why violence is sometimes met by violence. Use this opportunity to question who is seen as angry or violent and who is not. Chapter 8 elaborates on these tensions.

Teachers also have to consider and define clearly the process for earning or being entitled to respect. If you work from an authoritarian orientation, the teacher's authority and respect are required and demanded, not earned. While respect, responsibility, trust, and other pillars of character and community are important, in what ways do you tie these concepts to a philosophy of justice and equity? Who is required to earn respect and who is entitled to it automatically? Emdin (2016) argues that building relationships through dialogue is how teachers earn the respect of their students. Emdin's work is a recommended resource for both responsive approaches and the need for justice and equity across the curriculum.

Through his notion of reality pedagogy, Emdin advocates for teachers to meet students where they are. To Emdin, meeting students where they are doesn't mean low expectations or deficit views, but an authentic desire to learn from and about students' experiences both in and outside the classroom. One of Drew's teacher-colleagues explained, "It comes down to modeling what respect looks like and feels like. I never feel that students should respect me simply because I was their teacher or an adult, but rather because they felt I was a worthwhile person—just as they are."

Also note that the notion of respect and respecting elders is embedded in most cultures, but respect can look different in different contexts. Students of color may not see White teachers as elders worthy of immediate respect because history and experience tells them that Whites hold implicit biases about their families and communities and have been historically complicit in racial violence. Earning the respect of students in the classroom community does not diminish the expertise or knowledge of the teacher; rather, it calls for authentic respect-building among all members of the classroom community. Liberatory and restorative approaches build respect and trust among all community members. This respect and trust is embedded in Freire's notion of love, dialogue, and consciousness-raising practices. When teachers call attention to the injustices in society and allow for students to authentically engage in controversial conversations, it opens the space for students to make connections, share their experiences, and address real-world problems.

The following sections provide additional activities to support restorative, consciousness-raising, liberatory dialogue through activities grounded in a CRTA approach.

Activity 1: Community Audit

Based on the questions posed throughout this chapter, design a classroom community audit. Create a table, placing the questions in the far-left column and empty columns on the right. With your students, engage in a participatory action research (PAR) project (see Chapter 7), investigating the culture of your classroom. Include the questions posed about authoritarian orientations and token economies (e.g., extrinsic rewards, top-down or teacher-centered activities). Teachers can also evaluate their lesson plans. Begin by recording all activities you planned for one day. Create a code and mark activities that are student centered/student led, culturally responsive (authentically), how much time students were able to engage in extended discussion on authentic topics, and so forth. Also, record how you expect students to comport themselves during each activity in your lesson plan. What do you plan to do if activities go "off task"? What restorative practices can you implement to engage students and prioritize learning over discipline and punishment?

Activity 2: Get Political

Remaining silent about politics won't cultivate community. Instead, it allows students to be isolated in their own belief systems. It also prevents students from learning from one another, including where personal political stances might originate. Explore with your students the following questions: Where do political parties come from? What social, emotional, psychological, familial, regional, economic, racial, and cultural factors impact our political orientations historically and today? In what ways can we create a classroom community that allows for true dialogue? Teachers can also use a problem-posing approach (Smith-Maddox & Solórzano, 2002) to ground the conversation in race and immigration. What social, emotional, psychological, familial, regional, economic, racial, and cultural factors might contribute to someone supporting the building of a border wall between the US and Mexico?

Activity 3: Border Crossing Dialogue and Authentic Cultural Exchange

Discuss and create "border crossing" experiences for all students regardless of whether you see your classroom as diverse or not. What does it mean to cross national borders? What about metaphorical borders in our everyday lives? In what ways do we diminish borders through authentic cultural exchange that moves beyond what Sonia Nieto (2014) calls the "foods, festivals, folklore, fashion, and famous people" of culture (the 5 Fs)? How does this build community both in and outside of the classroom?

For example, invite members of the community to your classroom, conduct interviews in the community, or visit immigrant and refugee service agencies on field trips. Use Pat Mora's *Borders* (1986), Gloria Anzaldúa's *Borderlands* (1987), Jaqueline Woodson's children's book *The Other Side* (2001), and Gloria Anzaldúa's children's book *Friends From the Other Side* (1997) to explore notions of both physical and metaphysical borders. Find memoirs of immigrants or refugees, newspaper or magazine articles on the current struggles of immigrants and refugees, and what it means to cross borders and live transnationally (see Chapter 1).

Activity 4: Make Social Action a Key Part of Every Lesson

Identify social ills and challenges in your own community. Connect these ills to what you study in your classroom. For example, if you are studying the water cycle, research the water quality in your community by collaborating with the local water company (some offer test kits) and compare it to those in areas where immigrants live. Read about the ongoing atrocity of lead poisoning in the water supply in communities like Flint, Michigan, or food deserts in places like Camden, New Jersey. Also, explore in science how food gets from the farm to the table. Who picks the lettuce, and where does it come from? How much do workers get paid? Does this differ for documented and undocumented workers? Who pays them? Where do they live? What protections do workers have? Building classroom community involves the wider local, national, and global community. Study the ways local lives are impacted/connected to global lives through the economy, globalization, labor, the environment, and technology.

RECOMMENDED RESOURCES

Books and Articles

Kenney, M. (2014). Teaching the N-word. Retrieved from https://www.rethinkingschools.org/articles/teaching-the-n-word

Rich, M. (2015). Analysis finds higher expulsion rates for Black students. Retrieved from https://www.nytimes.com/2015/08/25/us/higher-expulsion-rates-for-black-students-are-found.html

Podcasts and Videos

Dos Vatos Productions and the Independent Television Service. (Coproducers). (2015). *Precious knowledge* [Motion picture]. Retrieved from https://vimeo.com/ondemand/preciousknowledge

Websites: Restorative Justice Practices

http://www.iirp.edu/pdf/beth06_davey2.pdf
http://restorativejustice.org/#sthash.JB0L0Son.dpbs

https://www.theatlantic.com/eduAcation/archive/2015/12/when-restorative-justice-works/422088/

REFERENCES

Ada, A. F., & Campoy, F. I. (2004). *Authors in the classroom: A transformative education process*. Boston, MA: Allyn and Bacon.

American Civil Liberties Union. (2018). *School to prison pipeline*. Retrieved from https://www.aclu.org/issues/racial-justice/race-and-inequality-education/school-prison-pipeline

Camera, L. (2017, May 9). *Black girls are twice as likely to be suspended, in every state*. Retrieved from https://www.usnews.com/news/education-news/articles/2017-05-09/black-girls-are-twice-as-likely-to-be-suspended-in-every-state

Emdin, C. (2016). *For White folks who teach in the hood . . . and the rest of y'all too: Reality pedagogy and urban education*. Boston, MA: Beacon.

Freire, P. (1968). *Pedagogy of the oppressed*. New York, NY: Seabury Press.

Fronius, T., Persson, H., Guckenburg, S., Hurley, N., & Petrosino, A. (2016). *Restorative justice in U.S. schools: A research review*. Retrieved from https://jprc.wested.org/wp-content/uploads/2016/02/RJ_Literature-Review_20160217.pdf

Gardner, T. (2016). *Discipline over punishment: Success and struggles with restorative justice in schools*. Lanham, MD: Rowman & Littlefield.

Gilliam, W. S., Maupin, A. N., Reyes, C. R., Accavitti, M., & Shic, F. (2016). Do early educators' implicit biases regarding sex and race relate to behavior expectations and recommendations of preschool expulsions and suspensions? *Yale Child Study Center*, A Research Study Brief.

Giroux, H. (1983). Theories of reproduction and resistance in the new sociology of education: A critical analysis. *Harvard Educational Review , 53*(3), 257–293.

Giroux, H. (1988). Education for Democracy and Empowerment. *Tikkun, 3*(5), 30–33.

Giroux, H. (2014). When schools become dead zones of the imagination: A critical pedagogy manifesto. *Policy Futures in Education, 12*(4), 491–499.

González, N. (2001). *I am my language: Discourses of women & children in the borderlands*. Tucson: University of Arizona Press.

Heath, S. B. (1983). *Ways with words: Language, life, and work in communities and classrooms*. Cambridge, England: Cambridge University Press.

International Institute for Restorative Practices. (2006). *Restorative justice and practices*. Retrieved from http://www.iirp.edu/pdf/beth06_davey2.pdf

Iselin, A-M. (2010). *Research on school suspension*. Retrieved from https://childandfamilypolicy.duke.edu/pdfs/familyimpact/2010/Suspension_Research_Brief_2010-04-27.pdf

Kohn, A. (1993). *Punished by rewards: The trouble with gold stars, incentive plans, A's, praise, and other bribes*. Boston, MA: Houghton Mifflin.

Kohn, A. (2006). *Beyond discipline: From compliance to community*. Alexandria, VA: ASCD.

Kohn, A. (2015). *The perils of "growth mindset" education: Why we're trying to fix our kids when we should be fixing the system*. Retrieved from https://www.salon.com/2015/08/16/the_education_fad_thats_hurting_our_kids_what_you_need_to_know_about_growth_mindset_theory_and_the_harmful_lessons_it_imparts/

Marian, V., & Shook, A. (2012). The cognitive benefits of being bilingual. *Cerebrum*. Retrieved from https://www.ncbi.nlm.nih.gov/pmc/articles/PMC3583091/

Marinak, B., & Gambrell, L. (2008). Intrinsic motivation and rewards: What sustains young children's engagement with text? *Literacy Research and Instruction, (47)*1, 9–26. http://dx.doi.org/10.1080/19388070701749546

Marquez, N., & Prandini, R. (2018). *The school to prison to deportation pipeline: The relationship between school delinquency and deportation explained*. Retrieved from https://www.ilrc.org/sites/default/files/resources/school_delinq_faq_nat-rp-20180212.pdf

Nieto, S. (2010). *Language, culture, and teaching. 2nd ed.* New York: Routledge.

Noddings, N. (2013). *Education and democracy in the 21st century*. New York: Teachers College Press.

Nouri, A., & Sajjadi, S. M. (2014). Emancipatory pedagogy in practice: Aims, principles and curriculum orientation. *The International Journal of Critical Pedagogy, 5*(2), 76–87.

Philips, S. U. (1992). *The invisible culture: Communication in classroom and community on the Warm Springs Indian Reservation.* Long Grove, IL: Waveland.

Price, S. (2011). Teaching the N word. *Teaching Tolerance, 40*. Retrieved from https://www.tolerance.org/magazine/fall-2011/straight-talk-about-the-nword

Smith-Maddox, R., & Solórzano, D. G. (2002). Using critical race theory, Paulo Freire's problem-posing method, and case study research to confront race and racism in education. *Qualitative Inquiry, 8*(1), 66–84.

Chapter Five

Critical Approaches to Curricular Change

With Contributions From Drew Gingrich

> I'm not interested in a curriculum of inclusion. What we need is a curriculum of liberation.
>
> —John Henrik Clarke

This chapter explores how to modify and decolonize the curriculum through a critical race teacher activism (CRTA) lens. Critical literacy practices are also discussed as a framework for designing literature-based theme units to engage teachers and students in critically analyzing and modifying curriculum to reflect mirrors, windows, and doors (Sims Bishop, 1990).

This chapter seeks to do the following:

- Support White teachers in decolonizing the curriculum
- Emphasize the responsibility of White educators to create more opportunities for windows, mirrors, and doors in the curriculum
- Explore ways the existing curricula are permeable to critical perspectives, including asking questions such as, what needs to be modified or abandoned in order to teach from a liberatory perspective?
- Support teachers in generating ideas for literature-based theme units around race and immigration in the classroom
- Dispel myths about the challenges of changing curriculum

Key Ideas and Terms

- Critical literacy
- Decolonizing the literature and curriculum canon
- Multiculturalism

Teachers experience both real and perceived boundaries to changing curriculum. Part 1 of this chapter clarifies conceptual and pedagogical perspectives of viewing curricula through CRTA, and Part 2 provides specific strategies that can support educators as they begin to modify and write their own curriculum. Chapters 8 and 9 of this book address specific ways to advocate for the changes we recommend in this chapter.

PART 1: DEFINITIONS AND BACKGROUND

What Is the Purpose of Schooling?

Questions about curriculum are inextricably linked to ideas about the purpose of schooling. Is the purpose of schooling to create citizens? If so, what kind of citizens? I advocate in this book that the purpose of schooling is to liberate and promote freedom. The CRTA framework is helpful because it requires both teachers and students to question the nature of knowledge and take action to disrupt systems of oppression. For example, what do we learn about in school? Why? For what purpose? Who gets to decide? Who benefits? Who is left out?

Education reformers and politicians tend to promote an instrumental rationale for education, that is, to advance the economic and social interests of a nation (Ladwig, 2010). Education at the federal level focuses primarily on academic and career pursuits ("College and Career Readiness"), which grounds the purpose of education in capitalism rather than a desire to cultivate informed citizens. The No Child Left Behind Act, Race to the Top, and other punitive-based education reform initiatives, for example, have led to classrooms where scripted, packaged curricula are the norm rather than the exception. At their roots, these scripted curricula are designed to be "teacher proof," that is, built upon the notion that a well-written curriculum can be taught by almost anyone. This dehumanizing process that envisions the curriculum as a product divorced from the teachers and students who interact with it undermines the profession of teaching and relegates students to mere widgets on an educational assembly line.

While opt-out testing groups and other grassroots organizations have sought to place curriculum decisions back into the hands of schools, classrooms, and communities, the reality is that many teachers are required or feel obligated to follow the district- or state-mandated curriculum and assessment practices. And while the desire to promote critical thinking seems to be a common trope in education, the proliferation of standardization at the local, state, and federal level suggests otherwise.

Standards: Do We Use the Standards or Do They Use Us?

To be clear, critiquing the standards is not intended to devalue the use of standards or assessments entirely, but rather to question the design and implementation of these standards and assessments without consideration for issues of justice, equity, and representation.

Chapter 1 addresses the problem of imagined histories of immigration in school curricula and the problem of misrepresenting or omitting stories altogether. Imagined histories become official narratives when colonizing nations—nations that wield power, erase the stories of the people who are marginalized and exploited. Decolonizing the curriculum means questioning and changing whose stories are told and who gets to tell them. Narrow interpretations of standards, which focus solely on what is scripted or prescribed, are an example of educators being used by the standards that are often grounded in a single story. Standards are intended to guide, rather than dictate, curriculum. Viewing the standards and curriculum as static and fixed entities creates missed opportunities for teachers to create critical, authentic, responsive, and meaningful learning experiences.

How can teachers decolonize the standards and curriculum? In the Common Core Standards of Pennsylvania, second graders are expected to learn to "identify how conflict is impacted by ethnicity and race, working conditions, immigration, military conflict, and economics" (Pennsylvania Department of Education, 2014). It is not unusual for this to be addressed through a lesson about Pennsylvania as an early colony formed by immigrants. What is often missed is a discussion of how Pennsylvania continues to be shaped by immigrants. Lancaster, Pennsylvania, for example, takes in twenty more refugees per capita than the rest of the United States (Fekos, 2017).

In fourth grade, a teacher in Pennsylvania is responsible for PA Common Core Standard CC.1.3.4.C. This standard states, "Describe in depth a character, setting, or event in a story or drama, drawing on specific details in the text" (Pennsylvania Department of Education, 2014, p. 13). Instead of addressing this standard through a prescribed, basal reader, teachers can select high-quality, multicultural literature. For example, *Inside Out and Back Again* (Lai, 2011) highlights the complexities of immigration through the experiences of a child emigrating from Vietnam.

Teachers can discuss the challenges faced by immigrants and refugees in adapting to a new community. How do refugee families find and access resources? What does it mean to live, work, and love in a new language? Designing or modifying a curriculum should be an iterative process that involves drawing from your students' and community's funds of knowledge, in addition to considering the standards, goals, and objectives of your grade level and content area. For White teachers working with White students, it involves actively looking for biases students hold about students of color and working to dismantle them. Once standards are identified, begin to consider the background information students need to engage successfully with the content of your unit. Predict the biases.

For example, do your students understand the impact of race on immigration experiences? What experiences do your students have with immigrants in your community? What do they know about the multiple paths to citizenship? Use these questions to develop essential questions and objectives. Teachers can envision essential questions and objectives as three pronged—what are the content objectives (specific knowledge related to immigration), what are the skills objectives (language and literacy skills required to access and successfully complete the lesson), and the CRTA objective (how are students engaged in authentic dialogue about inequity and taking [or preparing for] action to solve the problem?). Ideally, the CRTA objectives and essential questions are embedded into the content and skills objectives.

For example, CRTA content essential questions could include the following: What is citizenship? How does one attain it? What does it mean to become a citizen? What is the process, and how has this process changed over time? Is citizenship the same as being American? Why or why not? How do experiences of documented, undocumented, and refugees vary? What are the current policies to help or suppress immigration? In what ways can citizens advocate for just and equitable immigration processes? A CRTA objective could resemble the following: Students will identify their own biases about "Americanness" and citizenship by watching a YouTube video (see for example: https://www.youtube.com/watch?v=DWynJkN5HbQ) that illustrates how people of color are viewed as perpetual "Others." Or, students will practice persuasive language by writing a letter of advocacy for an issue facing immigrant families in their school or community.

Disrupting and Decolonizing the Canon

If imagined histories take center stage in most curricula, how can White teachers in predominantly White contexts interrupt a curriculum that so heavily centers on Whiteness? A CRTA lens provides opportunities for teachers to explore their hidden biases, views, and ideologies and to transform their ideas in ways that liberatory practices provide. The primary bias is the centrality of Whiteness in the literature and curriculum canon. Sensoy and DiAngelo (2012) explain:

> A critical component of school knowledge is not only what is taught, both explicitly and implicitly, but also what is not taught. School knowledge can also be thought of as canonized knowledge (or the canon). Canonized knowledge is knowledge that has been approved or officially sanctioned by the state, for example, through textbooks or on standardized tests. Once knowledge is canonized, it is presented as the objective truth. (p. 9)

An example of canonized knowledge might include the insistence that Shakespeare is always in the curriculum. Hirsch's (1988) book on cultural literacy is perhaps the most egregious example of canonized knowledge centered on colonialistic White, Eurocentric views. What examples of canonized knowledge can you identify in your own curriculum? How was the canon chosen, by whom, and for what purpose?

Imagined histories are born out of canonized knowledge. In predominantly White classrooms where children are only exposed to characters in books with situations and stories that are familiar to them, this White isolationism creates distorted views that normalize White, Western, Eurocentric, and heteronormative perspectives. Decolonizing the canon also includes questioning existing literature used in the classroom that claims to promote diversity, but perpetuates the "White savior" syndrome—the centering of Whites as the heroes in narratives where people of color are facing discrimination. Harper Lee's *To Kill a Mockingbird* (1960) is a prime example of a text that is promoted as a book about racial justice, but centers the experiences of the White characters and largely ignores structural and institutional racism.

In the 1990s, Rudine Sims Bishop (1990) developed the notion of privileging mirrors, windows, and doors in children's literature to combat this phenomenon. The notion of mirrors, windows, and doors within the framework of CRTA can be can be applied across the curriculum. Where do students have the opportunity to see themselves (mirrors), have a look into the experiences of others (windows), and step into someone else's world (doors) in your curriculum?

I interpret the door metaphor as the action step of CRTA. You can reflect on your own beliefs and also learn about the experiences of others, but until you engage yourself with another community and seek to join them in their quest for equity and justice, you have not met the complete requirement of modifying the curriculum through a CRTA lens.

Challenges: Real and Perceived

Real and perceived boundaries exist to modifying curriculum. Teachers engaging in CRTA practices take time to know and understand their community. Ladwig (2010) acknowledges that quests for designing curricula that center on justice and equity are often contested. What will students say? Will there be parent resistance or backlash? Will administrators be supportive? I urge teachers to consider instead what happens when teachers are neutral on matters of justice in equity. But, where do teachers start?

Because many schools have resorted to scripted and packaged curricula, educators—especially those who were educated under the No Child Left Behind Act themselves—have little experience in developing curriculum and instruction outside of the teacher's manual.

Teacher groups and unions, for example, are places of advocacy and support for students, parents, teachers, and schools and can provide a community of support for grassroots teacher activism. In Philadelphia, the Working Educators Caucus (WE) of the Philadelphia Federation of Teachers (PFT) worked for the second year in a row in January and February of 2018 to design a week's worth of curriculum for National Black Lives Matter Week of Action (http://www.workingeducators.org/racial_justice). Included in the curriculum and scheduled events were lessons and presentations related to the intersections of race and immigration.

The American Federation of Teachers (AFT) has links on their web page in support of the DREAM Act (Development, Relief, and Education for Alien Minors Act) (American Federation of Teachers, 2018). This legislative bill advocates for legal status for undocumented immigrants who were brought to the US as children. The AFT is also targeting legislators in advertisements to pass a replacement to Deferred Action for Childhood Arrivals (DACA) (Bakeman, 2018). Finding groups that are already engaged in antiracist practices is essential to the process of modifying curriculum through a CRTA lens.

Add-On Approaches Are Only the Beginning

For teachers who are hesitant to make sweeping changes to their curriculum, add-on approaches can serve as a strategy to pilot change and build a case for larger curriculum revisions. Simply adding new and diverse voices and experiences to the curriculum, however, is only the beginning of the process. There is a long history of critique in curriculum studies of using add-on approaches to address so-called multicultural issues (Banks, 2004, 2008). We write "so-called" because the use of the term *multicultural* can be problematic as it positions voices of color as something extra or outside of the standard curriculum. Even when people of color such as Martin Luther King Jr. or Cesar Chavez are present in the official curriculum, they are introduced during special weeks or months during the school year, and deep analysis of how these figures advocated for social justice is minimal.

An illustrative example can be found in how most curricula address Martin Luther King Jr.'s (1963) "I Have a Dream" speech. Most curricula highlight the following passage: "I have a dream that my four little children will one day live in a nation where they will not be judged by the color of their skin but by the content of their character." Teachers may use this quote to advocate for the color-blind approach critiqued in Chapter 2. Instead, a CRTA teachers can ask, "Who is King referring to when he says, 'four little children'?" What is the historical and social context of this speech? Teachers can also study how Dr. King is portrayed in the curriculum. Does the curriculum adequately show the depth of his radical work including the intersection of race and workers' rights? What about his critique of ongoing police brutality? If teachers choose to use the "I Have a Dream" speech, it should be studied in its entirety. For example, discuss the following passage:

> For many of our white brothers, as evidenced by their presence here today, have come to realize that their destiny is tied up with our destiny. They have come to realize that their freedom is inextricably bound to our freedom. We cannot walk alone. And as we walk we must make the pledge that we shall always march ahead. We cannot turn back. There are those who are asking the devotees of civil rights, "When will you be satisfied!" We can never be satisfied as long as the Negro is the victim of the unspeakable horrors of police brutality.

What is King asking Whites to know, do, and understand? He emphasizes that Whites' freedom is "inextricably bound to our freedom. We cannot walk alone." In this way, he is urging Whites to take up the issues facing Black communities as accomplices (see Chapter 8), not saviors.

Langston Hughes wrote about a dream deferred in his poems "Harlem" and "I, Too." How do these poems relate to what King said years after this work? What would King say today? How are these writers in conversation with the public about injustice? Teachers working from a CRTA perspective can connect Dr. King's speech to the Black Lives Matter movement, including the #sayhername hashtag. Who were the four little girls? What were their names? Why don't we learn them? #CynthiaWesley, #CaroleRobertson, #AddieMaeCollins, #DeniseMcNair.

Decolonizing the Curriculum Through Theme- and Literature-Based Units

Literature offers a way to share stories that might be missing from the curriculum or the everyday experiences of White students in predominantly White schools and communities. The use of CRTA-based themes to frame units also helps teachers make decisions about what types of literature to include. Examples of CRTA-based themes might be "Race and Diaspora" or "Border Walls and Cultural Exchange." Both of these themes have the potential to address any immigration-related requirements in the curriculum with the added component of grounding the discussion in the sociohistorical, social, political, and economic context.

Critical literacy scholars suggest that the use of literature in the classroom helps both teachers and students construct varying perspectives about their own roles in society and provides insight and understanding into the experiences of others (Botelho & Rudman, 2009; Lazar & Offenberg, 2011; Sims Bishop, 1990; Yokota, 1993).

Students can help in decolonizing and reimagining the curriculum by examining the types of literature used in the classroom. Teachers and students can use the tools of participatory action research (PAR), discussed in Chapter 7, to critically analyze the curriculum using CRTA curriculum audits or rubrics. These audits or rubrics should include an investigation of how the curriculum, including literature, provides opportunities for students to experience mirrors, windows, and doors. Students and teachers can also evaluate who is represented in the curriculum, who has the authority to speak on issues like race and immigration (e.g., if you have books on immigration, are the authors immigrants themselves or do they have appropriate proximity to immigration experiences?).

If, through your audits, you learn you do not have texts that relate to immigration or that the stories represent tokenized or stereotypical views of communities of color, design projects with your students to advocate for change in the curriculum. Teachers can also seek stories that illuminate related topics to immigration, such as diaspora, persistence, determination, or resistance.

PART 2: CLASSROOM ACTIVITIES

This section provides specific strategies and practices for modifying curricula from a CRTA perspective. We continue the discussion of using literature- and theme-based teaching to give students opportunities to experience mirrors, windows, and doors in the curriculum and to disrupt the single story.

The Value of Reading Aloud

Authentic, high-quality multicultural literature should be envisioned as the centerpiece of any curriculum. This means that students need to have multiple opportunities to read and interact with texts. Begin each literature-based theme unit with a read-aloud of a novel excerpt or poem. The read-aloud is used to gauge students' knowledge of the topic, explore initial interpretations, and provide students with necessary schema to engage in more critical conversations as the unit unfolds. The importance of read-alouds cannot be overstated as it is one of the most crucial activities for reading success (McCaffrey & Hisrich, 2017).

Read-alouds with authentic, high-quality literature also provide an opportunity to disrupt the impact of highly isolated and resegregated schools and communities. The stories told in literature can expose White students to multiple perspectives and ways of being. Howrey and Whelan-Kim (2009) found that preservice teachers who were given the opportunity to read and discuss high-quality multicultural literature through a social justice lens were able to better connect, relate, and identify with cultural groups other than their own.

The presence of diverse literature alone, however, is not enough to teach from a CRTA perspective. Read-alouds should not be a passive classroom learning activity. Fountas and Pinnell (2006) assert that read-alouds should be interactive and include connections beyond the text and can be used with any age or grade level.

In order to support teachers in selecting literature for read-alouds and asking CRTA questions, we draw from and expand the steps recommended by Howlett, Bowles, and Lincoln (2017) for successful K–12 read-alouds.

Step 1: Selecting Authentic, High-Quality Literature

Begin by familiarizing yourself with high-quality literature through book awards (e.g., Jane Addams Children's Book Award, Pura Belpré Award, Caldecott Medal, and Coretta Scott King Award) and diverse literacy initiatives such as #WeNeedDiverseBooks. Consider the literacy standards you plan to address and whether the book meets the needs of essential questions. What features of language and literacy are present in the text? In what ways do these features connect to the standards? Also, ask, in what ways does this book offer stories that are often untold? In what ways does the book represent and empower marginalized communities?

The texts used in a unit plan set the tone for a CRTA approach. Text sets are one powerful way to include counterstories into the curriculum. Text sets are "a collection of materials . . . composed of diverse resources on a specific subject matter, genre, or theme" (Tracy, Menickelli, & Scales, 2016, p. 527). Text sets offer multiple entry points into the same topic or theme and can include resources such as picture books, novels, academic articles, websites, film clips, periodicals, photographs, and artistic renderings. In classrooms with varying reading levels and background knowledge of the unit, teachers can include high-interest, low-vocabulary texts to help English language learners or readers who are challenged by the grade-level texts. Newsela (https://newsela.com/), a tool for adapting content to varying reading levels, can help students access content and participate fully in the lesson.

Multimodal texts such as photographs and art also help to provide multiple entry points for students with diverse abilities to make connections to content. The benefits of multimodal text sets include helping students adopt critical thinking skills. "When students must read and synthesize across texts, they begin to see how there may be conflicting information, different interpretations of events, and changing perceptions over time" (Tracy, Menickelli, & Scales, 2016, p. 528). Text sets can also be used as a strategy to begin decolonizing or modifying the existing curriculum. Providing counterstories to a required text about Ellis Island, for example, allows teachers to present multiple stories and perspectives and interrupt imagined histories.

Lupo, Strong, Lewis, Walpole, and McKenna (2017) recommend four types of text in a text set: "one that is challenging on—or above—grade-level text (the target text) and three other texts that build the background knowledge and motivation needed to comprehend the target text" (p. 436). Tschida and Buchanan (2015) recommend asking the following questions when searching for texts: "What are the questions that will intrigue students? What are the big ideas that students will uncover during their inquiry? Which voices are needed to tell a more complete story?" (p. 46). While these questions will be beneficial in finding texts, a more refined comb must be used to create a finalized list. To finalize your text set list, consider the reading level, overall quality of the text, the authenticity and accuracy of immigration content, and how various perspectives are represented throughout the text (Tschida & Buchanan, 2015).

Choose texts that challenge the single story by asking, what perspectives are needed to create a more diverse portrait of events and concepts? Find ways to identify "the silences to which we have become accustomed" (p. 45). Once objectives and essential questions are determined, engage in a review of scope and sequence for the unit. Students can also add to the text set as the unit unfolds. Table 5.1 represents a sample text set for an immigration unit, including a rationale for each text.

Step 2: Before Reading: Prediction and Preparation

Before reading, prepare possible questions students might ask related to the topic or genre. Reflect on natural places to pause during the reading to engage the class in discussion (Howlett et al., 2017). Before reading, allow students to examine the book cover, title, and illustrations, and make predictions (Howlett et al., 2017). Make your CRTA goals for the text explicit when appropriate. For example, "I chose this book because it offers us a different perspective on immigration than we typically see in the news or in our curriculum. I want us to consider multiple histories and viewpoints on the topics we study." Introduce how the reading connects to the overall theme of the unit.

Step 3: During Reading: Critical Moments

While reading to the class or while the students in your classroom are reading aloud, use your planned pauses to engage in conversation about the text. Listen and "read" students' reactions to identify when other pauses are needed and to elicit responses to essential questions. Also listen for opportunities for critical moments to address issues of justice and equity. Roy (2015) found that read-alouds provide possibilities for "border crossings" in the

Table 5.1. Sample Text Set: Refugee Displacement and Survival

Text	Citation	Description and Rationale
Picture book: *My Name is Sangoel* by Karen Lynn Williams and Khadra Mohammed	Williams, K., & Mohammed, K. (2009). *My name is Sangoel.* Grand Rapids, MI: Eerdmans Books for Young Readers.	*My Name Is Sangoel* is a refugee story told through the eyes of Sangoel, a young man leaving his homeland of Sudan with his mother and sister after his father dies in war.
Newsela Opinion Piece: Refugees Around the World Need Homes; U.S. Must Help More of Them by Rebecca Erbelding, (Adapted from *The Washington Post* by Newsela staff)	Erbelding, R. (2018). *Opinion: Refugees around the world need homes; U.S. must help more of them.* Retrieved from https://newsela.com/read/holocaust-promise-refugees/id/40108	This article adapted by Newsela addresses the politics of refugee relocation past and present. It challenges the notion that the US is or has been an ever-welcoming nation to refugees by drawing connections between WWII and the Holocaust and the present-day experiences of Syrian refugees.
Video: *Meet One of the Syrian Refugee Children*	UNICEF. (Producer). (2013). *Meet one of the Syrian refugee children* [Video file]. Retrieved from https://www.youtube.com/watch?v=xpG3jLGGkvc	This video provides a portrait of Aya, a Syrian refugee, who is living in a refugee camp. The video provides students with a window into what it is like to be denied asylum.
Photographs: Syrian Refugee and Syrian Environmental Climate	Billing, L. (2015). *These are the most powerful photographs of the Syrian refugee crisis in 2015.* Retrieved from https://www.buzzfeed.com/lynzybilling/these-are-the-most-powerful-photographs-of-the-syrian-refuge?utm_term=.vykpZZVE#.qc6JmmMX	These photographs show the harrowing realities of displacement. The photographs can be used to elicit conversations about the pain of displacement and the hardships associated with leaving your homeland.
Documentary: *Rain in a Dry Land*	Makepeace, A. (Producer). (2007). *Rain in a dry land* [Motion picture]. Retrieved from http://www.pbs.org/pov/raininadryland/	This film depicts the relocation experiences of Somali Bantu refugees from Kenya to the US. The full-length film or clips can be used to show the psychosocial, emotional, and economic challenges refugees face when acclimating to a new school and community.

classroom, especially when teachers are prepared to answer students' questions about the intersectional nature of race and immigration. The teacher in this study read *Grandfather's Journey* (1993) by Alan Say. The students noticed the author's use of colors to describe people, and the teacher used it as an opportunity to talk about the complex nature of racial labeling. Children notice race (Van Ausdale & Feagin, 2001). It is up to adults to cultivate healthy understandings of how racial labeling is grounded in systems of racial oppression and White supremacy. Teachers can guide students in understanding their role in disrupting that system.

Step 4: After Reading: Assessing and Connecting

After reading the text, prepare to formatively or summatively assess whether students met the lesson objectives. When summatively assessing students, there are multiple options that can be used depending on the pedagogy of your school. If your school requires an explicitly standard-based assessment, find two texts that are related to immigration. Using these articles, it is beneficial to create your own assessment. On the teacher-created assessment, students are asked to apply what they have learned throughout the unit on two previously unread articles. In creating the unit, you can be certain that all of the academic standards are assessed and ensure that students are applying their understanding in a new context.

Outside of an explicit, standard-based assessment, you could also consider student projects. These projects could be from a list of options or based on student interests and passions throughout the unit. Provide specific rubrics for students to use. Rubrics will help to ground the project in the standards and objectives of the unit plan. Also, compile a list of students' wonderings about the unit and your assessment of what they know about the intersections of race and immigration, for example. Extend the text by connecting it to the lived realities of children and families in the local and global context. Invite community members and parents to the classroom.

After the standards, essential questions, objectives, and texts are compiled and a scope and sequence is outlined, decide how students will be authentically assessed. Use both formative and summative assessments, but remember to test how you teach. For example, if unit lessons focus primarily on read-alouds, discussion, and written reflections, make sure your assessments evaluate these skills. A multiple-choice test, for example, would not represent an appropriate assessment unless you practiced this type of questioning throughout the unit.

Activity 1: CRTA Graphic Organizers

Explore the benefit of graphic organizers to building background knowledge and reflect on the learning process with students. Drew likes to ask his students to consider three surprising facts, two reframed opinions or ideas, and one humbling moment. This sets the expectation that opinions can be changed and expanded during the learning process. The humbling moment in particular acknowledges that learning sometimes requires us to be uncomfortable—to be in a state of disequilibrium as we grapple with ideas that contradict or bump up against our existing opinions and stances. Graphic organizers can serve as both learning tools and formative assessments.

Activity 2: Double-Sided or Two-Columned Notes

Double-sided or two-columned notes can be used to record wonderings about a text and find textual evidence to address those wonderings. Double-sided or two-columned notes are also ways to scaffold ethnographic field note-taking as described in Chapter 7. In this way, students can use one column to record notes and another column to identify key themes or ideas from their notes.

Activity 3: The People You Meet

Another way to use literature to build relationships, not walls, when discussing immigration is to include a thread throughout the unit titled "The People You Meet." This can consist of an author study highlighting authors included in the text set and the specific characters or real-life people or groups discussed in the unit. The People You Meet activity can also be used as a formative or summative assessment at the conclusion of the unit to review the events, stories, and experiences studied. Laura extends this activity by asking students to plan a dinner party with the people they met. Depending on the unit, students can decide which people they met would be good candidates for their presidential cabinet or local school board. Who can best weigh in on our school curriculum? Who would make the most just decisions in immigration policy?

RECOMMENDED BOOKS AND SOURCES

Books and Articles

Botelho, M., & Rudman, M. (2009). *Critical multicultural analysis of children's literature: Mirrors, windows, and doors.* New York, NY: Routledge.

Cai, M. (2008). Transactional theory and the study of multicultural literature. *Language Arts, 85*(3), 212–220.

Cirdiello, V. A. (2004). Democracy's young heroes: An instructional model of critical literacy. *The Reading Teacher, 58*(2), 139–147.

Fleming, J., Catapano, S., Thompson, C. M., & Ruvalcaba Carrillo, S. (2016). *More mirrors in the classroom: Using urban children's literature to increase literacy.* Lanham, MD: Rowman & Littlefield.

Iannelli, J. (2018). *Florida saw the nation's largest spike in immigration arrests in 2017.* Retrieved from http://www.miaminewtimes.com/news/florida-had-largest-ice-arrest-jump-in-2017-10068732

Sims Bishop, R. (1990). Mirrors, windows, and sliding glass doors. *Perspectives: Choosing and Using Books for the Classroom, 6*(3), ix–xi.

Taxel, J. (2002). Children's literature at the turn of the century: Toward a political economy of the publishing industry. *Research in the Teaching of English, 37*(2), 145. Retrieved from http://dbproxy.lasalle.edu:2048/login?url=https://dbproxy.lasalle.edu:6033/docview/215368958?accountid=11999

Thein, A. H., & Beach, R. (2013). Critiquing and constructing canons in middle grade English language arts classrooms. *Voices From the Middle, 21*(1). Retrieved from http://www.ncte.org/library/NCTEFiles/Resources/Journals/VM/0211-sep2013/VM0211Critiquing.pdf

REFERENCES

American Federation of Teachers. (2018). *Immigration.* Retrieved from https://www.aft.org/ourcommunity/immigration

Bakeman, J. (2018). *National teachers union targets south Florida republicans in DACA ad campaign.* Retrieved from http://wlrn.org/post/national-teachers-union-targets-south-florida-republicans-daca-ad-campaign

Banks, J. and Banks, C. (2010). *Multicultural education. 7th ed.* Hoboken, NJ: Wiley.

Banks, J. (2008). *An introduction to multicultural education. 4th ed.* Boston, MA: Pearson/Allyn and Bacon.

Billing, L. (2015). *These are the most powerful photographs of the Syrian refugee crisis in 2015.* Retrieved from https://www.buzzfeed.com/lynzybilling/these-are-the-most-powerful-photographs-of-the-syrian-refuge?utm_term=.vykpZZVE#.qc6JmmMX

Botelho, M., & Rudman, M. (2009). *Critical multicultural analysis of children's literature: Mirrors, windows, and doors.* New York, NY: Routledge.

Erbelding, R. (2018). *Opinion: Refugees around the world need homes; U.S. must help more of them*. Retrieved from https://newsela.com/read/holocaust-promise-refugees/id/40108

Fekos, K. (2017). *Watch: Lancaster city takes 20 times more refugees per capita than rest of US, BBC says.* Retrieved from http://lancasteronline.com/news/local/watch-lancaster-city-takes-times-more-refugees-per-capita-than/article_2f214950-e4fd-11e6-b5e0-a7db41900a2b.html

Fountas, I. C., & Pinnell, G. S. (2006). *Teaching for comprehending and fluency: Thinking, talking, and writing about reading, K–8*. Portsmouth, NH: Heinemann.

Hirsch, E. D. (1988). *Cultural literacy: What everyone American needs to know*. New York, NY: Vintage Books.

Howlett, K. M., Bowles, F. A., & Lincoln, F. (2017). Infusing multicultural literature into teacher education programs. *Multicultural education, 24*(3/4). Retrieved from https://search.proquest.com/openview/c6df6c92adb8f52fa138f61822df1d64/1?pq-origsite=gscholar&cbl=33246

Howrey, S. and Whelan-Kim, K. (2009). Building Cultural Responsiveness in Rural, Preservice Teachers Using a Multicultural Children's Literature Project. *Journal of Early Childhood Teacher Education, 30*(2), 123–137.

King, Martin L., Jr. (1963, August 28). "I Have a Dream" speech. Lincoln Memorial, Washington, DC.

Ladwig, J. G. (2010). Beyond academic outcomes. *Review of Research in Education, 34*, 113–141. http://dx.doi.org/10.3102/0091732X09353062

Lai, T. (2011). *Inside out & back again*. New York, NY: HarperCollins.

Lazar, A. & Offenberg, R. (2011). Activists, allies, and racists: Helping teachers address racism through picture books. *Journal of Literacy Research, 43*(3), 275–313.

Lupo, S. M., Strong, J. Z., Lewis, W., Walpole, S., & McKenna, M. C. (2017). Building background knowledge through reading: Rethinking text sets. *Journal of Adolescent & Adult Literacy, 61*, 433–444. http://dx.doi.org/10.1002/jaal.701

Makepeace, A. (Producer). (2007). *Rain in a dry land* [Motion picture]. Retrieved from http://www.pbs.org/pov/raininadryland/

McCaffrey, M., & Hisrich, K. E. (2017). Read-alouds in the classroom: A pilot study of teachers' self-reporting practices. *Reading Improvement, 54*(3). Retrieved from https://eric.ed.gov/?id=EJ1152775

Pennsylvania Department of Education. (2014). *Academic standards for English language arts: Grades preK–5*. Retrieved from http://static.pdesas.org/content/documents/PA%20Core%20Standards%20ELA%20PreK-5%20March%202014.pdf

Roy, L. (2015). Borders and Intersections of Possibility: Multilingual Repertoires of Refugee Families in the Southwest U.S. *Multicultural Perspectives, 17*(2), 61–68.

Sensoy, Ö. & DiAngelo, R. (2012). *Is everyone really equal? An introduction to key concepts in social justice education*. New York, NY: Teachers College.

Sims Bishop, R. (1990). Mirrors, windows, and sliding glass doors. *Perspectives: Choosing and Using Books for the Classroom, 6*(3), ix–xi.

Tracy, K. N., Menickelli, K., & Scales, R. Q. (2016). Courageous voices: Using text sets to inspire change. *Journal of Adolescent & Adult Literacy, 60,* 527–536. http://dx.doi.org/10.1002/jaal.613

Tschida, C. M., & Buchanan, L. B. (2015). Tackling controversial topics: Developing thematic text sets for elementary social studies. *Social Studies Research and Practice, 10*(3), 40–56. Retrieved from http://www.socstrpr.org/wp-content/uploads/2016/01/MS06651-Tschida.pdf

UNICEF. (Producer). (2013). *Meet one of the Syrian refugee children* [Video file]. Retrieved from https://www.youtube.com/watch?v=xpG3jLGGkvc

Van Ausdale, D., & Feagin, J. R. (2001). *The first R: How children learn race and racism.* Lanham, MD: Rowman & Littlefield.

Williams, K., & Mohammed, K. (2009). *My name is Sangoel*. Grand Rapids, MI: Eerdmans Books for Young Readers.

Yokota, J. (1993). Issues in selecting multicultural children's literature. *Language Arts, 70*(3), 156–167.

Chapter Six

Critical Media Literacy

Fake News, Trolls, and Memes

With Contributions From Drew Gingrich

> Media literacy is not just important, it's absolutely critical. It's going to make the difference between whether kids are a tool of the mass media or whether the mass media is a tool for kids to use.
>
> —Linda Ellerbee

This chapter explores the role media plays in shaping views of race and immigration. We explore how critical media literacy can serve as a key component of engaging critical race teacher activism (CRTA). The proliferation of social media platforms as a mode for producing and widely sharing content calls for both students and teachers to be able to critically read, interpret, evaluate, and synthesize information. We argue that critical media literacy offers a framework for critically consuming Internet and social media content in ways that question stereotypes, biases, and misinformation.

Key Ideas and Terms

- Literacy as a social practice
- Critical literacy
- Media literacy
- Fake news, troll factories, memes, and bots

PART 1: BACKGROUND AND DEFINITIONS

To explore the benefits of critical media literacy practices in classrooms, we begin by introducing and defining terms such as literacy, critical literacy, and critical media literacy and how these terms intersect with CRTA. In Part 2 of this chapter we provide recommendations and activity ideas for engaging in critical media literacy practices in the classroom and community.

What Is Literacy?

The definition of literacy has evolved beyond the cognitive ability to read and write to the understanding that literacy is a socially situated practice composed of multiple literacies used to read and interact with the world (Freire, 1968). How we read the world is grounded in our sociohistorical, cultural, and political orientations and experiences. Sluys, Lewison, and Flint (2006) contend that "becoming literate is about what people do with literacy—the values people place on various acts and their associated ideologies" (p. 199). In this way, reading and writing happen at the intersection of the "text" and the social world. The definition of "text" not only includes books, but other artifacts in our social world such as written and spoken discourses, art, photographs, memes, film, graffiti, and diagrams.

What Is Critical Literacy?

Critical literacy was born out of critical theory and critical pedagogy. Critical theory is the analysis and deconstruction of accepted truths and knowledge in society. Critical literacy, then, is the process of questioning how power plays a role in our socially situated ways of reading the word and world. Critical literacy requires recognition "that our world—geographically, environmentally, politically and socially—is not neutral or natural. It has been formed by history and shaped by humanity" (Janks, 2013, p. 227).

Critical literacy provides educators with an opportunity to consider moral and ethical stances related to human rights and democratic practices (Shor, 2014, p. 23). It rejects the notion that knowledge can be neutral and instead sets the stage for a learning environment where students are invited to reflect on and challenge their current accepted truths.

Janks (2013) explains that critical literacy practices in the classroom enable "young people to *read* both the word and the world in relation to power, identify difference and access to knowledge, skills, tools, and resources. It is also about *writing* and rewriting the world: it is about design and re-design" (p. 227). We contend that Janks's notion of "rewriting the world" is the essential component of action required in CRTA.

While teachers and students can employ critical literacy strategies in the classroom, critical literacy is not, in itself, a strategy, nor is it critical thinking. Critical literacy is a *framework* that requires the questioning of power and a commitment to action. Vasquez (2017) explains that critical literacy should not be confused with an add-on strategy or a box to check once or twice throughout the school year. If teachers want to "do" critical literacy, it should frame the events of the classroom.

What Is Critical Media Literacy?

Critical media literacy is a form of critical literacy designed to address widely shared media in both digital and analog formats. In other words, critical media literacy is a way of applying the critical literacy framework to the media that students are exposed to in both the public and private sphere. Shor (2014) suggests that critical literacy and critical media literacy "connects the political and the personal, the public and the private, the global and the local, the economic and the pedagogical, for reinventing our lives and for promoting justice in place of inequality" (p. 1) and promotes activism (p. 11). In this way critical literacy and critical media literacy can be envisioned as modes for enacting CRTA practices.

You cannot do critical media literacy without asking critical questions about power. Kellner and Share (2007) explain that critical media literacy involves reading and challenging dominant narratives in media content. It "involves cultivating skills in analyzing media codes and conventions, abilities to criticize stereotypes, dominant values, and ideologies, and competencies to interpret the multiple meanings and messages generated by media texts." It is a framework for helping "people to discriminate and evaluate media content, to critically dissect media forms, to investigate media effects and uses, to use media intelligently, and to construct alternative media" (p. 4).

Critical media literacy prepares both students and teachers to critically engage and stay current with the ever-changing world. Kellner and Share (2007) call attention to the generational disconnect between teachers and students in using and interacting with the digital world. "The twenty-first century is a media saturated, technologically dependent, and globally connected world" (p. 3). There is no sign of slowing down, either. A 2015 study found that teens are spending 9 hours or one-third of their days using media (Tsukayama, 2015). These trends have pushed state and national standards and curriculum developers to embed media literacy. The focus on the "critical," however, has yet to be seen. With this growing emphasis on media and technology, it is imperative for students and teachers to be savvy consumers of information.

Fake News, Troll Factories, Bots, and Meme Warfare

The ability to critically analyze media content is even more vital with the rise of fake news and "alternative facts" produced by Internet "troll factories," which mass-produce memes and use "bots" (robotic technology like "robotweets," for example) to sway public opinion. Fake news was brought to the forefront during the 2016 election when it was discovered that Russian-influenced operations were producing tweets by fake Americans. Troll factories in Russia and other Baltic states posed as individuals from prominent activist groups such as Black Lives Matter, for example, to incite division and stoke the fears of a US public historically biased against people of color. Russians have not cornered the market on producing fake news, however; troll factories producing malicious content to distort reality have been linked to US alt-right nationalist (White supremacist) groups and conservative news media outlets. These groups fan the flames of xenophobia with anti-immigrant tweets and fake news articles, for example.

People use social media to communicate beliefs through their posts and decode the beliefs posted by others. And, while people may have less time to read an article, or a book, they do have time to scroll through Facebook, Twitter, Instagram, or Snapchat. For this reason, critical media literacy is a necessity for learning how to actively read, deconstruct, and evaluate text, both digital and analog, to determine its validity and make informed decisions about whether to accept or reject the ideas presented. Troll factories and meme warfare depend on the public to share their content. The ability to identify patterns used in fake news—to develop that little voice that says, "Something seems off here," requires the critical framework that critical media literacy provides.

Social media also plays a role in not only reading and interpreting social issues, but in constructing and "writing" our own identities, both authentically and inauthentically. It provides an outlet for citizens to advocate policy and oppose policy, awaken friends and family members who scroll through their social media pages, or cause riffs among social media "friends." Teachers can ask themselves, "How does social media shape the ideas and opinions of the students in my classroom? How can I harness that influence to help students become better and more critical readers of the world?"

PART 2: CLASSROOM ACTIVITIES

This section explores how to use critical media literacy through a CRTA lens in the classroom. We emphasize the need for teachers and students to not only critically question media, but to find ways to take action in dismantling systems of oppression in classrooms, schools, and communities. Framing the classroom in a CRTA framework and engaging in critical media literacy first involves educating students and their families on the importance of criticality in the education process. Use this book as a resource for sharing background information and defining concepts for students and families. We emphasize that teachers should consider how to build *with* parents and the community in order to promote critical literacy both inside and outside of the classroom walls. This involves communicating your goals to families and allowing them to be part of the process. Parents are less likely to object to critical activities if they have an understanding of the context and rationale. Set the tone during teacher conferences and events like "Back to School Night." Give a snapshot of activities you have already tried in previous years (or examples from other teachers) to give them a taste of what critical literacy and critical media literacy look like. Communicate in notes home whenever possible. For example, teachers can write:

> In our classroom, we encourage students to be critical "readers of the world." Since the Internet is such a powerful source of information, we value skills that help students to read, interpret, and evaluate Internet and social media content. During the school year, your child may be asked to engage in some "critical reading" of the world. Our goal is for students to be educated, critical consumers of information. This week's activity is: ________[briefly explain the activity]. We encourage you to participate and join in on the conversation by ________[briefly explain how you'd like parents to contribute].

Critical media literacy in school has the potential to impact families and communities. Reassure parents that critical literacy and critical media literacy are not designed to indoctrinate or sway students toward an opinion. Critical literacy and critical media literacy do the opposite. They provide a framework for questioning and seeking more information to confirm or disconfirm ideas.

When making decisions about homework to encourage critical literacy and critical media literacy activities, make sure the work is purposeful. All too often, homework activities become cumbersome and interfere with families' choices about how to spend their time together. Select critical media literacy activities that can be accomplished while grocery shopping, walking around the mall, watching TV, or traveling to and from extracurricular activities. Environmental print like billboards are ripe with opportunities to engage in critical media literacy activities. Ask students to read the billboard, both words and images. What does the billboard say or not say? What images are presented? Who (what population) is the billboard trying to reach? Who paid for the billboard? What is their involvement or investment in the issue or product?

McLaughlin and DeVoogd (2004) recommend the following questions when analyzing billboards or other texts such as social media feeds, songs, television shows, movies, video games, comic books, or photographs:

- Who is in the text/picture/situation? Who is missing?
- Whose voices are represented? Whose voices are marginalized or discounted?

- What are the intentions of the author? What does the author want the reader to think?
- What would an alternative text/picture/situation say?
- How can the reader use this information to promote equity? (p. 44)

Critical Media Literacy in the Classroom

This section provides examples of what critical media literacy can look like in a classroom. When practicing critical media literacy through a CRTA lens, ask the following questions of your planned lessons: "In what ways does this lesson provide an opportunity for students to address real-world issues? What social issues are connected to this lesson and how do these issues play out in the media content students are exposed to? How does the lesson contribute to a critical understanding and questioning of power relationships? How do these questions help me to address the standards and objectives of the lesson and curriculum?"

The following lesson exemplar gives an overview of how teachers can engage in critical media literacy through a CRTA lens in a literature-based, theme unit. Refer to Chapter 5 for additional information about the importance of using text sets and multimodal resources when designing units.

Begin with the picture book *Super Cilantro Girl* (Herrera, 2003). This book can be used in grades K–12 with age- and grade-appropriate standards, objectives, essential questions, and activities. With upper grades, picture books offer students an opportunity to analyze how social issues are addressed through multiple modes. The shorter text provides an access point to complex issues such as race and immigration. Teachers can ask their middle and high school students, "What are the hidden complexities of picture books? In what way do the words and illustrations convey complex messages in ways other texts can't? Why did the author write this children's book?" With middle and high school students, *Super Cilantro Girl* can provide an entry point for the topic of immigration and transnationalism. For elementary students, it can serve as the core or focal text. The next few paragraphs provide options and possibilities how CRTA can go above and beyond the standards, and how to include CRTA-based essential questions, and resources to include in a text set.

The following two standards present in the Pennsylvania Common Core Standards could be used for a lesson on immigration, with subthemes such as separation, diaspora, and displacement: Pennsylvania Common Core Standards (Pennsylvania Department of Education, 2014): Standard CC.1.2.5.G, addressing informational texts, requires students to "draw on information from multiple print or digital sources, demonstrating the ability to locate an answer to a question quickly or to solve a problem efficiently" (p. 10) and standard CC.1.2.5.C, which requires students to "explain the relationships or interactions between two or more individuals, events, ideas, or concepts in a text based on specific information in the text" (p. 8). The text set in particular provides ways to address these relationships and interactions between people, events, and ideas.

These standards taken alone do not require nor do they explicitly advocate for critical media literacy or CRTA. Critical media literacy through a CRTA lens allows teachers to meet and exceed the standards in ways that are engaging and authentic for students. The critical media literacy and CRTA lens can support teachers and students to compare, contrast, and critique depictions of immigrants and their experiences in the US.

Teachers can craft their essential questions to reflect a critical media literacy, CRTA lens. For example, instead of simply asking students to identify textual evidence, discuss what textual evidence is. What does it mean to find "evidence" in a text? What is it evidence for—the author's ideas? How do you represent the ideas of others when citing textual evidence? In what way does textual evidence represent truth? In what ways can texts be used to persuade and sway opinion? How can we use textual evidence from multiple sources and evaluate the validity of those sources? As teachers, remember not to only "do" critical media literacy, but talk about what it is with students. Use essential questions such as, "How does using critical media literacy change the way we find textual evidence?"

As we discussed in Chapter 5, text sets provide ways to modify the existing curriculum. If your existing curriculum only explores immigration through the experiences of immigrants coming through Ellis Island, use other text to supplement and connect the conversation to modern immigration. For example, to promote the use of multiple literacies, use the following video clip that shows the reality of deportation experiences in the US: https://www.youtube.com/watch?v=kpAEAYg2JTw. In the video, Jorge Garcia is deported after living in the US for more than 30 years. He must leave his family and return to a country he barely remembers. *Super Cilantro Girl* shows how children internalize this very real fear of deportation and the trauma of separation. To compare immigration then and now, ask, "How do these modern examples of immigration and deportation compare to the experiences of immigrants in the early 20th century?"

In addition to the literacy standards addressed in these texts, teachers can incorporate social studies content. Explore policies and legislation related to immigration over time. What is DACA? What is the Dream Act? Ask students to consider the relationship between the video and *Super Cilantro Girl*—what was the author's intent in producing both texts? What position may the author have as it relates to DACA or the Dream Act? What about other policies and practices in US history such as the Braceros Program, the Immigration Act of 1965, the Immigration Reform and Control Act of 1985, or the Enhanced Border Security and Visa Entry Reform Act of 2002? (See the following timeline for more information: http://www.emmigration.info/us-immigration-laws-timeline.htm.) How do these policies and practices impact real human beings?

In order to teach from a CRTA perspective, action-oriented activities that promote justice and equity, not just questions, must be included as an integral part of the lesson or unit. "How do we create a more just world? What does youth activism look like?" Teachers can guide students in researching the stances of local and state representatives on issues of immigration. Students can write letters or request a phone call or virtual meeting with their representatives to share their opinions and ideas using evidence from their text set resources. Teachers and students can also attend grassroots organizing events, protests, and community or legislative meetings to learn more. This provides a real-life, authentic connection to content.

In this way, students reach the mastery required in the standards and, at the same time, become an active part of democracy. The following activities can also be used to support action. The activities can be modified to include in an immigration unit or across the curriculum in any type of related unit to engage critical media literacy through a CRTA lens.

Activity 1: Textual Analysis of Memes

Social media posts and memes, in particular, can provide opportunities to deconstruct texts with students through a critical media literacy framework. The Facebook post that appeared in the *Time* article written by Ashley Hoffman (2017) and shown in Figure 6.1 was used by Russian operatives to influence the 2016 election.

After reading the post and the meme, ask the students, "Who wrote the post, why, and for what purpose? Who is the intended audience? What are they trying to accomplish with this meme?" Include in this conversation an analysis of discourse. That is, ask what words and phrases are used to divide, create affiliation, or marginalize. If you are not familiar with Texas, research the slogan, "Don't mess with Texas." How does the use of this slogan appeal to certain audiences? What about the invocation of God in the meme? Who are the meme producers trying persuade by saying, "Guided by God"? Who is positioned as *not* being guided by God? In what ways were the troll factories capitalizing on conservatives' fears of border security in this meme? What about the language used in the text such as "illegal alien"? Are the claims made about crimes committed by immigrants accurate? What happens when this meme is shared? Have you ever shared a political meme? Did you know where the meme originated from? How do you find out? These are critical questions teachers and students should explore together.

Teachers can also work with students to generate a list of ways to identify fake news. For example, teachers and students should ask, "Where is the

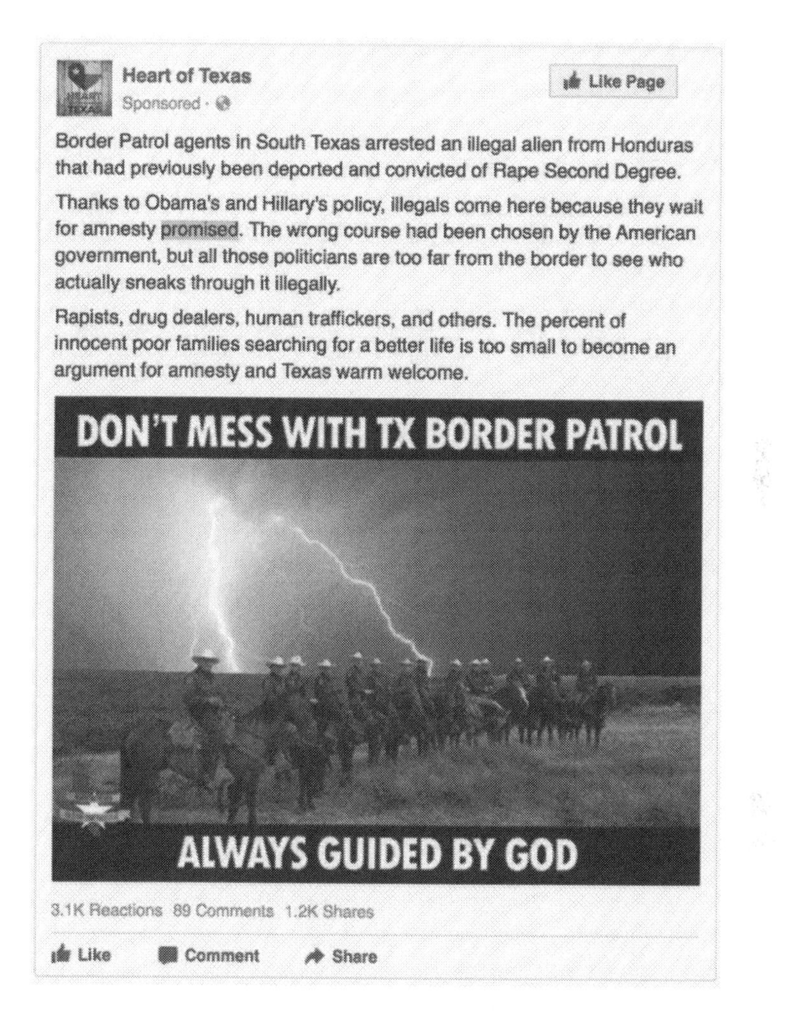

Figure 6.1. Anti-immigrant Facebook post created by Russian trolls. https://www.washingtonpost.com/graphics/2017/business/russian-ads-facebook-targeting/?utm_term=.82dd47865c49

article, meme, or post from? Who wrote it? What website published it? What other articles do they publish? What is the publication date? If it is an article, how does the headline match with what is written in body of the article?" Students can also consider to what degree the potential fake news artifact confirms or disrupts their current viewpoint. How does this sway their willingness to share? In what ways can we avoid confirmation bias—believing fake news because it affirms the stances we already hold?

Activity 2: Art as Text

Art can be used to promote critical literacy and critical media literacy in the classroom. Artists concerned with justice and equity see their artistic creations as a form of activism. The Parsons School of Design, for example, recently featured an exhibit titled *State Exception/Estado de Excepción* (Cotter, 2017). This exhibit shows the belongings of immigrants as they made their journey through the Sonoran Desert in Arizona. Whether you have access to exhibits that could offer such a display or you simply have access to the images posted online of this specific exhibit, you can engage students in an analysis of images as a text in your immigration unit. Use the link provided to discuss and consider with students the intentions of the artist in collecting and compiling the pieces and displaying them. How does the art installation promote awareness and activism related to immigration?

Exploring activism art can also lead to a discussion of questioning the types of art that are privileged in mainstream society—that is, why we study particular works of art by particular artists in school, and why some art garners millions at auction and some does not. What does this say about which works of art (and artists) are valued by society? The Guerrilla Girls, a group of women donning gorilla masks who anonymously educate the public on how museums almost exclusively privilege White, male artists, create new forms of radical art to inspire these questions. They distribute flyers, create billboards, write Op-Eds, and project counterstories on the side of well-known art museums to educate and inspire action. Visit their website to find more images to analyze with students: https://www.guerrillagirls.com/. Examples of quotes from their posters include: "You're seeing less than half the picture." These words are written in bold on the right side of the poster with a large blank space on the left. At the bottom, the poster reads, "without the vision of women artists and artists of color." Another poster lists all the well-known art museums with less than half of the art representing women artists. Students can research other works by the Guerilla Girls and make their own posters representing counterstories in the media.

Related to the issue of art, culture, and media is the problem of cultural appropriation. Cultural appropriation is the process of adopting, using, stealing, and/or capitalizing on elements of a minority group's culture by the dominant group. This is especially evident in the fashion industry where designers visit poverty-stricken areas and copy the prints and designs of indigenous populations. They then incorporate these sometimes sacred designs into mainstream, Western fashion, without permission from the artists or communities who created them. The selective import of cultural goods, with the rejection of the human beings who created them, is also a form of imperialism and colonialistic exploitation. Use this link to explore how the US appropriates cultural goods: http://acclaimmag.com/style/cultural-appropriation-in-fashion-is-nothing-new/#1. How does this conversation connect to what the Guerilla Girls are trying to achieve? What is art? How is it commodified? Who benefits? Who doesn't?

Activity 5: The Mask We Wear in Social Media

Laura asks her students to use the tools of discourse and theme analysis (see Chapter 7) to explore the "masks we wear" in social media. Students, K–12 to grad school, explore how their social media profile pictures and posts represent their identities, both public and private. For example, teachers can ask, "How does your profile picture represent or hide your beliefs about the world? And, how does it 'market' who you are? What's your brand?" Students can thematically analyze their social media feeds for frequently appearing words, ideas, or themes. "What social issues most frequently appear in my social media feed?" In addition to looking at content, students can analyze the types of advertisements pushed by various social media outlets, examine privacy settings, discuss net neutrality, and talk about online safety. Critical media literacy conversations around social media do not always have to be negative. How can students make use of the Internet and social media to share and shape ideas, engage in grassroots organizing, and make change? This article from *Education Week* is a helpful resource for exploring how net neutrality impacts educators and students committed to social justice: https://www.edweek.org/tm/articles/2018/02/07/students-cant-afford-to-lose-net-neutrality.html.

Emdin (2016) argues that schools can play a role in teaching students how to craft their online identities and what it means to have an online presence. In this way, students can be savvy producers of their own lives and identities in ways that promote entrepreneurship and networking. Students can use these virtual spaces to build *with* and advocate *for* marginalized communities.

RECOMMENDED BOOKS AND SOURCES

Books and Articles

Cotter, H. (2017). For migrants headed north, the things they carried to the end. Retrieved from https://www.nytimes.com/2017/03/03/arts/design/state-of-exception-estado-de-excepcion-parsons-mexican-immigration.html

Herrera, J. F. (2003). *Super cilantro girl*. New York, NY: Children's Book Press.

Thomas, J. R. (1994). *Lights on the river*. New York, NY: Hyperion.

Torres, M., & Mercado, M. (2006). The need for critical media literacy in teacher education core curricula. *Educational Studies, 39* (3), 260–282.

Warikoo, N. (2017). ICE defends deportation of immigrant in U.S. nearly 30 years. Retrieved from https://www.usatoday.com/story/news/nation-now/2018/01/17/ice-defends-deportation-immigrant-u-s-nearly-30-years/1043110001/

Podcasts and Videos

Center for Economic Progress (CEP). (Producer). (2010). *Kid's talk: The stories of refugee children.* [Video file]. Retrieved from https://www.youtube.com/watch?v=3uoUXlGHWts

Donoghue, M., & Stuckwisch, K. (Producers), & Whitmore, T. (Director). (2016). *Immigrants (we get the job done)* [Music video]. United States: Atlantic Records.

Glass, I. (Producer). (n.d.). *This American Life Podcast* [Audio podcast]. Retrieved from https://www.thisamericanlife.org/listen

REFERENCES

Cotter, H. (2017). For migrants headed north, the things they carried to the end. Retrieved from https://www.nytimes.com/2017/03/03/arts/design/state-of-exception-estado-de-excepcion-parsons-mexican-immigration.html

Emdin, C. (2016). *For White folks who teach in the hood . . . and the rest of y'all too: Reality pedagogy and urban education.* Boston, MA: Beacon.

Herrera, J. F. (2003). *Super cilantro girl.* New York, NY: Children's Book Press.

Hoffman, A. (2017, November 1). *Here are the memes that Russian operatives shared to influence 2016.* Retrieved from http://time.com/5006056/russia-election-2016-memes/

Janks, H. (2013). Critical literacy in teaching and research. *Education Inquiry, 4* (2), 225–242. Retrieved from http://www.lh.umu.se/digitalAssets

Kellner, D., & Share, J. (2007). Critical media literacy, democracy, and the reconstruction of education. In D. Macedo & S. R. Steinberg (Eds.), *Media literacy: A reader* (pp. 3–23). New York, NY: Peter Lang.

McLaughlin, M., & DeVoogd, G. L. (2004). *Critical literacy: Enhancing students' comprehension of text.* New York: Scholastic.

Merriam, S. (n.d.). *Qualitive research and case study applications in education. 2nd ed.* San Francisco: Jossey-Bass Publishers.

Pennsylvania Department of Education. (2014). *Academic standards for English language arts: Grades preK–5.* Retrieved from http://static.pdesas.org/content/documents/PA%20Core%20Standards%20ELA%20PreK-5%20March%202014.pdf

Shor, I. (2014). What is critical literacy? In S. Totten & J. Pedersen (Eds.), *Educating about social issues in the 20th and 21st centuries: Critical pedagogues and their pedagogical theories: Vol. 4.* Charlotte, NC: Information Age.

Sluys, K. V., Lewison, M., & Flint, A. S. (2006). Researching critical literacy: A critical study of analysis of classroom discourse. *Journal of Literacy Research, 38*(2), 197–233. Retrieved from http://journals.sagepub.com/doi/pdf/10.1207/s15548430jlr3802_4

Tsukayama, H. (2018). *Teens spend nearly nine hours every day consuming media.* Washington Post. Retrieved from https://www.washingtonpost.com/news/the-switch/wp/2015/11/03/teens-spend-nearly-nine-hours-every-day-consuming-media/?noredirect=on&utm_term=.729e6b5df75f

Vasquez, V. M. (2017). *Critical literacy across the K–6 curriculum.* New York, NY: Routledge.

Part III

What Disruption Looks Like: Supporting Teacher Activism

Chapter Seven

Teacher Research as Activism

> There's really no such thing as the "voiceless." There are only the deliberately silenced, or the preferably unheard.
>
> —Arundhati Roy

This chapter focuses on the liberatory possibilities of teachers engaging in original research in their classrooms, schools, and communities. This book includes a chapter on research because educators are continuously inundated with claims of research-based best practices in pedagogy and curricula and data-driven assessment practices, but are rarely called upon to critique, understand, and validate these claims.

I propose that a critical race teacher activism (CRTA) lens has the potential to support teachers in critically questioning the merit of some so-called research-based assertions and data-driven practices. This chapter focuses on using the tools of critical ethnography (CE) and participatory action research (PAR) to operationalize CRTA and help teachers analyze and critique systems of power, including questions about who is positioned as a knower or expert in educational research. The primary goal of this chapter is to engage teachers in research for liberation by providing tools for examining the intersections of race and immigration with "new eyes" (Frank, 1999).

This chapter focuses on the following goals:

- To question the notion of data and problematize so-called research-based practices that are promoted by curriculum publishers
- To reframe the lens through which educators view immigrant and refugee children and families by using the tools of the critical ethnographer (CE) and participatory action researcher (PAR)
- To provide activities that support educators in practicing critical observation, analysis, and interpretation of multiple forms of data

- To privilege teachers, students, and community members as knowers, experts, and co-researchers in solving educational issues
- To explore how tools of CE and PAR can enhance and strengthen pK–12 praxis
- To envision teacher research as a liberatory practice

Key Ideas and Terms

- Ethnography
- Critical ethnography
- Participatory action research
- Data for liberation

PART 1: DEFINITIONS AND BACKGROUND: WHAT'S THE RELATIONSHIP BETWEEN RESEARCH AND PRACTICE?

Not all research is equal, and some claims about research-based practices are questionable. How can teachers evaluate these claims? How do teachers know what constitutes good research? How can teachers use research to improve practice? Textbook and curriculum publishing companies often tout their products as "research based," but what does that really mean? How do teachers know what research the products draw from, and whether it is the best choice for their school or classroom? If teachers must make data-driven decisions in the classroom, what actually constitutes data? How do teachers distinguish between anecdotal data and hard facts? Is there a difference?

Before reading on, think about the types of data you collect about the students in your classroom. How do you make use of this data? Is this research? What is research anyway? Part 1 of this chapter explores some basic definitions of research tools and practices in order to support teachers in exploring the possibilities of using the tools of critical ethnography (CE) and participatory action research (PAR) to make pedagogical and curricular decisions. Part 2 invites teachers to use the tools of CE and PAR to engage in their own research by providing examples of teacher research projects and how teachers worked through complexities of using research to engage CRTA.

I encourage you to explore the resources at the end of this chapter for in-depth explanations of different research approaches. I do not expect, nor is it possible for, you to be an expert in CE, PAR, or other approaches after reading this chapter; rather, this book is designed to convey the way certain tools support educators in employing CRTA. In the sections that follow, I provide a working definition of CE and PAR and provide a discussion of how these approaches align with CRTA.

What Is Research? What Is Data?

Research is generally understood to be a systematic process of investigation designed to inform existing knowledge or draw new conclusions. Research projects typically have a theoretical framework: a theory or combination of complementary theories from which the research is grounded; and methods: the practices and procedures associated with collecting, analyzing, and drawing conclusions about data.

Data are the units of analysis, the collection of artifacts analyzed to draw conclusions in relation to the research questions. Research is often defined as quantitative (dealing primarily with numerical data), qualitative (dealing primarily with data that is nonnumerical, such as themes, ideas, characteristics, and phenomena), or mixed methods (a combination of quantitative and qualitative approaches).

When designing a study, researchers select methods that best enable them to investigate the problems or answer the questions they are interested in. There are a myriad of possible approaches and methods to choose from when designing a research study, which may feel daunting to the novice researcher. In this chapter, the focus is on CE and PAR as a point of entry for teacher research. I endeavor to engage teachers in authentic research to disrupt the current education reform movements that distort notions of data and research to promote neoliberal and corporate-based educational practices (Saltman, 2014). CE and PAR tend to be qualitative in nature, but mixed methods, drawing from both quantitative and qualitative methods, are possible depending upon what you plan to study.

What Is a Theory?

We all have "theories" about how the world works. Some of those theories are grounded in scientific evidence and others are not. A true theory is based on principles set forth by a field of scientific study, a collection of evidence that leads to potential assumptions grounded in conclusive evidence. True theories are more than just hunches or speculation. When designing a research study, the theories represent the researcher's lens. For example, if you choose to study classroom literacy practices through a critical feminist lens, your research question(s) and data collection will likely center on issues of power and gender in literacy practices. A possible research question might be, "In what ways are literacy practices gendered in the elementary classroom?" This question allows the teacher researcher to consider collecting data on gender representation and bias in classroom library collections, classroom talk related to gender positioning, or gendered classroom participation expectations.

Reliability, Validity, and Bias

In research, reliability is determined by its replicability. In other words, if the same study is conducted again, are the results the same or similar? Validity is determined by a study's credibility, namely, whether the study produces results that match up with the real world. Reliability and validity go hand in hand. If a study confirms knee replacements are effective, for example, but the study only included male participants, the reliability and validity could be questioned. The ACT and SAT tests discussed in Chapter 3 are another example of tests that have questionable reliability and validity. If the purpose of the ACT and SAT is to determine college readiness and success, but the tests are found to not actually predict success, we would say that these tests are unreliable and invalid measures of college success.

No research approach, qualitative or quantitative, is free from bias. As Chapter 3 addressed, the orientation of the researcher(s) and the research questions asked greatly influence the study findings. The social and political climate of the time also impact how research is conducted and how it is interpreted by the public. That is to say, research is often politicized, especially when it contradicts the historical, social, and political leanings of those in power.

Consider a hot-button topic such as climate change. The existence of climate change is supported across the globe. A statement written by 18 prominent scientific associations reads, "Observations throughout the world make it clear that climate change is occurring, and rigorous scientific research demonstrates that greenhouse gases emitted by human activities are the primary driver" (American Association for the Advancement of Science, 2009). The statement is also supported by NASA and the majority of the American public, but companies that contribute to the emissions, including energy companies and the automobile industry, have lobbying power with politicians. The research is valid and reliable, but it is marginalized in place of corporate interests.

Representation in Research

Understanding how research comes to be is imperative for teachers who want to develop a CRTA approach in their classrooms. Using the tools of CE and PAR can help to disrupt racism and White supremacy by shifting the power relationships in the classroom and school. Further, engaging students in CE and PAR as co-researchers teaches valuable skills of observation, critique, and using evidence-based claims—all skills required in local, state, and national standards.

Just as there is a lack of diverse representation in authorship of children's and young adult literature and curriculum as described in Chapter 5, there is a lack of diverse representation in education research. How does research get published? Who gets to decide what articles appear in academic journals? Who has access to and reads these journals? If it is important for scholarly articles to be "peer reviewed," what does this mean? Who are considered peers?

While this book may not be able to dive deeply into these questions, they are presented to encourage teachers to consider the nature of how knowledge is valued and transmitted in the field of education. Who do curriculum developers rely upon to make decisions about books to include in a curriculum? When a curriculum is touted as "research based," what does that actually mean? Whose research and why?

When educational researchers conduct a research study and write up the results, they generally submit their papers to an academic journal. Though processes vary by journal, the manuscript is typically sent to several academics (i.e., professors) who are considered "experts" in the subject, theoretical framework, and/or methodologies used in the study. These reviewers provide feedback to the editor of the journal, and then the editor and/or editorial board makes decisions about whether further edits are needed prior to publication. The idea is that by having multiple experts' eyes on the research, potential biases or weaknesses in the research will be identified and addressed or acknowledged.

Once final edits are made, the study is published in an academic journal. Journalists from a variety of news outlets are sometimes assigned to read these journals and synthesize the information for the general public in print and digital media. Digesting large studies into news "bites" can run the risk of oversimplifying or misrepresenting results or implications of a research study. Critical literacy practices as described in Chapter 6 provide a framework for questioning media content.

Even highly regarded peer-reviewed journals pose challenges in how research is disseminated. White, cisgender, heterosexual male scholars are more likely to be tenured, which means they are more likely to maintain longevity in their given field and thus produce more of the published research and serve as editors and experts who determine what gets published. This has consequences for the type of research published. For example, *The Journal of Political Philosophy* in June of 2017 published a themed issue related to the Black Lives Matter movement with only White authors contributing to the issue. This was followed by critique, from both scholars of color and White scholars.

The critique was not designed to dissuade White authors from writing about or contributing to the scholarship related to Black Lives Matter, as this too is important, but rather to urge White scholars who are in positions of decision-making power to consider representation in academic spaces. Similar critiques could be made, for example, of a themed journal issue devoted to women's issues written entirely by men. As discussed in Chapter 8, it is imperative for people who benefit from the larger system of power to consider ways to be allies and accomplices in the pursuit of justice and equity. This means asking questions and taking action when diverse voices are not represented.

The for-profit publication of research is also important to consider. Most academic journals do not pay scholars for contributing and thus the only monetary benefit is perhaps increased chances for tenure and/or notoriety in the field. This does not eliminate bias altogether, but it does shift the motivation somewhat from a fully commissioned study or non-peer-reviewed source.

Book and curriculum publishing companies vary in their processes for seeking peer review and are generally working for profit rather than for the sake of scholarship or altruism. It is often up to the author to ensure books are grounded in peer-reviewed sources. This is not to say that commissioned studies or books and curricula published by for-profit companies are not reliable sources; rather, it provides rationale to question the process and product through a CRTA lens in order to make informed decisions.

Another way research has adjusted to address justice-related concerns is through an official review process. Research conducted in modern-day scientific communities must undergo a rigorous review process before "human subjects" (people) can be included in research projects. Universities, research institutes, and many government organizations have institutional review boards (IRBs). This independent review entity is required to review the proposed research project to determine and prevent potential harm and ensure the rights and welfare of research subjects.

IRB procedures were first developed in 1947 as a result of the Nazi medical research atrocities revealed during the Nuremburg war crimes trials. IRB protocol was further refined in 1974 with the National Research Act and in 1983 with the US Department of Health and Human Services Policy for the Protection of Human Subjects. They continue to be updated.

Educators engaging in research should review IRB guidelines with a university professor and their school community in order to determine whether or what type of IRB approval is needed. This can help educators distinguish between using the tools of the researcher for pedagogical purposes and conducting official research in their classroom, school, or community. While IRB processes can sometimes be tedious, they are an important component in considering power and adhering to principles of justice and equity.

CRITICAL ETHNOGRAPHY (CE) AS TEACHER RESEARCH

Ethnography was born out of the field of anthropology and can be viewed as both a theoretical and methodological approach. It is longitudinal in nature and requires the researcher to be immersed in the research context. Kirkland (2013) describes ethnography as "a scholarly approach to inquiry aimed at understanding cultural phenomena." He goes on to say that "ethnography, like the telling of stories, is not always considered scientific by some. It can be messy and personal, a science that emerges from real relationships where very real circumstances lead to very real consequences" (p. 2).

CE pays careful attention to relationships between the wider sociohistorical, social, political, and economic context in which the study is conducted. Thomas (1993) explains that "the critical ethnographer contributes to emancipatory knowledge and discourses of social justice" (p. 5). CE also requires consideration of how researchers' own stories, realities, and lived experiences intersect with the community they are studying.

This consideration of self in ethnography is called positionality. Positionality is defined by Sensoy and DiAngelo (2012) as "the recognition that where you stand in relation to others in society shapes what you can see and understand about the world" (p. 8). Including a statement of positionality in the write-up of a CE makes transparent the researcher's "position(s)" in relation to the study. It is also a good place to start when engaging in CE to identify potential biases and the impact of researcher identity on the study design. The introductory chapter of this book serves as our positionality statement to readers. Here is an example of a positionality statement from a practicing teacher's CE in one of my graduate courses:

* * *

"As veteran educator with more than 25 years of experience in elementary school settings, I approached the study of the welcoming and unwelcoming aspects of my school community through new eyes. Growing up as a White woman in a small town in southeastern Pennsylvania, I always had the impression that our community was the friendly, all-American town with mom-and-pop businesses, houses with unlocked doors, and kids riding their bikes until the street lights came on.

"A few years ago, we were redistricted and many of the children of migrant worker parents were enrolled in the local elementary school. I was surprised to learn how the children were being treated by other kids, community members, and even teachers. It changed my perception of our 'friendly' town. I didn't see it happening in our neighborhood because our community was so segregated.

"I enrolled in this course to learn how my school could better serve our children of migrant workers who are predominantly Spanish speaking from Mexico. These experiences and questions led me to focus on the following research questions: How do perceptions of 'friendliness and welcoming' change or evolve around issues of race or immigration status in schools that experience an influx of immigrant students? What role can teachers play in shifting negative and deficit perspectives of immigrant children in predominantly White elementary schools?"

* * *

In this positionality statement example, the teacher reveals her own identities: a White teacher and veteran educator who has lived in the same small town for the majority of her life. She also reveals her initial impressions of the research context as an insider and how her perceptions changed over time based on her everyday observations and lived experiences. She shares her personal experience, observations, and lived experiences to set the stage for how she arrived at her research questions and study. In this way, she demonstrates a meaningful rationale for seeking new knowledge about her context through planned research and, at the same time, is transparent about her potential biases and motivations in engaging this work. An advanced critical ethnographer could also use his or her own perspectives as a unit of analysis in the work. This is sometimes called an autoethnography.

The positionality statement disrupts the notion that research methods can be wholly objective and allows the reader of the research to critique or draw new or different conclusions by having all of the information. It also has the potential to address the past challenges in ethnography and research in general, where White researchers intentionally or unintentionally misrepresented and/or exoticized their research participants. Early European ethnographers, for example, traveled to regions in Southeast Asia and Africa and portrayed the people inhabiting these lands as uncultured, primitive, and savage. The people studied were not consulted or given access to the research prior to publication. And, the subsequent publication of this work, which was consumed by primarily Western audiences, inculcated deficit views of communities of color, which are ever present in historical and scientific research today.

Modern ethnographies are not immune to this critique, nor is any research that is not carefully examined for bias. Approaching ethnography from a critical perspective has the potential to ameliorate this bias and contribute to the emancipatory possibilities. CE requires the researcher to have immense concern for the integrity of the people and places being studied. It emphasizes the questioning of power relationships in how systems and institutions influence how we read the word and world. Moreover, it more deeply considers the impact of these systems and institutions on research practices, moving beyond a single story told by one researcher to considering multiple perspectives and histories.

Making the Strange Familiar and the Familiar Strange

To begin practicing the tools of the critical ethnographer and to consider their own positionality, teachers can attempt to make the strange familiar and the familiar strange (Miner, 1956/2012). This means considering your own identity and lived experiences in relation to the phenomenon and context you are researching. It is the process of trying to understand and make familiar that which is outside of your own experience while, at the same time, distancing yourself and attempting to take an outsider perspective on what is familiar to you. For example, if you are a teacher conducting research in a school, you are an insider to "schooling" and "doing school." If you are conducting research in your own classroom, your insider status becomes even more salient. In ethnographic research, this insider or "within social group" perspective is called the emic perspective.

The opposite of emic is etic. A White, female Christian teacher conducting research in a community of Muslim refugees from Iraq would be working from an etic perspective and from a position of power since the majority of the teacher population is White, female, and Christian. There are also examples of researchers working from both an emic and etic perspective. Teachers who work in a traditional public school who are conducting research in a Friends Quaker school may represent both an emic and etic perspective: emic because they are teachers and familiar with teaching and learning, and etic because the philosophy of teaching might differ from their own classroom or school.

A proficient ethnographer continuously works to consider how emic and etic perspectives influence the assumptions and conclusions made in the study. For example, what do you see and know about your classroom that a parent may not see or know? If you identify as a woman, how would a man experience your daily lived experiences? What insider knowledge do you have as a teacher who teaches in the town where you grew up? What if you are a teacher who is also a recently arrived immigrant? How and in what ways does insider knowledge help or hinder your perspective on any given situation? Activities are included at the end of this chapter to hone your CE observation skills.

PARTICIPATORY ACTION RESEARCH (PAR AND YPAR)

This book introduces another approach, participatory action research (PAR), to the CRTA educator's research toolbox because like CE, PAR considers notions of power and privilege in research. PAR is also a form of activism scholarship in that PAR studies seek to find solutions to injustice and inequity. PAR is fluid in the type of data and data collection methods required. PAR can be qualitative, quantitative, and/or ethnographic. The two primary functions of PAR are a careful consideration of who participates in designing and conducting the research and a focus on taking action.

In PAR, participants are seen as co-researchers in the process of identifying a problem and engaging in collective inquiry to work toward a solution. Fine (2008) describes PAR as a "radical epistemological challenge to the traditions of social science, most critically on the topic of where knowledge resides" (p. 215). Engaging in youth-led PAR is called Youth Participatory Action Research (YPAR). Caraballo, Lozenski, Lyiscott, and Morrell (2017) describe YPAR as "a critical research methodology that carries specific epistemological commitments toward reframing who is 'allowed' to conduct and disseminate education research with/about youth in actionable ways" (p. 313). The engagement of youth in investigating the educational and social problems that impact them in the community and classroom is a key tenet of YPAR. For example, a teacher who wanted to learn more about reading motivation could engage in traditional qualitative research on their own build a research group with students to post questions about literacy learning. With PAR and YPAR, the teachers and students are co-researchers who gather and analyze data, and write up the results together.

In this scenario, teachers and students would engage in a critique of the sociocultural, historical, and political factors at work in planning and designing literacy instruction. Depending on the age of the students, the teacher might assume a larger role in facilitating the research. When working with older students, colleagues, or community members, the power can be more equitably distributed. In this way, it is possible to have a lead researcher(s) in PAR/YPAR, but the nature of the approach requires constant consideration of power relationships and questions about who is considered a knower and expert. This is emancipatory because it rejects the idea that knowledge moves unidirectionally whereby expert researchers "read" a context, draw conclusions, and disseminate to the lay and scholarly community what they learned.

Translate this way of thinking into the classroom. Are you assessing students as "subjects" to be evaluated and "filled" with official knowledge provided by a standard set of competencies? Or, are you colearners and assessors in a classroom where the curriculum is permeable enough to allow for multiple interpretations of the world? Are you an enforcer of knowledge or a coconstructor of knowledge with students and families?

CE AND PAR RESEARCH TOOLS

The tools of CE and PAR can be borrowed to complement other forms of research. In these cases, the researcher could write, "This quantitative study also draws from the tools of the ethnographer, including participant observation to inform data collected from quantitative surveys at teacher in-service days." Or, "This quantitative study draws from youth participatory action research (YPAR) by including students in the process of designing, evaluating, and creating culturally responsive assessment tools in the classroom." The iterative nature of CE and PAR is what makes them so thorough and rich.

The primary tools of the ethnographer are participant observation and ethnographic field note-taking (Spradley, 1980). These tools can also be used in PAR/YPAR, especially if teachers and students work together to practice these tools and engage in co-research projects. Participant observation is observation with the recognition of the researcher's role in the research context. If you are a teacher conducting research in your own classroom, you are both a researcher and participant as you have an impact on the results and findings. Even an outside researcher conducting research in your classroom is a participant as their presence in the classroom alters the events and interactions in that space.

Ethnographic field note-taking can take a variety of forms, but should involve an attempt at "thick description" (Geertz, 1973). This thick description is aimed at capturing the depth of stories, identities, and practices in the research context. The activities at the end of this chapter provide practice and examples of both participant observation and field note-taking.

CE and PAR also require elements of "member checking" and triangulation of data. Member checking is the process of returning to your participants (members) periodically to check assumptions or assertions about the data (Merriam, 1998). Member checking helps to avoid bias or misrepresentations of your participants. Multiple interpretations of the same event by participants should not be seen as a flaw in the findings, but rather, a part of your findings that illuminate the multiple interpretations of events.

Triangulation of data is a companion to member checking. It is the process of seeking multiple data sources to confirm assumptions or assertions both pre- and postanalysis of data. Member-checking and co-research projects can support CRTA because they disrupt the idea that the researcher is the sole knower and interpreter of data. The language used in employing CE and PAR is designed to disrupt power relationships. Namely, individuals or groups are labeled as participants or co-researchers rather than "subjects." Recall from Chapter 3 the importance of how language use can frame and convey practices and perspectives. Not only reconsider your practice but reconsider the language you use to describe your practice.

A CRTA lens can be used to evaluate quantitative, qualitative, or mixed-methods research. Ask questions about who created the data collection instrument, how the data were collected and analyzed, who collected and analyzed the data, and who wrote the final interpretations and findings. Each of these touchpoints offers a place to learn, understand, and critique the final conclusions of a study. CE and PAR have the potential to support teachers in exploring how histories are situated within the historical, social, and political realities of everyday life.

Begin with the assessments you use in your own classroom. Consider the stakes. . . . What conclusions are drawn based on this limited knowledge? What are the consequences for children? Consider how adding the tools of CE and PAR to your existing assessments could enrich your ability to understand the full range of students' knowledge and experience.

PART 2: CLASSROOM ACTIVITIES: PEDAGOGICAL POSSIBILITIES FOR CE AND PAR

Educators can explore CE and PAR through both formal research projects and everyday classroom practices, but what are the benefits that can accrue? The use of CE and PAR in schools has the potential to disrupt institutionalized power and reclaim educator voice.

- Educators can read and interpret research in new ways in order to make more informed decisions in the classroom.
- Educators can use CE and PAR to justify practices to administrators and colleagues.
- Educators can join and contribute in the professional and scholarly community by contributing original research to the field.
- Educators can use the tools of CE and PAR to critique and modify assessment practices.
- Educators can cocritique books, curricula, and other educational texts with students to promote multiple perspectives and critical thinking.
- Educators can learn more about their students and communities in order to make better decisions about praxis.

Getting Started With a Research Question (RQ) and Data Collection

To study a particular phenomenon in your classroom, school, or community, begin with a research question or questions. Research questions are challenging to write. Good research questions not only define the aim and scope of the study, but also align with the chosen methods. In CE and PAR, research questions rarely have "yes" or "no" responses. Once you have your research question(s), decide on the type and source of your data. Data is typically defined as the unit or units of analysis, the actual pieces of information gathered to answer your research question(s).

Consider beginning with the tools of the critical ethnographer by engaging in participant observation and ethnographic field note-taking. Depending on your question, you may want to collect classroom discourse (oral and/or written) such as classroom interactions, assignments, projects, assessments, lesson plans, or curricula. The following are examples of possible research questions (RQs) teachers and students could use to begin to engage in CRTA. With each question are examples of possible data to be collected.

RQ: What are the welcoming and unwelcoming aspects of my school (or classroom or community) for immigrant and refugee students?

Data Sources: Environmental print, linguistic landscape, teacher or administrative discourse related to immigrant and refugee children and families, culturally responsive curricula (or lack thereof), interviews with teachers, students, families, or community members.

RQ: What role does teacher discourse play in positioning immigrant and refugee students as insiders and outsiders in my classroom?

Data Sources: Audio or video recordings of classroom discourse, analysis of discourse such as the use of pronouns to affiliate with or distance students of color (e.g., using "we" to refer to White people and "they" or "those people" to refer to people of color). Deficit and microaggressive discourses, including labeling (see Chapter 3) could also be used to explore this question.

RQ: What are teachers' (or students' or community members') perspectives on bilingualism? Newcomers? Language services? Immigration policies?

Data Sources: Seek existing survey instruments related to attitudes and perspectives on these topics. If necessary, modify the survey for your own purposes. Conduct observations and take field notes to confirm, disconfirm, or elaborate on what you learn from the surveys. For example, do teachers in your school present positive attitudes toward bilingualism, but suppress the use of languages other than English in their classroom in both explicit and implicit ways? Engage in a critical race audit of your classroom that focuses on how the relationship between race, dialects, accents, and official languages are positioned in the curriculum.

RQ: Whose voices are heard or silenced in school curricula, including children's literature?

Data Sources: Classroom library or justice inventories, discourse analysis of curriculum, theme analysis sampling of new library books or curriculum. This research project lends itself well to PAR. In addition to building students' research skills, library and critical literacy skills are inherent in these projects.

Both CE and PAR allow for flexible research questions that can be modified along the way. While this process might feel messy, it does not mean it is less rigorous. An ethnographer is transparent about these changes. For example, in an ethnographic study, you could find the following written in the "study background" and/or methods section of a research paper:

> My initial research focused on Somali Bantu refugees' storytelling practices in the classroom, but initial observations revealed that students had few opportunities to respond or contribute through oral or written discourse in the classroom. For this reason, the study evolved into an investigation of storytelling practices used in the school and how these aligned or misaligned with practices in the Somali Bantu homes and communities.

Unlike the fixed nature of many quantitative studies, the ethnographer uses methodologically sound choices to make changes to the original research questions. These changes are described and justified in the write-up of the research.

Analyzing the Data

The theoretical framework or lens, methods, research question(s), and data all inform decisions about how to analyze the data and draw conclusions. Some theoretical frameworks or lenses require or lend themselves to a particular type of analysis. For example, if you are studying language practices in the classroom that socialize children to gender, theories of language socialization and discourse analysis are likely candidates for your theoretical framework and methodological approach.

Choose a peer-reviewed journal article or articles as mentor texts for determining what types of methods to use for analysis. As a novice, begin with a basic theme analysis of the data you collect. Review your data and search for themes described in your mentor texts or new themes that emerge based on your analysis. For example, "welcoming and nonwelcoming" aspects for immigrants and refugee families in a school community might be an overarching theme related to your questions and overall study.

When you analyze your data, look for particular themes related to these overarching questions and ideas. For example, you may find that environmental print such as multilingual signs and posters represent visual and linguistic notions of welcoming, but the lack of books in multiple languages or use of students' home language in classroom discourse promotes unwelcoming or unsupportive examples of students' lived experiences and realities. Once you have themes, engage in member checking and triangulation of data to determine whether your themes hold up. If the example above seems to be a strong theme, what conclusions can you draw about a school? The next section shows how positionalities, preconceived notions, and actual data points intersect to change teachers' views of a school community.

CE and PAR: Changing Perspectives of Immigrant and Refugee Communities

Taking a CRTA approach in the classroom by engaging in CE and PAR can help to dispel the myths of Black and Brown communities and challenge majoritarian narratives. Students in one of my classes were able to question single-story narratives by practicing the tools of CE through critical mini-ethnographies.

I elect to use the critical mini-ethnography as a pedagogical tool instead of case study research in order to firmly ground the practices in the tools of the ethnographer and to emphasize the questioning of power relationships in the research. "Mini" is used here because the students used the tools of the ethnographer like participant observation and field note-taking but were unable to study the school community longitudinally as the research assignment could only span the length of a 16-week undergraduate course.

* * *

Students were asked to work in groups and use the tools of the ethnographer to observe the four to five blocks surrounding a school. They were unable to observe schools in which they were familiar (e.g., schools they attended, lived near, or had personal connections to), and all high-performing schools with predominantly White student populations were removed from the list of possible observation sites. One group of four undergraduate women, two who identified as Latina and Mexican American and two who identified as White, all of whom were from upper-middle-class backgrounds, decided to drive to a school community on the "Southside": a predominantly Black, Brown, multilingual, and poor neighborhood in a city in the southwest US.

The group expressed their apprehension and fear of this neighborhood in their reflections. "We were locking our car doors and worrying about getting back before dark," one student wrote. Another student wrote, "We made jokes about whether we needed to 'pack heat' for our observations." Despite their preconceived notions and hesitations, the group set out to conduct their required observations.

During their first trip to the neighborhood, they got a flat tire. "We freaked out," one woman said. "We were afraid to get out of the car." Instead of their fears of crime and violence coming true, several men from a local shop noticed their situation and offered to change their tire. The group acquiesced, but also called one of their boyfriends to pick them up.

As the men were changing the tire, the conversation turned to the group's school project: observing a school community and learning about the assets and resources available for bilingual families. The men shared their concern about the lack of health care facilities and community resources and directed the women to a corner café run by one of the men's wives. After the spare tire was safely affixed, the women walked across the street to the café where they were treated to lunch and stories about the history of the neighborhood, community arts initiatives, bilingual resources, and many ways the community works together to support those in need and advocate for more resources. The groups' fears were debunked.

In their final critical mini-ethnography, the group wrote, "We held deficit views of this community and others like it, but through ethnographic observation and analysis, we learned how the community has been historically marginalized through discriminatory housing policies and divestment. The families in this neighborhood, like all families, deserve to have a high-quality education." One member of the group applied for and accepted a job in the school community upon graduation.

* * *

The experience of this group is not unusual. While they were the only group in my class to get a flat tire while conducting ethnographic field observations, the experience of having biased, deficit perceptions that were overturned through "ethnographic eyes" is a common experience. Adding community members as co-researchers in a long-term PAR project would have likely further enhanced these students' experiences.

The use of first person in research writing has become a matter of preferred style depending on the audience or venue for your writing (e.g., a particular university course, academic journal, and/or field of study). Research writing, just like all conventions of writing, is ever evolving. In ethnographic and PAR research, first person is typically used in writing the positionality statement. There is a distinction, however, in the difference between writing in first person and expressing *personal opinion* in research writing:

a. First-person research writing example: "I used language socialization as a theoretical framework and discourse analysis as the methodological approach to examining gender identities in the elementary, English language arts classroom."
b. Opinion in research writing example: "I think language socialization and discourse analysis should be used to examine gender identities in the elementary, English language arts classroom."

Example A uses first person as a matter of style preference to describe the theoretical and methodological approach used by the researcher. Example B provides an opinion about the methods without including supportive evidence. A better way to write Example B could be, "I assert that discourse analysis is an apt method for examining gender identities in the classroom because it illuminates macro-level ideologies through micro-level talk." The researcher in this case should also cite the claim or reference previous studies that have used this framework and methodology. In this way opinion and editorializing are replaced by evidenced-based language.

Embracing the Messiness of CE and PAR Research

* * *

A kindergarten teacher enrolled in my graduate literacy research course was focusing on examining the welcoming and unwelcoming aspects of her school for a critical mini-ethnography project. One requirement of the project was to pay particular attention to the "linguistic landscape" of the school. In doing so, the teacher noticed that the multilingual signs that once adorned the walls of her school a year or two ago were no longer present. She recorded this in her field notes.

As part of her proposed data collection, she planned to interview the principal. In the interview, she asked about the multilingual signs in addition to other questions. The next week, the teacher entered the building and saw the multilingual signs had been rehung. When the teacher returned to my class the following day, she lamented, "I feel like this messed up my study. When I first conducted my observations, I already recorded that no signs were present in the school. My conversation with the principal reminded her about the signs. Did that skew my findings? Now I don't know what to write about!"

* * *

This example demonstrates ingrained views about the nature of research. The teacher was still imagining a controlled study in which the researcher attempts to remain neutral without influencing the data. Consider this scenario: Let's say the researcher was not a teacher, but an outside observer who visited the school one time before the signs had been replaced and recorded the information and wrote it up as part of a research project. The findings would show no multilingual signs, and thus might contribute to an overall assumption about the school related to the valuing of multilingualism.

An ethnographer or PAR researcher, however, recognizes the role of the researcher, the importance of longevity in the research context, and the power of action in making change. Without multiple perspectives the researcher would not have known that the signs were removed for summer painting. This is not to say that one situation or the other "proves" particular findings about the valuing of multilingualism in the school; rather, the collection of data points can be used to explore the impact of educators in shaping the welcoming and unwelcoming aspects of the school community.

The teacher included the following in her write-up:

> Initial observations in the school revealed no environmental print representing multiple languages, even though many languages and dialects are represented in the school. Given that multilingual signs were present in the school during previous academic years, a question about the signs was included in the interview with the school principal. One week following the interview, the multilingual signs were returned to the hallways. The principal explained that the signs had been put in storage when the hallways of the school were painted over the summer. In this way, the researcher and research impacted the linguistic landscape of the school.

Later, in the discussion, the teacher wrote:

> Given that a simple conversation with the principal during the administrator interview portion of this study made an immediate impact on the linguistic landscape of the school (i.e., existing signs were relocated and rehung), findings show how teachers who evaluate the welcoming and unwelcoming aspects of their schools for immigrant and refugee students can advocate for and make change. In this case, it only required a simple reminder that the multilingual signs existed.

Practicing the Tools of CE and PAR With Teachers and Students

Ethnographic field notes are the written record of your observations. Writing ethnographic field notes involves a complex process of recording sights, sounds, activities, events, and discourses. Using the ethnographic field notes example at the end of this chapter, engage in the following activities.

Ethnographers use a field notebook. It may be helpful to divide your notes into columns. In the first column record any relevant temporal information such as dates, times, or categories for activities (e.g., 8:00 a.m.: Morning meeting). You can also record changes in location, context, or participants (9:34 a.m.: Science club group returns to classroom).

It takes time and practice to know what information is important to record in your field notes. It also depends on your research questions and what you hope to learn from your study. Sometimes, ethnographers audio- or video-record their research context. This allows them to return to the scene and analyze events more closely. If you are unable to audio- or video-record, do your best to record the sights, sounds, talk, movements, or events that seem relevant. Field notes may also consist of excerpts of talk, drawings, or mapping the physical space or movements of people. How is the room designed? How are people situated in relationship to one another? How does this change as the events unfold?

The following activities are designed to provide practice for ethnographic field observations and note-taking. These activities can be used for both teachers and students to develop their own observation and note-taking skills through a CE and PAR lens.

Activity 1: "Reading" Film: Pear Film Viewing

I use this activity, which is extended from an activity used by one of my mentor-professors, Juliet Langman. Engage in this activity first with a friend or group of coworkers. Then, try it out with your students to build their observation skills.

- Access the Pear Film on YouTube: https://www.youtube.com/watch?v=bRNSTxTpG7U.
- Watch the film and take limited notes.
- Watch the film again and try to include more details in your notes.
- Before discussing the content of the film, compare the format and style of your notes with your friends or coworkers. Did you write them in narrative form? List form? Did you focus your notes on events? Descriptions of people? Sights? Sounds?
- What assumptions did you make about the events or people in the film? Where did the film take place? What language(s) do the people speak? How do you know? What clues led you to these conclusions?
- Share your interpretation of the film with your friends or coworkers. How did your accounts differ? Do you disagree on any of the events? Did you choose to focus on different aspects of the film or events than your peers? Note: When you do this activity with students, some students may focus on aspects of cinematography such as camera angles or foci that engage story elements such as foreshadowing. You can connect observations such as these with literary devices used to do the same.
- If you wrote in your notes, for example, that "the little boy stole the pears," what "indexed" stealing to you? In other words, what actions, expressions, or contextual cues did you use to draw this conclusion? For example, if you thought the little boy was being "sneaky," what actions, body movements, or facial expressions, index "sneakiness"? Explore questions like these for all assumptions or assertions you made about the

film. This exercise provides practice in critiquing assumptions and assertions and making evidence-based claims.

Activity 2: Participant Observation and Field Note Practice

Select one of the following contexts to explore:

- Coffee shop or café: Sit in a coffee shop or café. What are the norms and practices in this space? How do visitors to the coffee shop or café know or understand how to participate in this environment? Does anyone seem out of place? What type of language practices are needed to interact proficiently in this space? What are the patterns of communication among employees and customers? What are the consequences of breaking these norms, patterns, or practices? What are the varying levels of participation in the space?
- Lunchroom at your school: Find a place to discreetly observe a group of students in the lunchroom. Practice taking ethnographic field notes, exploring the events, discourses, physical space, and movement occurring during a 15- to 20-minute observation. When you conclude your observation, return to your notes and fill in any information you need to while it is fresh in your memory. In the third column of your field notes, record your wonderings, assumptions, questions, or connections to what you observed. Who sits next to whom? What are the discursive practices? What role do power dynamics play in this space? What role do teachers play in this context?
- Observe a student while the student takes a test, reads a book, or works on an assignment. Record in your field notes the sights and sounds in the room. For example, you may consider: Are the lights buzzing in the room? Are kids playing outside the window or in the hall? Is someone tapping a foot? What is the lighting like in the room? Is there natural light? Next, consider the actions, movements, body language of the student. Is the student shifting in his or her seat? Squinting his or her eyes? Focused solely on the paper in front of him or her or looking around the room?

Once you conclude your observations and note-taking, review your written record of events for biases. For example, if you identified someone as rude or pushy, what evidence can you provide? In what ways are your interpretations grounded in your own cultural practices and preferences?

Research is messy. My preservice and in-service teachers often lament this challenge, especially in a world where data is defined almost entirely within the positivist tradition. Using the tools of the critical ethnographer and PAR can reveal the beauty of the mess and provide an in-depth look at an educational problem.

RECOMMENDED RESOURCES

Books and Articles

Caraballo, L., Lozenski, B., Lyiscott, J., & Morrell, E. (2017). YPAR and critical epistemologies: Rethinking educational research. *Review of Research in Education, 41*(1), 311–336.

Frank, C. (1999). *Ethnographic eyes: A teacher's guide to classroom observation*. Portsmouth, NH: Heinemann.

Goessling, K., & Doyle, C. (2009). Thru the Lenz: Participatory action research, photography, and creative process in an urban high school. *Journal of Creativity in Mental Health, 4*(4), 343–365. https://dx.doi.org/10.1080/15401380903375979

Grieve, G.P. (n.d.). *How to write field notes*. Retrieved from http://www.gpgrieve.org/PDF/How_to_write_Field_Notes.pdf

Kirkland, D. (2016, Spring/Summer). Overcoming the tradition of silence: Toward a critical bilingual education for the voiceless. *The NYSABE Bilingual Times*, pp. 4–7.

Koirala-Azad, S., & Fuentes, E. (2009–2010). Possibilities and constraints of participatory action research. *Social Justice, 36*(4), 1–5.

Langhout, R. D., Collins, C., & Ellison, E. R. (2014). Examining relational empowerment for elementary school students in a yPAR program. *American Journal of Community Psychology, 53*(3–4), 369–381. https://dx.doi.org/10.1007/s10464-013-9617-z

Wolfinger, N. H. (2002). On writing fieldnotes: Collection strategies and background expectancies. *Qualitative Research, 2*(1), 85–95. https://dx.doi.org/10.1177/1468794102002001640

Websites

About data for Black lives. (n.d.). Retrieved from http://d4bl.org/about.html

To learn more about anthropology and the roots of ethnography: Anthro flashcards quiz: Sunflower333445. (n.d.). *Anthro*. Retrieved from https://quizlet.com/7429675/anthro-flashcards/

University of North Carolina at Chapel Hill. (n.d.). *A sample of recorded ethnographic observations*. Retrieved from https://www.unc.edu/courses/2006spring/anth/010/001/fieldnotes_sample.pdf

REFERENCES

American Association for the Advancement of Science. (2009). [Statement of Climate Change from 18 scientific associations]. Retrieved from https://www.aaas.org/sites/default/files/migrate/uploads/1021climate_letter1.pdf

Caraballo, L., Lozenski, B., Lyiscot, J., & Morrell, E. (2017). YPAR and Critical Epistemologies: Rethinking Education Research. *Review of Research in Education, 41*(1), 311–336.

Fine, M., Tuck, E., & Zeller-Berkman, S. (2008). Do you believe in Geneva? Methods and ethics at the global local nexus. In N. Denzin, Y. Lincoln, & L. T. Smith (Eds.), *Handbook of critical and Indigenous methodologies, reprinted ed.*, pp. 157–180. Thousand Oaks, CA: SAGE.

Frank, C. (1999). *Ethnographic eyes: A teacher's guide to classroom observation*. Portsmouth, NH: Heinemann.

Geertz, Clifford. (1973). *The Interpretation of Cultures*. New York: Basic Books.

Kirkland, D. (2013). *A search past silence: The literacy of young Black men*. New York, NY: Teachers College Press.

Merriam, S. (1998). *Qualitive research and case study applications in education*. San Francisco, CA: Jossey-Bass Publishers.

Miner, H. (1956/2012). *Body ritual among the Nacirema*. Retrieved from https://msu.edu/~jdowell/miner.html. Reprinted from *American Anthropologist, 58*(3), 1956.

Saltman, K. J. (2014). Neoliberalism and corporate school reform: "Failure" and "creative destruction." *Review of Education, Pedagogy, and Cultural Studies, 36*(4), 249–259. http://dx.doi.org/10.1080/10714413.2014.938564

Sensoy, Ö. & DiAngelo, R. (2012). *Is everyone really equal? An introduction to key concepts in social justice education*. New York, NY: Teachers College.

Spradley, J. P. (1980). *Participant observation*. New York, NY: Holt, Rinehart, and Winston.

Thomas, J. (1993). *Doing critical ethnography*. Newbury Park, CA: Sage Publications.

Chapter Eight

Allies and Accomplices

What White Teachers Should Know and Do

> You have to act as if it were possible to radically transform the world. And you have to do it all the time.
>
> —Angela Davis

This chapter focuses on the activism component of critical race teacher activism (CRTA) and what White teachers in particular need to know and do in order to advocate for immigrant and refugee children and families and join people of color in the fight to dismantle systems of oppression. This chapter seeks to explore what is activism and what is an ally? How does the role of an ally differ from that of an accomplice? What role can and should White people play in advocating for immigration rights? What responsibility do White teachers have in the fight against racism? I invite teachers to become active agents of change in dismantling the system of racism and White supremacy by engaging in radical, liberatory practices grounded in a CRTA framework.

I recently had the opportunity to interview activist and actor Diane Guerrero about her book *In the Country We Love: My Family Divided* (2016) in front of 300 students, faculty, and staff. In her book, Diane shares the heartbreaking story of her family's deportation despite their efforts to obtain legal, US citizenship. Diane, who was born in the US, was left alone to fend for herself at 14 after her parents were deported to Colombia after being detained for months in separate US immigration detention prisons.

At the conclusion of the interview, Diane fielded questions from the audience. A student of undocumented parents had tears in her eyes as she asked Diane for advice about how to cope with the constant fear of her own parents being deported. Another student shared her experiences with immigrant families in the area and mentioned names of local organizations that help immigrants find safe and legal paths to citizenship. Toward the end of the Q&A session, a young White woman raised a question about an earlier part of the discussion when Diane spoke about Black and Brown solidarity in activism. She asked, "Why are you leaving White people out of this conversation?" This chapter builds from this White student's question. What role should White people play in activism and solidarity with Black and Brown communities? Part 1 of this chapter provides background and definitions related to teacher activism. Part 2 provides specific activities for cultivating activism literacies in the classroom.

PART 1: DEFINITIONS AND BACKGROUND

What Is Activism? What Is Teacher Activism?

Activism is the process of taking action to make change. Activism is most often associated with working toward *social* change in particular. This book advocates for a particular type of activism, especially as it relates to White teachers teaching about immigration: critical race teacher activism (CRTA).

Critical race teacher activism is centered at the intersection of critical Whiteness studies (CWS), critical race theory (CRT), and teacher reflection (Matias & Liou, 2015). At its core, CRTA draws from "communities of color epistemologies," which recognize privilege and power, reject deficit notions of communities of color, and engage teachers in activism at the level of pedagogy, curriculum, personal/reflective, and leadership levels. Race is at the center of this notion because of the powerful presence of institutional and systemic racism in the US.

Critical race theorists position race as an intersectional notion inextricably tied to other identities such as language, religion, and immigration status. Because the system of White supremacy and racial oppression plays such a powerful role in anti-immigrant policy and rhetoric, it is impossible to address immigration in the classroom without the discussion of race. And, it is impossible to teach an immigration unit without taking a political stance on immigration. In other words, if you choose to teach the curriculum that is given to you, you are taking a political stance of inaction. If you choose to question that curriculum and change it, you are also taking a political stance. White teachers must be clear about the path they are choosing and the implications for that choice.

Teacher activism can take many forms. CRTA involves a multilayered approach to making change. It requires teachers to move beyond disrupting the curriculum to actively engaging students, colleagues, and community in an effort to dismantle racism at the institutional level.

What Is an Ally? What Is an Accomplice?

Teachers working from a CRTA perspective challenge themselves to interrogate power relationships in society and challenge their own notions of activism. The word *ally* in social justice work is often used to describe those who join an effort to help a marginalized group or advocate for an issue of justice. The term *accomplice* is preferred to *ally* because it makes clear the power dynamic.

To be an accomplice, you must work alongside, not for or on behalf of, a group. As Baldwin (1965) wrote in "The American Dream and the American Negro," "I am not an object of missionary charity." He is asking White Americans to invest themselves in the struggle without attempting to save, fix, or critique people of color. To be an accomplice, you must position yourself as a colearner and coconspirator who is in a perpetual state of learning and becoming, privileging the knowledge and practices of the community which you are supporting, and engaging in meaningful action-oriented steps to make change.

As an accomplice, it is important to understand the difference between nonracist and antiracist work. Nonracist work attempts to be neutral and passive. Antiracist work centers action against the system of White supremacy and racial oppression. For Whites engaging in antiracist work, it involves a process of shedding and decentering Whiteness. That is to say, recognizing the problematic and divisive history of White supremacy in the US and the world and embracing transformation. It requires decentering the comfort of the White population and instead working to fix the system. The system of White supremacy thrives on the denial of its existence. A dismantling of this system involves recognizing history, privileging the voices of people of color, and supporting movements for Black and Brown liberation. I agree with Matias and Liou (2015), who assert that White educators who seek to decenter Whiteness and work from a CRTA perspective can do the following:

> a. See and feel the world through the eyes and hearts of their low-income Asian, Black, Latino/Latina, and Native American students;
> b. Emotionally invest in a mutual project of racial justice with urban students of color and their communities from within the community;
> c. Critically interrogate the normalcy of their ideology of White superiority and how it impacts how People of Color experience race on a daily basis;
> d. Have a critique of racial hegemony and commit to working toward systemic change as an activist through teaching and learning. (Matias & Liou, 2015, p. 606)

DEVELOPING YOURSELF AS A CRITICAL RACE TEACHER-ACTIVIST

Previous chapters provided a guide for understanding the system of White supremacy and racial oppression. The following sections of this chapter seek to build teachers' activism literacies in moving toward changing this system.

"Getting Woke": What It Means to Be a Critical Race Teacher-Activist

How do you become a critical race teacher-activist? The notion of getting and staying "woke" is not new, but it gained traction during the birth of the #BlackLivesMatter (see also #staywoke) movement following the murder of Michael Brown by a White police officer in Ferguson, Missouri. The notion of "getting woke" (or staying woke) is defined as being acutely aware of racial and social injustice—not just awareness and acknowledgment of isolated incidents, but awareness from a position of understanding systemic and institutional racism.

This chapter includes a discussion on getting and staying woke because of its current popularity and subsequent critique. The notion of getting woke encapsulates the first stage of becoming an accomplice in addressing the system of racism, but like any term, once it becomes popular, it becomes overused and the term loses some of its meaning. Critics of White allies who appropriate this term or who claim to be "woke" raise the issue of "faux wokeness."

Faux wokeness is the act of identifying yourself as an ally to people of color, but supporting color-blind, savior, or colonialistic approaches to activism. Faux wokeness ignores the intersectional, systemic, and institutional functions of racism. White accomplices should strive to be woke enough not to call themselves woke and instead strive to embody this state of being by building *with* people of color.

To support teachers in embodying the key tenets of CRTA, I include a checklist of considerations for being an accomplice to people of color in addressing issues of injustice and oppression. The first checklist, "Check Yourself," is designed to check your perceptions and expectations of accomplice work. The section that follows, "Check Your People," provides suggests for White teachers to check other White people, including White, K–20 students.

Check Yourself

1. *Educate yourself:* Learn about history from multiple sources. Study social movements, especially the roots of current movements like #BlackLivesMat-

ter and #ImmigrationReform (see recommended resources at the end of this chapter). Read articles, listen to podcasts, and connect yourself with mentors who are already teacher-activists. Be in a perpetual state of learning and be woke enough to know that you are never woke enough. If you cannot envision yourself as a perpetual learner in this process, you cannot be an accomplice.

2. *Understand your privilege:* Review Chapter 1 and 2. Recall that while you may support paths to citizenship and do not actively discriminate against immigrants and refugees (nonracist), you are still part of a larger system that privileges European immigrants and Eurocentric views. If you cannot understand, accept, and work to dismantle privilege, you are not an accomplice. Find ways to be actively antiracist.

3. *Critique the system, not the movement:* Avoid critiquing how marginalized groups choose to engage in activism (e.g., perceptions of violent vs. peaceful protests). Instead, use the chapters of this book to explore why social movements related to issues such as race and immigration occur. Ask the larger questions in your classroom about systemic and institutionalized racism. Listen, hear, and be willing to be uncomfortable. Accept anger. Fighting for justice does not always sound polite.

Consider, for example, how social movements and activists of color are portrayed in the media. Ask questions like, why are some activists' actions labeled "protests," while others' are labeled "riots"? Who gets to decide about these labels? Support your students in critiquing a system that privileges White, middle-class norms. If you focus on critiquing the movement rather than educating yourself and questioning the larger system, you are part of the problem and are definitely not an ally or an accomplice.

4. *Listen and believe:* When people of color point to the problem or examples of racism, listen and believe them. Psychological studies reveal the impact racism has on people of color (see, for example, Carter, 2007; Sue, Capodilupo, Torino, Bucceri, Holder, Nadal, & Esquilin, 2007). The denial of the system of racial oppression and White privilege on the part of White people is an act of racial violence. Privilege is not finite. Poking holes in the system of privilege benefits everyone, including White people. If you are skeptical of the existence of widespread, systemic racism, you are not an accomplice.

5. *Defer to the community: be mindful when taking leadership roles:* Part of being an accomplice is knowing when to sit down, shut up, and listen. Realize that you may not know what is best for a given community. Ask how you can help, but do not place the burden of your own education and awakening in the hands of marginalized communities (see point 1 above, "Educate yourself"). Recognize marginalized communities as knowers and leaders and find ways to amplify their voices. If you want to take a leadership role, focus on taking cues from the community you are working with. If a person of color critiques how you are fighting injustice, listen to that person. Whenever

possible, focus on using your leadership and privilege to persuade White peers to understand and fight injustice. If you believe you know what is best for marginalized communities, you are not an accomplice.

6. *Don't always take White privilege personally, but don't ignore it:* Do not make this about you or your hardships. That is an example of centering Whiteness. For example, if a parent who is an immigrant shares an experience of discrimination, do not use this as a cue to describe the struggles of your own immigrant ancestors. Everyone experiences oppression in some way, but in order to be an accomplice, you must put your individual experiences aside and consider the larger system of privilege that is grounded in White supremacy. If you are left out of a conversation, do not take it personally. Instead, recognize your own identity and experiences, and ask how you can help. If you privilege your personal feelings over the understanding of systemic and institutional privilege, you are not an accomplice.

* * *

Early in my educational career, I was working with a Latinx youth mentoring program. The program was designed to work collaboratively with K–12 schools and a local university to socially, emotionally, and academically support Latinx youth on a pathway to college. One day, I received a phone call from the mother of one of the students in the program. She was angry and wanted to know what I, as a White woman, could possibly know about helping her Puerto Rican son.

It caught me off guard and, at first, I felt hurt because I thought I was doing good work. I had been working with schools and nonprofits in Latinx communities for several years, I grew up in a small town with a large Latinx population, and I saw myself as an ally to the Latinx community. I wanted to defend myself, but, then I also thought, "She's right. What do *I know?"*

I knew I still had a lot to learn, and I also knew that it was likely that her experiences with the White community were negative; she was protecting her son and her family by making this call. So, I listened. I told her she had every right to question me. I agreed that perhaps my position should be held by someone from the Latinx community, but I also shared why I chose to work for the program and why it was important to me. I acknowledged that as much as I wanted to be an ally (I was still learning how to be an accomplice), I was still an outsider to the community. I explained that I wanted to support the goals she had for her son and asked her if she'd be willing to meet in person sometime. I also did some research on my own to find better ways to connect with parents.

It took some time, but I eventually earned her trust and respect. She became a powerful supporter of the program. I often reflect on how I could have messed this up. I could have been defensive, I could have taken it personally, and I could have withdrawn from the situation or given up, but I chose not to. I should also mention, there are plenty of examples where I messed up when trying to do justice work; there have been plenty of times where I've had to check myself or be checked by others.

As a beneficiary of racial privilege, I have to remind myself every day to recognize the ways privilege manifests in both overt and implicit ways. And, as an accomplice, I have to commit to listen to critique and use my privilege to disrupt power and make change, including reconsidering the leadership roles and positions I take.

* * *

7. *Be aware of how your contributions are/are not recognized:* Chapters 1 through 3 address how histories and contributions of people of color are erased, omitted, or misrepresented in school curricula (and elsewhere). In the same way that men are often lauded for work that women do every day, so too are White, middle-class people lauded for accomplishing strides in civil rights when people of color have historically led the way. For example, Abraham Lincoln often gets credit for the Emancipation Proclamation and Lyndon Johnson for signing the Civil Rights Act of 1964, but it was the tireless work of scholars, activists, and communities of color who drafted these demands and advocated for their signing. If your satisfaction in doing justice work comes from praise and recognition, you are not an accomplice. In fact, finding ways to honor and recognize the work of people of color should be a priority for White accomplices.

Check Your People

This section urges White people to focus their activism energy on dismantling the system of White supremacy and White privilege by "checking" other White people at both the interpersonal and institutional level. This is perhaps the most important section of this book.

1. *Speak up:* Have you ever heard a racist joke about immigrants or people of color told in an all-White setting? Speak up. Have you ever heard a colleague make disparaging remarks about immigrant students? Call that person on it. Have you ever been on a predominantly White hiring team, curriculum committee, or professional learning community? This is your chance to ask, "Are we interviewing any people of color? Are we including and privileging diverse voices in this conversation?" If no people of color apply to a position, ask questions such as, "Why might people of color want or not want to work here? What are *we* doing wrong? What could we do better?" Watch for practices in your school and community that seem to disproportionately affect people of color and say something.

* * *

I attended an assembly at an elementary school with a high population of Black and Brown students, many of whom were recently arrived immigrants. During the assembly, a children's book author and poet of color was presenting her work to students. I watched as teachers pulled students from the audience to punish them for talking. Not one White student was pulled from the audience, although many White students were also talking.

* * *

Watch for these occurrences. Is there a pattern? Notice and ask questions. We already know that students of color, including immigrant students, are much more likely to be disciplined and suspended from school than White students engaging in the same behavior. Is this happening in your school? What can you do about it? Speak up.

2. *Focus on institutional change whenever possible:* Part of checking your peers involves checking their ideas when the issue of "diversity" arises. Workshops addressing diversity can serve a purpose, but rarely do they result in large, systemic change. Also, the very idea of focusing on diversity and inclusion often subverts the conversations from addressing the real issue, which is the system of White supremacy and racial oppression. Diversity activities often focus on deficit or stereotypical views of communities of color and/or superficial notions of inclusion rather than questioning the system. Do not be afraid to use words like White supremacy and racial oppression when pointing to the problem. Discuss what racism looks like, including deficit and microaggressive discourses, and social and economic inequities that contribute to school underachievement. Focus on fixing the system, not the children and families of color.

3. *Educate others to disrupt and recognize how power works:* From the school assembly example above, you may be thinking, "But I've seen Black and Brown teachers overpunish kids too." Power and oppression is perpetrated by both the oppressor and the oppressed; that is the reality of how oppression is internalized by all. In other words, sometimes people of color are complicit in the marginalization of their own community. This is a testament to the powerful and insidious nature of racism, but it is not the accomplice's role to critique or police. As a White accomplice, focus on checking your White peers only.

4. *Play the race card:* People of color and/or other marginalized groups often get accused of "playing the race card" when they speak out against injustices. Part of being an accomplice is playing the race card too. That is, talk about the system of racism and White supremacy so people of color are not the

only people speaking up. Take the burden of pointing to racism off the communities it impacts. In addition to listening and believing, make other White people listen and believe too.

5. *Create accomplice networks:* Speaking up is step one. Organizing and taking action is step two. Encourage your peers to check their privilege. Create a cadre of accomplices who study the system of White supremacy and work to disrupt it. Always focus on taking action through institutional and systemic change.

Questions to Consider With Yourself and Your Students

Now that you have read the list for "checking yourself" and "checking your people," how would you respond to the White student in the beginning of this chapter who asked, "Why are you leaving White people out of this conversation?" What advice do you have for her? How could the student reframe her question if her intention is to truly embody the qualities of a White accomplice to Black and Brown communities? For example, was she really left out? Perhaps a better question to Ms. Guerrero could have been, "What should White people take away from this conversation? How can we better help to address the issue of criminalizing immigrants?"

COMMUNITY AND SELF-CARE FOR CRITICAL RACE TEACHER-ACTIVISTS

The quote by Angela Davis at the beginning of this chapter embodies the nature of activism and accomplice work; the struggle is ongoing and you have to do it all the time. Antiracist work can be socially, emotionally, psychologically, and physically taxing as the system of White supremacy is ever evolving. People of color face this system every day. Teachers who take on activist work, whether they are of color or White, run the risk of burning out without a strong network of allies and accomplices committed to the same cause. The sections that follow focus on developing an ethos of self-care for your students, colleagues, community members, and yourself in order to sustain long-term activism work.

Relationships Transformed? Friends, Family, and Peers

> I'm trying to free your mind. But I can only show you the door. You're the one who has to walk through it.
>
> —Morpheus, *The Matrix*, 1999

Once you are aware of injustices, it becomes difficult to ignore them. *The Matrix* (1999) is a dystopian science fiction film written and directed by the

Wachowski brothers. The film chronicles the experiences of humans living in an artificial world created by machines (the Matrix). The main characters find a way to "unplug" from the Matrix, but in doing so are forced to grapple with the now known reality: that Earth is now run by machines that use humans as sources of energy; they are essentially batteries. Try as they may, they are unable to physically or mentally "plug back into" the Matrix to resume a state of ignorance to the atrocities of the past and present.

As a critical text for the classroom, this film is a helpful metaphor for studying how the system of White supremacy and racial oppression works. When you are part of the system, you are shielded from the realities of injustice. When you are oppressed by the system and become aware of the injustices of the system, it becomes difficult to return to a state of ignorance and inaction. The film can be read as a text for exploring what it means to get woke and disrupt the system. Just as Neo experiences tension with his crew-mates, actively working to make people aware of the system of White supremacy and racial oppression can cause conflict or tension with friends, family, or coworkers.

Students in my courses often explain, "I can't see the world in the same way anymore and it drives me crazy that my friends can't see it." While activist work does involve carefully picking your battles, consider the stakes of remaining silent. Consider your own journey in learning about the intersection of racism and immigration and the time it takes to develop critical consciousness. Focus your energy on making systemic and institutional change with like-minded individuals or groups and share this work with your friends, family, and coworkers. You won't be able to change their minds right away. As Morpheus says, "You have to understand: Most people are not ready to be unplugged and many of them are so injured, so hopelessly dependent on the system, that they will fight to protect it" (*The Matrix*, 1999).

* * *

"I have friends and family members who I know their favorite ice cream flavors, the places they like to shop, and their hobbies, but I know very little about why they practice a particular religion or vote for a particular candidate. These relationships are built on polite conversation with the old adage of 'Never talk politics or religion at dinner' (or anywhere, it seems!). I know my political views are different from theirs, but it seems difficult to engage in dialogue without the conversation becoming heated or hurtful.

"Over time, I've learned to pick my battles: sharing the work I'm doing in the classroom and in my life, asking questions and pushing when I think I can get away with it. I don't write anyone off because I want to be open to all discussion and learning something new, but I focus my activist work on

making change in my school and community. I'm persistent with friends and family whenever possible, because if I don't do it, who will?"

—Drew Gingrich

* * *

Community and Self-Care

The best way to engage in community and self-care is to develop a community of like-minded friends and coworkers. Find your tribe and create a functioning support network committed to action. You may not immediately find this group at your own school. If you are in a graduate program, form a support group with classmates and professors. You do not have to focus all your time in these groups on activist work. Connect with good-humored people who care about social justice and equity and who you can share other interests and activities with too.

Consider joining a professional organization or teacher-activist group. The National Council of Teachers of English (NCTE), the American Education Research Association (AERA), the Literacy Research Association (LRA), and the National Association of Multicultural Education (NAME), for example, all have special interest groups and publications devoted to racial justice, immigrant and refugee education, teacher activism, and social justice. These groups can provide both professional and community support to your activism work. Local union and organizing groups or nonprofits like the YMCA/YWCAs are also sites for finding like-minded peers and support.

Another important aspect of self-care is knowing your own personal and professional threshold for stress. Begin with areas of your personal and professional life where you feel change is possible. Make space for interests, hobbies, and activities that relieve stress and bring you joy.

Professionally, you may have to make some tough decisions about where you work. For example, do you work or are you applying for a job in a school that is a philosophical match? If not, to what degree are you willing to lead the charge for activism and accomplice work in this context? Are you willing to leave a position or turn down a job offer for this reason? These are decisions you have to make based on the impact you want to make and your self-care needs. If you are concerned with making systemic changes, in what way are you complicit in the system if you continue to work for a school that rejects or ignores principles of social justice and equity?

PART 2: CLASSROOM ACTIVITIES: TEACHING ABOUT ACTIVISM, GETTING YOUR WHITE STUDENTS INVOLVED

Once you understand your role and how you want to engage a CRTA stance, you can support your students in becoming accomplices and activists in the fight for justice. The following activities provide an entry point for cultivating activism literacies related to race and immigration in the classroom. As suggested in Chapter 5, changing your pedagogy and curriculum can begin with add-on approaches and activities, but must eventually entail a rethinking of the way you approach knowledge and content. Explore ways to incorporate the following activities into your classroom:

Activity 1: Read Critical Multicultural Literature

Read literature focused on issues of social justice, racism, and immigration issues. See for example, use the work of Duncan Tonatiuh. While his books are considered picture books and are most often used in elementary classrooms, upper-level teachers can use them in text sets to supplement instruction and conversation on immigration.

Activity 2: Engage With Social Media

Follow social media hashtags related to immigration as a class. Consider following hashtags that are supportive of immigration reform and social justice (e.g., #ImmigrationReform, #stopIslamophobia, #refugeeswelcome, #nobannowall), those that are not (e.g., #AmericaFirst, #whitegenocide, #buildthewall), and those that give general entre into the current conversation (#fakenews, #citizenship, #immigration). Compare, contrast, and engage in dialogue about these critical issues. Keep in mind that new hashtags and social media movements change and evolve daily. Research and use what is most current.

Activity 3: Connect Literacy Learning and Social Justice

Social justice issues can easily support and extend literacy standards. Janet Wong, a prolific author and poet, blogs about "Poetry Power: Poetic Language in Signs" (http://penciltipswritingworkshop.blogspot.com/2017/04/poetry-power-poetic-language-in-signs.html). In her work, Wong engages issues of justice through interdisciplinary lessons on poetry and science. Explore resources from Rethinking Schools and Teaching Tolerance focusing on activism work in schools and communities (for example: https://www.tolerance.org/classroom-resources/tolerance-lessons/using-photographs-to-teach-social-justice-exposing). Commit to the #dailyaction movement (e.g., volunteering for the immigrant rights movement, writing letters, or making phone calls to your congresspeople, and/or participating in local or national protests).

Activity 4: Explore Ally, Accomplice, and Activism Work

Use the checklists provided in this chapter with students as a way to engage in dialogue about becoming an activist and accomplice. Ask students to find examples of websites, dialogue, books, or other texts that support or hinder activism work. Study White abolitionists and explore whether their work was colonial work or liberation work (see Chapter 2).

Activity 5: Draw From Existing Resources as Mentor Texts

Beginning in January 2017, Philadelphia teachers created a Black Lives Matter Week that became a national event the following year. Teachers, community members, and university professors met outside of the school day to create lesson plans grounded in state standards that addressed intersectional issues of race and racism, including immigration reform and supporting immigration students in schools. This resource can be accessed here: https://docs.google.com/document/d/1UHtJqY8xdDOZM5QY39aRgQURRu-9jZhXQxUe_T2yYG0/edit. They also scheduled free community events to educate the public and build support for issues around Black lives.

Activity 6: Invite Speakers and Stories

Invite immigration lawyers, immigrant parents or community members, storytellers, or researchers to speak in your classroom and school. Resistance to having controversial conversations is sometimes grounded in the unknown. Putting a face to an issue, showing how something impacts a friend or colleague, can humanize issues of justice and promote understanding.

Activity 7: Engage Your Students in the Community

Integrate community engagement and activism into your curriculum. Ask students to interview a recently arrived immigrant, assign community-based research projects, critical mini-ethnographies, and youth participatory action research. Avoid engagement in the community that resembles savior perspectives—think horizontal, not vertical action. Privilege the "accomplice" language and the importance of hearing and learning from and with communities.

Activity 8: Plan Field Trips Related to Activism

Attend a protest with your students, visit civil rights museums or sites, visit your local polling or political organizing locations, get a tour of a local nonprofit focused on immigration support. Interview teachers or community members who are engaged in activism.

Activity 9: Watch *The Matrix*

Search for other quotes from the film. Talk about how these quotes can be used as metaphors for understanding the system of White supremacy and racial oppression:

- *"You've already made the choice. Now you have to understand it."*
- *"The Matrix is everywhere. It is the world that has been pulled over your eyes to blind you from the truth."*
- *"What is real? How do you define 'real'? If you're talking about what you can feel, what you can smell, what you can taste and see, then 'real' is simply electrical signals interpreted by your brain."*
- *"The Matrix is a system, Neo. That system is our enemy. But when you're inside, you look around, what do you see? Businessmen, teachers, lawyers, carpenters. The very minds of the people we are trying to save. But until we do, these people are still a part of that system and that makes them our enemy. You have to understand, most of these people are not ready to be unplugged. And many of them are so inured, so hopelessly dependent on the system that they will fight to protect it."*

RECOMMENDED RESOURCES

Books and Articles

Bond, B., & Exley, Z. (2016). *Rules for revolutionaries: How big organizing can change everything*. White River Junction, VT: Chelsea Green.
Chang, Jeff. (2016). *We gon' be alright: Notes on race and resegregation* [Audio book]. Audible Studios on Brilliance Audio.
Davis, A. Y., & Barat, F. (2016). *Freedom is a constant struggle: Ferguson, Palestine, and the foundations of a movement*. Chicago, IL: Haymarket.
Taylor, K.-Y. (2016). *From #BlackLivesMatter to Black liberation*. Chicago, IL: Haymarket.

Podcasts and Videos

Activist Radio. (2018). Retrieved from https://player.fm/series/activist-radio
AERA, Division G. (2018). Webinars and Podcasts. Retrieved from https://aeradivg.wordpress.com/divgpodcasts/
McKesson, D. (2018). *Pod save the people*. Retrieved from https://player.fm/series/pod-save-the-people

Smith, K. (2017). *Ten great podcasts on activism, movements, and social change*. Retrieved from http://www.globaljustice.org.uk/blog/2017/aug/18/ten-great-podcasts-activism-movements-and-social-change

The Wachowski Brothers (Director). (1999). *The Matrix*. United States: Warner Bros.

REFERENCES

Baldwin, J. (1965). The American dream and the American Negro. *The New York Times*. Retrieved from https://archive.nytimes.com/www.nytimes.com/books/98/03/29/specials/baldwin-dream.html

Carter R. T. (2007). Racism and psychological and emotional injury: Recognizing and assessing race-based traumatic stress. *Counseling Psychologist, 35*, 13–105.

Guerrero, D. (with Burford, M.). (2016). *In the country we love: My family divided*. New York, NY: St. Martin's.

Matias, C. E., & Liou, D. D. (2015). Tending to the heart of communities of color: Towards critical race teacher activism. *Urban Education, 50*(5), 601–625. http://dx.doi.org/10.1177/0042085913519338

Sue, D. W., Capodilupo, C. M., Torino, G. C., Bucceri, J. M., Holder, A. M. B., Nadal, K. L., & Esquilin, M. (2007, May–June). Racial microaggressions in everyday life: Implications for clinical practice. *American Psychologist, 62*(4), 271–286.

Chapter Nine

Making Your Case

Building Relationships, Not Walls

With Contributions From Drew Gingrich

Voyager, there are no bridges, one builds them as one walks.

—Anzaldúa (2012)

Teachers have the potential to be intellectuals, artists, and researchers in their own schools and classrooms. Teachers' professional knowledge and decision-making should be privileged. This chapter builds on the liberatory possibilities of teacher research discussed in Chapter 7 and the accomplice work described in Chapter 8 to support teachers in advocating and making a case for doing antiracist work through a critical race teacher activism (CRTA) lens. A step-by-step process for building relationships with administrators, peers, parents, and students is presented. Suggestions for how to craft a verbal and written proposal and maintain ongoing support is also discussed.

Key Ideas and Terms

- Building relationships, not walls
- "Yeah, but . . ." syndrome
- The elevator speech

In this final chapter, Drew and I focus on building relationships, not walls. We use this metaphor of wall-building to highlight our rejection of the physical building of walls, such as the proposed border wall between the US and Mexico. Instead, we advocate for the crossing of borders and the breaking down of walls, both physical and metaphorical, in the classroom, school, and community in order to make change.

Making a case for CRTA in the classroom can be challenging in schools where criticality is not the norm. New teachers may feel vulnerable due to their pretenure status, and experienced teachers may feel reluctant to change their existing practices or identity at their school. In both cases, we recognize teachers are faced with a myriad of mandates including, but not limited to, district policies and guidelines, state and national standards and assessments, ongoing curriculum initiatives that are adopted and abandoned, and unfair value-added teacher evaluations that link student performance on standardized exams to teacher effectiveness, not to mention low pay and lack of adequate benefits.

These pressures can lead to what we call the "yeah, but . . ." syndrome. The "yeah, but . . ." syndrome occurs when teachers learn about critical practices, feel inspired to make change, but feel constrained or blocked by the aforementioned pressures. For example, teachers might feel compelled to incorporate high-quality, multicultural picture books with immigration stories into their curriculum after learning how it can dispel myths of immigrant experiences ("yeah!"), but abandon the idea because their school or district requires the use of district-provided basal reader programs ("but . . .").

Other concerns or "buts" involved with teaching from a CRTA perspective might include: the misconception that current issues related to immigration policy or immigrant experiences are too heavy, complex, or controversial; the fear of parents viewing a critical discussion on today's immigration to be "indoctrination" or part of a political agenda; a feeling of being ill-equipped to teach about immigration due to lack of experience, knowledge, or exposure to the issues.

Some teachers who decide to teach from a critical perspective, but still worry about how people will react, choose the "close your door and teach" method, absconding their practices from the potentially critical eye of the administration. As we addressed throughout this book, inaction and hiding critical work is a political act that contributes to the system of racism and White supremacy. The following sections invite you to consider moving past the "but" and opening your door despite the fears, challenges, and obstacles associated with critical, social justice work. We advocate for teachers to dismantle walls and build relationship bridges.

Building a Relationship With Data: Knowing Your Audience and Your Community

In order to begin teaching about race and immigration from a CRTA perspective in your classroom, school, and community, begin by educating yourself and collecting data about your classroom. Chapter 7 questions conventional data collection practices in schools and provides a guide for educators to become critical researchers in their own school communities. Viewing your school community from a critical, ethnographic perspective may prompt you to explore the following:

- What books in the school library depict the experiences of immigrants? Whose immigrant stories are told in these books?
- How many books in my classroom or school library are written by authors of color?
- Whose stories and voices are omitted, misrepresented, or silenced in the school curriculum?
- How do US-born White students and colleagues in my school talk about immigrants and immigration?

Other potential research questions can be found throughout this book. Use the data you gathered from this exercise to begin forming a rationale for your case—the rationale for using CRTA approaches.

Building on the recommendations from Chapter 5 of this book, consider conducting a few mini-lessons to "try out" teaching race and immigration from a CRTA perspective. Find ways to modify, extend, or supplement your current curriculum related to immigration themes. Consider ways to address some of the challenges you identified about the unwelcoming or welcoming aspects of your school. Take detailed notes about your pedagogical or curricular change and gather pre- and postdata of student work to show how standards were addressed and objectives were achieved. Keep in mind that the first time you implement a lesson that addresses a critical, social justice issue, it may not go as planned. Allow yourself time to learn and practice. This data will be vital in laying the groundwork for your case and writing a proposal to educate and persuade your students, colleagues, and the parents of your students.

Building a Relationship With Yourself and Your Knowledge

Before you address peers, administrators, and parents, build a relationship with yourself and your own knowledge. Be authentically *reflexive* and *reflective* in your teaching. Reflexivity is the process of noticing, reflecting, and evaluating yourself while you are teaching. Reflection is the process of looking back on your teaching after the fact. Review the chapters in this book related to privilege, power, and immigration. What do you know? What don't you know about immigration? Where can you find resources and answers to your questions? Search for newspapers, magazines, podcasts, websites, and radio programs to get informed. Study White abolitionists, the challenges they faced, and the missteps they made in advocating for justice. Decide what level of advocacy and activism you are ready to employ and make a commitment. Evaluate your own "yeah, buts" and use this chapter to dispel or address the real or perceived challenges.

Paulo Freire (1968) asserts that education is a political act and that teachers can never truly be neutral. Choosing to *not* teach something you consider to be "too political" is, in itself, a political act. For this reason, ask yourself, "What kind of teacher do I want to be? Do I want to teach in a school that marginalizes the voices of immigrants and refugees? Do I want to be responsible for leaving White students unprepared to engage issues of justice in their everyday lives? Is my silence contributing to White students' lack of preparedness to value and support all people?" Your responses to these questions should guide you in an effort to better understand yourself and the case you make to others.

Building a Relationship With Research: Supporting Your Claims

Once you have an understanding of your own teaching context, personal beliefs, and preparedness to engage CRTA, build a relationship with research to support your goals and claims. Learn how research comes to be, how to read and interpret research, and how it applies to your teaching. Teachers are often inundated with standards and curricula that claim to be research or evidenced based.

Placing language like "research based" and "evidenced based" on prepackaged curricula is used by publishers to sell a product and make a profit. Paulo Freire suggests that prepackaged curricula marginalizes both teacher and student knowledge and succeeds only in reproducing authoritarian practices.

Critical Questions for the Classroom

Answer the following questions about curricula and pedagogical practices that are labeled as "research based" or "evidence based":

- What evidence is provided when something is labeled as evidence based? What do they really mean by "evidence"?
- Does the evidence come from academic, peer-reviewed sources? How do you know?
- Do you need prepackaged curricula? Why or why not?
- Do the standards, objectives, and assessments in your classroom privilege equity?
- In what ways do the standards, objectives, assessments, and overall curriculum privilege the cultural and linguistic resources and knowledge of communities?

If you are unsure of how to read and interpret research to support your work, continue to build your relationship with research in the following ways:

- If you are enrolled in university coursework, take advantage of access to academic databases and journals.
- If you are not enrolled in courses, visit a local university or community library and seek help from the librarian or a university professor who conducts research on the intersectional issues of race, social justice, equity, and/or immigration.
- Join, present, or get involved with a national professional organization. National professional organizations are powerful resources for supporting your practice (e.g., National Council of Teachers of English [NCTE], National Association of Multicultural Education [NAME], American Education Research Association [AERA], and Literacy Research Association [LRA]).

Building Relationships With Administrators, Peers, Parents, and Students

Once you have asked these critical questions of yourself and your context, begin taking steps to convince your administrators, peers, and parents/guardians in your school community. The following steps focus on how to work from a CRTA perspective within the existing system to advocate for change.

Making Your Case to Administrators

Administrators are faced with a myriad of pressures related to local, state, and national standards; ongoing curricular initiatives, and pressures from the superintendent and school board to raise test scores, to name a few. Anticipate these pressures when making your case and be prepared to show how critical conversations about immigration can support the mission, goals, and strategic plan of the school.

For example, what does an administrator need to know in order to support a CRTA approach to teaching immigration? How does your proposed change meet and exceed local, state, and national standards? What research supports CRTA practices in the classroom? What are the costs or benefits that may accrue as a result of implementing this curricular change or pedagogical practice? How will you address student, parent, and community concerns related to content they might consider controversial? The best way to answer these questions is to create a verbal and written proposal. The following sections provide suggestions for how to address these questions and strengthen your proposal.

Preparing a Formal Proposal

Building relationships and advocating for change through everyday conversation is important, but a formal proposal is an important step in making long-term, institutional change. Prepare both a verbal and written proposal addressing the predicted questions and concerns of the administrator. The proposal to your administrator can be modified and can evolve over time to make your case to peers, parents, students, and even community stakeholders.

Just as teachers must use their professional expertise to design pedagogy and curriculum, they must use their expertise to make decisions about how to best approach peers and administrators. Depending on your administrator, decide whether to begin with an informal conversation or to provide the full proposal with a brief one-page summary prior to a formal meeting.

Write Your "Elevator Speech"

An elevator speech is a quick and concise description of your proposed change. It usually consists of (a) a statement related to the issue you are attempting to address, (b) one or two big issues that will be solved and/or benefits that will accrue if your proposal is implemented, and (c) a brief description (with examples) of what you plan to do. It is called an elevator speech because it is a short pitch designed to be communicated in the time it takes to share an elevator ride with your target audience. Constructing an elevator speech also helps to refine ideas and create a clear, concise rationale.

Addressing Administrators' Questions in Your Proposal

Your written proposal should clearly address the primary questions of the administrator in short sections with clear headings. Administrators have a lot on their plate, so a clear and easy-to-read proposal will be most effective. Begin your proposal with a short rationale, a few words about your philosophy of teaching and why your work is important to you, and sections addressing potential questions that are important to your administrator. To guide you in this process, we have provided some suggested questions and considerations for your proposal.

1. *How does your work meet or exceed state or national standards?* Prepare sample lessons or a unit plan with a detailed list of standards, assessments, and activities that will be covered. Provide a strong rationale for any conversations, texts, or resources that will be used in the lessons or unit. Use the data you collected from Chapter 7 to support your change with samples of mini-lessons and student work and growth connected to standards. Example sentence: "Recently, I have

read about critical race teacher activism (CRTA) and how it helps teachers meet and exceed the standards, and at the same time, attend to many of our district's concerns about diversity and inclusion."

2. *What research supports your practice?* Support your change with studies from peer-reviewed, academic journals. Find at least 5 to 10 of these sources to support your claims. Since administrators are accustomed to "big data" and quantitative studies, find resources that draw from a variety of methodological approaches if possible. Example sentence: "CRTA is supported by research in the following ways. . . ." Fill in the ellipses by using quotes from this book and the recommended resources that best fit your context. If you know the concerns of your district, including the strategic plan, show how CRTA can address each part of the plan. Emphasize CRTA as a framework, not an add-on strategy.
3. *What are the costs or benefits that may accrue as a result of teaching about race and immigration from a CRTA perspective?* Provide examples from your own teaching in order to show the benefits of CRTA. Be strategic by researching the district's areas of need/low-performing areas and speak to how your classroom activities and lessons address these needs. Administrators are largely concerned with test scores. While we do not advocate for this to be the primary rationale for engaging in critical work, we do recognize the importance of speaking the language of the administrator in your advocacy. Show how test scores can be impacted. For example, one of Laura's students chose to use Zinn's *A People's History of the United States* (2003) in her classroom. Until then, she was having trouble getting her high school students to relate to the history content and engage in discussion. When she assigned the first chapter, the students arrived in class with so many questions and comments, she could hardly keep up. The students did better on their weekly quiz than they ever had before. In this way, talking about injustice does not have to be unpleasant. It can engage students in the content and inspire them to learn more and make change. If Laura's student teacher was writing a proposal to make a case for CRTA, she could include this as a vignette in her proposal. She could also interview her students and include their feedback as a rationale for using critical content.
4. *How will you address student, parent, and community questions and concerns?* Create a detailed plan of how parent and community concerns will be addressed. Provide examples of other teachers, districts, or communities that have used and benefited from CRTA-related practices (e.g., critical literacy, critical social justice pedagogy, antiracist practices). This is also an area to be strategic. Consider which schools or districts your school attempts to emulate. If they are not

doing CRTA work, discuss how your school can lead the way and surpass approaches at high-performing schools. Find other resources that help to provide the language needed in your proposal. For example, this resource from Coalition for Community Schools discusses the value of community-school models that involve parents and communities as an integral part of the school: http://www.communityschools.org/resources/part_one_the_advantages_of_community_schools_.aspx.

After you have written a strong draft of your proposal, decide whether you want to present the proposal with your peers or on your own. Schedule a meeting with your school administrator(s). Begin the meeting with your elevator speech, and then list the two to three changes you wish to implement. Emphasize again that you are not proposing add-on strategies, but a framework that is woven throughout the school. In this way, teachers can learn the framework and use their professional knowledge to choose activities and strategies that align with the framework. This makes the job of the teacher much easier.

Next, present your proposal. Take notes during the proposal meeting, including comments, questions, and feedback from the administrator. End the meeting by reviewing the content that was covered, questions that need to be addressed, and agree to clear action items for moving forward.

Making a Case to Peers and Building a Network for Support

Find strategic partners, allies, and accomplices in your school to gain support for CRTA work. Seek feedback from these strategic partners and allies (e.g., mentor-teachers, grade-level peers, curriculum directors, reading specialists, ESL/bilingual specialists, and university professors). Enlist their help in writing and modifying curriculum, advocating to administrators, and creating resources for parents. As Emdin (2016) advises:

> The kind of teacher you will become is directly related to the kind of teachers you associate with. Teaching is a profession where misery does more than just love company—it recruits, seduces, and romances it. Avoid people who are unhappy and disgruntled about the possibilities for transforming education. They are the enemy of the spirit of the teacher. (p. 208)

It is important to find strategic partners, allies, and accomplices who excel in areas in which you do not. For example, if research writing is challenging, find peers who excel in this area and work together on the proposal. If you struggle with public speaking, find someone who is an engaging speaker. If you have little experience in organizing, find someone who is skilled at bringing people together to solve a problem. Your peers also serve as a self-care mechanism. Engaging in this work often goes beyond the everyday assigned duties of the educator and thus burnout is always a concern. Chapter 8 expands on the notion of self-care for teacher-activists and provides suggestions to cultivating activism within these peer groups.

Gaining peer support can begin with grade-level meetings, team-level meetings, and/or casual conversations both in and outside of school. Begin with an appeal to people who are most likely to understand and support you. Once you have their support, you can expand to making your case with other grade levels or subject areas. Prepare for the presentation or conversation in the same way you prepare for addressing your administrator. Begin by anticipating their concerns or "yeah, buts" and hone your elevator speech. For colleagues, it is especially helpful to provide sample lessons, mentor texts, or resources that clearly show how you intend to teach intersectional issues of race and immigration. Provide information about standards, assessments, and any other concerns when applicable.

Making a Case to Parents

You may ask yourself, "How will parents respond to lessons on undocumented immigrants? What if parents complain to the administration? How do I respond to politically charged comments about immigration in my classroom? How will parents and the community respond to social justice conversations in a predominantly White classroom? What if I have one or two immigrant students in my classroom? How do I make sure their and their parents' experiences are honored without singling them out?"

Parents, families, and community members play a vital role in the school. They can be the toughest critics or staunchest supporters for critical work. Consider the role of power and privilege when working with parents. Gather information on which parents are involved in the school, how they are involved, and for what purpose.

Check your own assumptions about why certain parents are "involved" and certain parents are not. For example, it is not uncommon for parents of immigrant students to be less present or involved in school than parents of US-born, White parents, especially in affluent districts. White, upper-middle-class parents often have jobs with more flexible schedules or one parent who is able to stay home. Are these the parents who carry the decision-making power in your school? In what ways could they serve as allies? How can you educate all parents on CRTA? If you have immigrant or refugee parents in your school, in what ways do they have access or power in decision-making at your school? In what ways could they serve as partners, allies, or accomplices?

The following suggestions are designed to support teachers in making a case to parents:

1. *Create community and address concerns from day one and beyond:* Chapter 4 supports you in creating a welcoming community from day one of the school year. Communicate this intent in an introductory letter to parents before the school year begins, at parent-teacher conferences, and in ongoing communication. Chapter 4 includes sample wording for this letter.
2. *Show parents who you are:* Share your teaching philosophy in as many ways as possible. For example, create a short Q&A about CRTA and why you teach from a critical perspective. Questions might include: "Why do I teach? What do I believe about teaching and learning? What do kids say about my teaching? What do parents appreciate most about my teaching? Why do I think it is valuable to practice having tough conversations in school?" Be transparent in describing the benefits of critical conversations.
3. *Focus on what matters to parents:* Parents want to know their kids are receiving the best possible education. Just as you did for administrators, explain how you are exceeding the required standards and objectives through CRTA. Highlight the rigor of teaching from a critical perspective and the emancipatory possibilities of an informed citizenry.
4. *Plan events around immigration and issues of justice and equity for parents:* Provide orientations and information nights around race and immigration issues. Allow students to create town halls for their parents. Create gallery walks or presentation nights where parents can view students' work on race, immigration, and social justice.
5. *Engage parents in the work:* Find ways to involve parents in the classroom activities. If they cannot participate during the school day, ask parents to share resources or provide input, or ask students to interview their parents about class topics. Also, provide parents with resources they can use to continue critical conversations at home. This also helps to keep parents informed and involved. The critical media literacy activities in Chapter 6 are a great way to begin these critical conversations.
6. *Create a loop of communication and support:* Make sure parents are aware of administrator support and vice versa. Communicate the standards or skills that are being addressed. Make them aware of in-class objectives and learning activities, and keep parents informed regarding in-class conversations. Some teachers like to write blogs or newsletters for parents. Remember to keep them short and concise (or provide some bullet points first).

Making a Case to Students

Students, just like administrators, peers, and parents, need time to struggle with a new idea or concept. Teachers who are adverse to controversy or critical conversations in the classroom tend to provide avenues for an easy exit, rather than engaging anti-racist pedagogies. Silencing rather than addressing examples of racism in schools and classrooms allows racism to persist. For example, around the time of the 2016 election, immigrant children in a central Pennsylvania school were met with anti-immigrant "Trump chants" during lunch and recess. Rather than addressing the issue, the principal banned teachers and students from discussing politics in schools. Silence and inaction against hate sends a very clear message to students and families about whose lives are valued and whose are not.

While the intention of this decision was to reduce tension, it was a missed opportunity for learning and failed to address the racial violence enacted on immigration students at school. How will students learn how to discuss race, politics, or religion, for example, if these conversations are not modeled at school or at home? What expectation do we have for eradicating racism if we never allow opportunities to discuss what it really looks like, sounds like, and feels like? Students of all ages are capable of complex conversations if given the opportunity.

Students can serve as powerful partners, allies, and accomplices in making your case for CRTA. In Chapter 7 we discussed the benefits of engaging students in research to discuss and respond to why they value these types of discussions. Share their comments with administrators, peers, parents, or community members or, even better, allow the students to share their work themselves.

The Struggle Is Ongoing: Making Your Case Long Term

The struggle for teaching from a CRTA perspective is ongoing. Rarely is there a case where full acceptance and support is achieved. There are steps you can take to ease the process. Whether you are making your case over time to administrators, coworkers, and parents on the credibility of discussing rights, for example, being transparent and keeping all stakeholders informed is vital.

Administrators must be continually informed on parent communication and concerns, student performance, and current events related to immigration experiences and policies. Share student work and parent feedback. When a lesson or unit is going well, enlist parents to share your success with the administrators. On the other hand, if a parent is contacting you with a concern, let your administrator know so he or she is aware of how you are addressing it. For example,

> Principal Maxwell, I am writing to share some feedback I have received on a lesson focusing on modern immigration, including the Dream Act. A parent was concerned that conversations in the classroom were getting too political. I reached out to the parent with a sample of the lesson and provided some bullet points about the benefits that accrue when kids are informed about real-world events. I also invited the parent for a one-on-one meeting. I just wanted you to be aware of the communication. I will keep you in the loop on how it develops. Please let me know if you have any questions. Sincerely, Ms. Tremblay

Coworkers must also remain informed. Use your network of support to help you in this process so you are not doing it alone. Regularly contact parents with information about instructional objectives, student performance and growth, and the topics you are addressing in your classroom. Post examples of classroom activities on your blog or in your newsletter. Highlight the ways students are engaging in dialogue even when they disagree on an issue. This also keeps parents informed on how the information is presented in your class. This type of transparency will support you in making and maintaining your case over time.

In conclusion, we cannot emphasize enough the need for teachers, especially White teachers, to educate themselves on systems of oppression that form the foundation of the social, educational, economic, and critical justice systems in the US. Students spend the majority of their waking hours in schools. Teachers must ask if those hours are spent inculcating and perpetuating systems of oppression or educating and empowering students for freedom. It is time to shed the myth that education can ever be neutral. It is time for teachers to take an active role in the pursuit of racial justice and equity in their schools and communities.

RECOMMENDED RESOURCES

Books and Articles

Zinn, H. (2003). *A people's history of the United States*. New York, NY: Harper.

Websites

Coalition for Community Schools (2018). Retrieved from http://www.communityschools.org/resources/part_one_the_advantages_of_community_schools_.aspx

REFERENCES

Anzaldúa, G. (2012). *Borderlands: The new mestiza = la frontera*. San Francisco, CA: Aunt Lute.

Emdin, C. (2016). *For White folks who teach in the hood . . . and the rest of y'all too: Reality pedagogy and urban education*. Boston, MA: Beacon.

Freire, P. (1968). *Pedagogy of the oppressed*. New York: Bloomsbury Publishing.

Additional Recommended Resources

MENTOR TEXTS

K–4 Mentor Texts

Anzaldua, G. (1995). *Friends from the other side.* New York, NY: Children's Book Press.
Argueta, J. (2007). *Alfredito flies home.* Toronto, ON: Groundwood.
Badoe, A. (2009). *Nana's cold days.* Toronto, ON: Groundwood.
Barasch, L. (2007). *Hiromi's hands.* New York, NY: Lee & Low.
Buitrago, J. (2016). *Two white rabbits.* Toronto, ON: Groundwood.
Bunting, E. (1998). *Going home.* New York, NY: HarperCollins.
Bunting, E. (2006). *One green apple.* New York, NY: Clarion.
Cheng, A. (2005). *Shanghai messenger.* New York, NY: Lee & Low.
Danticat, E. (2015). *Mama's nightingale.* New York, NY: Dial.
Dismondy, M. (2015). *Chocolate milk, por favor.* Wixom, MI: Cardinal Rule.
Dooley, N. (1992). *Everybody cooks rice.* Minneapolis, MN: Carolrhoda.
Eggers, D. (2017). *Her right foot.* San Francisco, CA: Chronicle.
Elya, S. M., & Davalos, F. (2002). *Home at last.* New York, NY: Lee & Low.
Farish, T. (2016). *Joseph's big ride.* Toronto, ON: Annick.
Farqui, R. (2015). *Lailah's lunchbox.* Thomaston, ME: Tilbury House.
Frederick, M. (2008). *Kamal goes to Trinidad.* London, England: Frances Lincoln Children's Books.
Hest, A. (2003). *When Jessie came across the sea.* Somerville, MA: Candlewick.
Keats, E. J. (1999). *My dog is lost!* Topeka, KS: Topeka Bindery.
Kim, P. (2014). *Here I am.* Mankato, MN: Picture Window.
Kobald, I. (2015). *My two blankets.* Boston, MA: HMH Books for Young Readers.
Lee, M. (2006). *Landed.* New York, NY: Farrar, Straus & Giroux.
Levine, E. (1995). *I hate English.* New York, NY: Scholastic.
Maestro, B. (1996). *Coming to America: The story of immigration.* New York, NY: Scholastic.
McCarney, R. (2017). *Where will I live?* Toronto, ON: Second Story.
Medina, M. (2015). *Mango, Abuela, and me.* Somerville, MA: Candlewick.
Recorvits, H. (2014). *My name is Yoon.* New York, NY: Square Fish.
Ruurs, M. (2016). *Stepping stones: A refugee family's journey.* Custer, WA: Orca.
Saenz, B. A. (2008). *A gift from Papa Diego.* El Paso, TX: Cinco Puntos.
Sanna, F. (2016). *The journey.* London, England: Flying Eye.
Say, A. (2008). *Grandfather's journey.* Boston, MA: HMH Books for Young Readers.

Schimel, L. (2011). *Let's go see Papa!* Toronto, ON: Groundwood.
Surat, M. M. (1989). *Angel child, dragon child.* New York, NY: Scholastic.
Tonatiuh, D. (2013). *Pancho rabbit and the coyote: A migrant's tale.* New York, NY: Abrams.
Tonatiuh, D. (2014). *Separate is never equal: Sylvia Mendez and her family's fight for desegregation.* New York, NY: Abrams.
Williams, K. (2009). *My name is Sangoel.* Grand Rapids, MI: Eerdmans.
Williams, M. W., & Christie, R. G. (2005). *Brothers in hope: The story of the lost boys of Sudan.* New York, NY: Lee & Low.
Wolf, B. (2003). *Coming to America: A Muslim family's story.* New York, NY: Lee & Low.
Wong. J. S. (2006). *Apple pie Fourth of July.* Boston, MA: HMH Books for Young Readers.
Yaccarino, D. (2014). *All the way to America.* New York, NY: Dragonfly.
Yep, L. (1991). *The star fisher.* London, England: Puffin.

Grade 5–8 Mentor Texts

Alvarez, J. (2010). *Return to sender.* New York, NY: Random House Children's Books.
Applegate, K. (2014). *Home of the brave.* New York, NY: Feiwel & Friends.
Argueta, J. (2007). *A movie in my pillow.* New York, NY: Lee & Low.
Blohm, J. M., & Lapinsky, T. (2006). *Kids like me: Voices of the immigrant experience.* Boston, MA: Intercultural.
Buss, F. L. (2002). *Journey of the sparrows.* London, England: Penguin Putnam.
Choi, Y. (2003). *The name jar.* New York, NY: Penguin Random House.
Danticat, E. (2004). *Behind the mountain.* New York, NY: Scholastic.
Denenberg, B. (2000). *One eye laughing, the other weeping: The diary of Julie Weiss, Vienna, Austria to New York, 1938.* New York, NY: Scholastic.
Diaz, A. (2016). *The only road.* New York, NY: Simon and Schuster.
Engle, M. (2016). *Enchanted air: Two cultures, two wings.* New York, NY: Atheneum Books for Young Readers.
Fleischman, P. (2004). *Seedfolks.* New York, NY: Harper Trophy.
Freedman, R. (2014). *Angel Island: Gateway to Gold Mountain.* New York, NY: Clarion.
Hobbs, W. (2006). *Crossing the wire.* New York, NY: HarperCollins.
House, S., & Vaswani, N. (2011). *Same sun here.* Berryville, VA: Candlewick.
Jaramillo, A. (2008). *La linea.* London, England: Macmillan.
Lai, T. (2011). *Inside out and back again.* New York, NY: HarperCollins.
Levine, El. (1994). *If your name was changed at Ellis Island.* New York, NY: Scholastic.
Pellegrino, M. (2014). *Journey of dreams.* London, England: Frances Lincoln Children's Books.
Perez, A. R. (2013). *My diary from here to there.* New York, NY: Lee & Low.
Prince, B. (2004). *I came as a stranger: The Underground Railroad.* Toronto, ON: Tundra.
Raphael, M. (2013). *A boy from Ireland.* New York, NY: Persea.
Takaki, R., & Stefoff, R. (2012). *Different mirror for young people: A history of multicultural America.* New York, NY: Seven Stories.
Temple, F. (1997). *Tonight, by sea.* New York, NY: HarperCollins.
Weaver, L. Q. (2014). *Enrique's journey.* New York, NY: Random House.

Grade 9–12 Mentor Texts

Ali, M. *Brick lane.* New York, NY: Simon and Schuster.
Bode, J. (1991). *New kids in town: Oral histories of immigrant teens.* St. Louis, MO: Turtleback.
Budhos, M. (2007). *Ask me no questions.* New York, NY: Atheneum.
Cofer, J. O. (1996). *An island like you: Stories of the barrio.* London, England: Puffin.
Corbett, D. (2010). *Do they know I'm running?* New York, NY: Ballantine.
Danticat, E. (1998). *Breath, eyes, memory.* New York, NY: Ballantine.
Danticat, E. (2004). *Behind the mountains.* New York, NY: Scholastic.

Diaz, J. (2008). *The brief wondrous life of Oscar Wao.* New York, NY: Penguin Putnam.
Eggers, D. (2009). *Zeitoun.* San Francisco, CA: McSweeney's.
Engle, M. (2016). *Silver people.* Boston, MA: HMH Books for Young Readers.
Grande, R. (2007). *Across a hundred mountains.* New York, NY: Simon and Schuster.
Hidier, T. D. (2014). *Born confused.* New York, NY: Scholastic.
Marshall, P. (2006). *Brown girl, brownstones.* New York, NY: Feminist Press at SUNY.
Nunez, E. (2009). *Anna in-between.* New York, NY: Akashic.
Satrapi, M. (2007). *The complete Persepolis.* New York, NY: Penguin Random House.
Son, J. (2004). *Finding my hat.* New York, NY: Scholastic.
Veciana-Suarez, A. (2003). *Flight to freedom.* New York, NY: Scholastic.

TEACHER REFERENCE BOOKS

Bigelow, B. (2002). *Rethinking globalization: Teaching for justice in an unjust world.* Milwaukee, WI: Rethinking Schools Publication.
Bigelow, B. (2006). *The line between us.* Milwaukee, WI: Rethinking Schools Publication.
Flaitz, J. J. (2006). *Understanding your refugee and immigrant students: An educational, cultural, and linguistic guide.* Ann Arbor: University of Michigan Press.
Igoa, C. (1995). *The inner world of the immigrant child.* London, England: Taylor & Francis.
Olsen, L. (2008). *Made in America: Immigrant students in our public schools.* New York, NY: New Press.
Stewart, J. (2011). *Supporting refugee children: Strategies for educators.* Toronto, ON: University of Toronto Press.
Thorpe, H. (2017). *The newcomers: Finding refuge, friendship, and hope in an American classroom.* New York, NY: Scribner.

ARTICLES

Cotter, H. (2017). For migrants headed north, the things they carried to the end. Retrieved from https://www.nytimes.com/2017/03/03/arts/design/state-of-exception-estado-de-excepcion-parsons-mexican-immigration.html
Tang, T. (2017, December 28). Judge blocks Arizona ethnic studies ban he found was racist. Retrieved from https://www.usnews.com/news/best-states/arizona/articles/2017-12-28/judge-blocks-ban-on-ethnic-studies-in-tucson-school-district

WEBSITES

Teaching Tolerance (2018). *Immigration.* Retrieved from https://www.tolerance.org/topics/immigration

VIDEOS, DOCUMENTARIES

Al Jazeera. (Producer). (2007). *Walls of shame* [Video file]. Retrieved from https://www.youtube
Bailey, S. (Producer). (2015). *Between borders: American migrant crisis* [Video file]. Retrieved from https://www.youtube.com/watch?v=rxF0t-SMEXA
Center for Economic Progress. (Producer). (2010). *Kid's talk: The stories of refugee children.* [Video file]. Retrieved from https://www.youtube.com/watch?v=3uoUXlGHWts

Comedy Central. (Network). (2012). *Tucson's Mexican-American studies ban* [Video file]. Retrieved from http://www.cc.com/video-clips/ovmyo9/the-daily-show-with-jon-stewart-tucson-s-mexican-american-studies-ban

Couto, M. S. (Producer). (2014). *Risking it all: Children at the border* [Video file]. Retrieved from https://www.youtube.com/watch?v=5aSFVMNvQkc

Dissard, J., & Peng, G. (Directors and Producers). (2013). *I learn America* [Video file]. Retrieved from http://ilearnamerica.com

Dos Vatos Productions and the Independent Television Service. (Coproducers). (2015). *Precious knowledge* [Motion picture]. Retrieved from https://vimeo.com/ondemand/preciousknowledge

Eaton, L., & Lindsay, J. (Executive Producers). (2012). *Homeland: Immigration in America.* [Motion picture]. Retrieved from http://www.pbs.org/show/homeland-immigration-america/

Espitia, D. (Producer). (2012). *Illegal movie* [Motion picture]. Retrieved from Illegalmovie.org

Fink, M. (Director and Producer). (2016). *Beyond borders: Undocumented Mexican Americans* [Video file]. Retrieved from http://www.beyondborders.tv

Germano, R. (Producer). (2010). *The other side of immigration* [Video file]. Retrieved from http://www.theothersideofimmigration.com

Makepeace, A. (Producer). (2007). *Rain in a dry land* [Motion picture]. Retrieved from http://www.pbs.org/pov/raininadryland/

Mazzio, M. (Director). (2014). *Underwater dreams* [Motion picture]. Retrieved from https://www.underwaterdreamsfilm.com/about-the-film/

Muccino, G. (Director). (2006). *The pursuit of happyness* [Motion picture]. Retrieved from http://www.imdb.com/title/tt0454921/

Pérez Arellano, R. (Producer). (2014). *Undocumented and underage: The crisis of migrant children* [Video file]. Retrieved from https://www.youtube.com/watch?v=HVHqV0ibCWI

Public Broadcasting Service (Producer). (2013). *My American girls: A Dominican story* [Motion picture]. Retrieved from http://www.pbs.org/pov/myamericangirls/

Rigby, T. (Director). (2010). *Sin pais (without country)* [Motion picture]. Retrieved from https://www.newday.com/film/sin-pa%C3%ADs-without-country

Robertson, S. (Producer). (2015). *Immigration battle* [Motion picture]. Retrieved from https://www.pbs.org/wgbh/frontline/film/immigration-battle/

Scholastic Rock, Inc. (Producer). (1977). *The great American melting pot* [Video file]. Retrieved from https://www.youtube.com/watch?v=5ZQl6XBo64M

Serrano, M. (Producer). (n.d.). *Forbidden: Undocumented and queer in rural America* [Motion picture]. Retrieved from http://www.forbiddendoc.com

Seven League Productions. (Producer). (1981). *Against wind and tide: A Cuban odyssey* [Video file]. Retrieved from https://archive.org/details/againstwindandtideacubanodyssey

Shwer, M. (Director and Producer). (2015). *Don't tell anyone (no le digas a nadie)* [Motion picture]. Retrieved from http://www.pbs.org/pov/donttellanyone/

Snyder, K. A. (Director). (2011). *Welcome to Shelbyville* [Motion picture]. Retrieved from http://www.pbs.org/independentlens/films/welcome-to-shelbyville/

Teplitsky, M. (Producer), & Bastidas, B. (Director). (2014). *New American girls—Kassandra* [Motion picture]. Retrieved from http://www.pbs.org/video/pbs-new-american-girls-kassandra/

Vargas, J. A. (Director and Producer). (2014). *Documented: A film by an undocumented American* [Motion picture]. Retrieved from http://documentedthefilm.com

Vice. (Producer). (2012). *Illegal border crossing in Mexico* [Video file]. Retrieved from https://www.youtube.com/watch?v=BH_Z5BEZ5ts&t=189s

PODCASTS

Glass, I. (Producer). (n.d.). *This American Life Podcast* [Audio podcast]. Retrieved from https://www.thisamericanlife.org/listen

Gonzales, R. (2017). *Federal investigation finds "significant issues" at immigrant detention Centers* [Audio podcast]. Retrieved from https://www.npr.org/sections/thetwoway/2017/12/14/570984026/federal-investigation-finds-significant-issues-at-immigrant-detention-centers
Jacobs, E. (2017). *When immigration detention means losing your kids* [Audio podcast]. Retrieved from https://www.npr.org/2017/12/08/565426335/when-immigration-detention-means-losing-your-kids
Vedantam, S. (2018). *The huddled masses and myth of America* [Audio podcast]. Retrieved from https://www.npr.org/2018/01/15/578169724/the-huddled-masses-and-the-myth-of-america

About the Author and Contributor

Laura Roy (PhD, University of Texas at San Antonio) is associate professor and chair of education at La Salle University in Philadelphia, Pennsylvania. Laura's program of research is interdisciplinary, drawing primarily from critical and sociocultural theories in order to examine the places where new and existing communities meet and intersect. At the core of her work is a concern for and commitment to equity, social justice, and antiracist teacher activism. Her record of publication centers primarily on the classroom and community experiences of refugee and immigrant populations in the US, examining the intersections of race, culture, language, and other markers of identity. She is particularly interested in the discursive practices in the classroom that cultivate or marginalize students' unique cultural and literate histories. Her work has appeared in journals such as *The Harvard Educational Review*, *Urban Review*, and *The TESOL Journal.* As a teacher educator, Laura is committed to supporting teacher research and teacher voice, including collaboration on research projects and copresenting at national conferences.

* * *

Drew Gingrich (BS, Penn State University) is a fifth-grade teacher at Nova Southeastern University School in Davie, FL. Previously, Drew taught fourth grade at Cornwall Elementary of the Cornwall-Lebanon School District in Lebanon, Pennsylvania. As a teacher, Drew believes in teaching and facilitating a classroom community where all are accepted and welcomed. It is Drew's hope that, through education, students can foster a more accepting and socially just world.

Made in the USA
Columbia, SC
14 November 2018